Jack Cavanaugh

D1013599

EXTREME
RIGHTEOUSNESS

Seeing Ourselves in the Pharisees

EXTREME RIGHTEOUSNESS

TOM HOVESTOL

MOODY PRESS
CHICAGO

ISBN: 0-8024-6696-6

1 3 5 7 9 10 8 6 4 2

Printed in the United States of America

To my parents,
Harold and Virginia Hovestol

You humbly cast yourself on the
mercy and grace of God alone;
you were not afraid to admit fault
as you pursued faithfulness;
you lived by the Word and loved the Lord; and
you unconditionally loved all eight of us
and prayed constantly for our spiritual welfare.
Because of you I have been given
the background to understand the Pharisees,
the grace to look humbly in my own soul, and
the courage to challenge the status quo for Christ's sake.

CONTENTS

"THE RIGHT WAY" ARTICLES

ACKNOWLEDGMENTS

Many kind and giving people have helped me in putting in your hands this book with its message of hope and freedom. I acknowledge each as friends and helpers in this project.

My special thanks to Gwynne Johnson for being my main sounding board. You are a true comrade in the pursuit of truth and an untiring encourager. You and Don are my mentors and dear friends.

In assembling the material, I must thank several people. To Pat Brunner, thanks for correcting my grammar and encouraging my heart. To the staff and friends at Calvary Church (Jeff, Scott, Steve, Margie, Joyce, Patty, Deb, Dan, Jay, Walt, and Anahid), thanks for your research, constructive comments, skilled fingers, and invaluable assistance behind the scenes. To the members and friends of Calvary Church, thank you for the freedom to speak boldly and the freedom in Christ you have shown me. Your love and prayers have given me more than I can ever repay. And to my Sunday school class, thanks for your insights and encouragement as we discussed Pharisaism for a year together.

I am also grateful to Craig Blomberg of Denver Seminary for his God-honoring scholarship and passion for the truth and balance in studying God's Word and John Knight, MD., for suggesting the title of this book.

My appreciation also to Greg Thornton, Bill Thrasher, and Jim Vincent at Moody Press. Thanks for your enthusiasm for an idea, your believing in me, and your patience to see me through.

Finally, my thanks to my family and my Lord. To my seven supportive siblings. To my wife, Carey, and our five children—

Nathan, Christian, Susanna, Priscilla, and Seth—a big thank you for graciously setting me free to write, and for being the greatest human beings of my life. And to my Lord Jesus Christ, thank you for loving Pharisees like me.

Chapter One
BLIND GUIDES

I wasn't searching for a soul-shaking revelation or a life pursuit that evening in June of 1975 when I opened my Bible looking for something, anything, to share with a captive audience group of African students. As a teacher at a mission school, scheduled to speak in a chapel session, I flipped frantically through the pages of Scripture, begging God to give me some glimmer of what to say. Not receiving any immediate enlightenment, I decided to employ the "open Bible, point finger" method. I let the Bible flop open before me, pointed, and then started reading, hoping something would "hit me." Within a day or so I would have to stand before a few hundred Swazi High School students in our chapel service and teach them something about God. But what?

My Bible opened to the early chapters of Matthew. I began reading and soon became engrossed in the narrative. I didn't stop until I had read most of the Gospel. Nothing in particular about the life of Jesus nor the disciples struck me that day. None of the great events and miracles in Jesus' ministry caught my eye. Nor did I focus on His teaching or parables. Surprisingly a group of people mentioned almost as often as the disciples captured my attention, the Pharisees. I knew they were never named in the Old Testament. But in Matthew's Gospel they were ubiquitous. Who were these Pharisees? Where did they come from? What were they like? What did they believe? How did they behave? Instinctively I knew I did not like them, whatever they were like, and I was certainly not like them!

And so, at age twenty-three, trying to prepare a message for my Swazi students, I wrote the following in my journal:

> The purpose of the Bible is not just to convey a message but also to reflect an image. The images of the Bible are presented primarily through the lives of its characters. These images are not only to be hung on a wall like a portrait to show me what I should look like, but also like a mirror, to show me what I actually look like. If I do not see myself reflected in the Bible, then its value to me is greatly diminished or lost entirely.
>
> As I read the Bible I should compare and contrast myself with the various characters within. On occasion I may see myself in a disciple, an obedient or disobedient follower, a simple believer, a defender of the faith, or a repentant sinner like David.
>
> But do I ever compare myself with a Pharisee? No, that would be unthinkable. There are no Bible characters who are so scathingly exposed by Jesus for their wickedness. No others anger me as much as those scheming, self-righteous, envious, murderous, proud, hate-filled, hypocritical Pharisees. Jesus reserved His most acidic and condemnatory remarks for them. They acted religious and claimed to know God, and yet didn't. They preached and practiced and proselytized their religion, yet they knew neither themselves nor God. Could I be a Pharisee? Never!!! Jesus calls them fools, murderers, hypocrites, serpents, and tomb-like. It is unthinkable to imagine that I could resemble one of them!!!
>
> Perhaps I fail to see that the Pharisees are the Bible characters whose background is most like mine. I'm afraid that the Pharisees may be more like me than I care to admit. Did the Pharisees cease existing 2000 years ago? I fear they are alive and flourishing today!

ULTIMATE BAD GUYS

I had concluded from my extensive church background that the Pharisees were the Bible's ultimate bad guys. They were the ones primarily responsible for the crucifixion of Christ. They were the recipients of Jesus' harshest words and most acrid condemnations. They were the ones scorned in my church as the epitome of *other* religious people with whom we did not agree. As far as I knew, they were Satan personified.

But were my conclusions about the Pharisees correct? I did not know. I never remember anyone telling me where the Pharisees came from or what they were like. I just assumed they represented the essence of theological badness. I recall many people and groups being likened to Pharisees. And I have an overwhelming sense that they were vociferously condemned whenever they came up in Bible teaching and preaching. But what haunted me in that little tin-roofed, single-room house in Mhlosheni, Swaziland, that night was the question, "Why would God devote so much space in His Word to such worthless people?" God does not waste words, and I was convinced that all the words of the Scriptures are profitable (2 Timothy 3:16-17). Surely the Pharisees had very little, if anything, to teach me about godliness. Many questions flooded my mind. Why didn't God simply make brief mention of them for historical accuracy and then focus on the interaction between Jesus and the disciples? Why not tell more about what Jesus did and said? Why not devote more space to describing the intricacies of discipleship and disciple-making? Why not reveal more truths that are directly relevant to my life? Why devote so much space to the Pharisees?

For some reason God had placed these scoundrels near the center of the gospel message. That night I concluded my journal entry with these words:

> I need to take a closer at the Pharisees and at myself, but not to ridicule them and pat myself on the back. I think Jesus wanted there to be no mistake about His attitude toward external religiosity. Unfortunately, the Pharisees are often so scathingly caricatured that I cannot bring myself to see myself in them. If I see myself only in the noble or semi-noble characters of the Bible, perhaps I do not really see myself at all. The Spirit of God prevents me from being too harsh on the Pharisees for I am potentially more like them than anyone else in the entire Bible!

A HAUNTING QUESTION

That night I formulated the question that has haunted me for over twenty years: *"Why, God, did You place these scoundrels so central to the message of the Gospels?"* Surely God did not intend for people like me to laugh at them, accuse them, or ignore them. Then I simply began to ask the next, logical questions, *Who were the Pharisees, anyway? What do You want me to learn from them?*

With the few resources that I had available to me in Swaziland, I began to dig into the background on the Pharisees. As I began piecing together the facts of their lives, I was stunned and profoundly affected. Armed with a fresh perspective I reread the text of Matthew. Now I was seeing myself in the interactions between Jesus and the Pharisees, noting the parallels. They were frightening, yet also strangely freeing!

Since that time the subject of Pharisees continues to attract me more than any other in the Bible. But more importantly, they have done more to transform my life and ministry than any other single theme. And, as I have shared these thoughts with people from less rebellious backgrounds than mine, they told me that once they came to Christ they too quickly began to fall prey to many of the same characteristics of the Pharisees that plagued me.

Let me take you back prior to that 1975 chapel service in Africa to show why I had identified so strongly with the Pharisees. I now call the Pharisees my friends. For they, more than any disciple or deadbeat, are the "blind guides" who have helped me find my way. As I look back, I might have titled my early years, "The Subtle and Unseen Dangers of Being Good."

MY SPIRITUAL ROOTS

Deeply committed Christian parents nurtured me in the Christian faith from day one. When asked how I was converted, I sometimes facetiously reply, "I was born a Christian." This response often raises the eyebrows of the orthodox who expect to hear, "I went forward and asked Jesus into my heart." Though I do not remember a definitive time, date, and place, I "became a Christian" early in life. From talking to many who were raised as I was, I have discovered that my experience is not unique.

My spiritual roots have some built-in advantages. Christian truth about God, myself, the world, and eternity was etched deeply into my soul at an early age. This Christian training has provided me with a worldview that makes sense and fits reality. However, there are also potential dangers that are often overlooked. Though we say, "God has no grandchildren"—that each person must make his own personal decision—many of us, if we are honest, would have to admit that we came into Christianity on the spiritual coattails of our parents. And though it is exceedingly subtle, it is easy to acquire an underlying attitude of self-righteousness.

My background is as profoundly and pervasively religious as anyone I have met. My parents took seriously the mandate of Deuteronomy 6 to teach the Christian faith in every possible way. They expected church attendance every time the doors opened. I remember being removed from Little League games midstream to attend, still in my uniform, Wednesday evening prayer meetings. Daily we had family devotions after breakfast and supper. My parents also encouraged personal daily devotions.

Our home was a veritable feast of Christian truth. Just as many homes today are bathed in the sounds and sights of the television, our home was filled with the sounds of Christian radio. Ranger Bill, Aunt Bee, and "Unshackled" were family favorites. I was exposed to voluminous amounts of Christian literature, including missionary biographies; Christian novels; *Pilgrim's Progress;* and my favorite, *Foxe's Book of Martyrs.* Christian hymnody pervaded our home, and I imbibed it naturally. To this day I can usually quote the words to hymns as they are played—even ones that only the old-timers know.

This Christian culture enveloped my life. In addition to my parents, numerous other Christian adults influenced my Christian growth. I can still quote tidbits of their wisdom. Missionaries were among the most special people in my life, particularly those who served in "darkest Africa." Their stories always fascinated me.

DO'S AND DON'TS

To help me walk the "straight and narrow" I had a list of do's and don'ts (mostly don'ts) that were strictly enforced. You could call them the "Dirty Dozen." The list of taboos included dancing, smoking, drinking, card playing, swimming on Sunday and listening to rock music. Separation from "the world" was a concept often taught and compliance was expected.

Not everything was negative; there were some do's. Do love God and hate sin. Do attend church (even on vacation). Do have a "Daily Quiet Time." Do memorize the Bible (in the King James Version, of course). Do pray every day. Do respect your elders. Do witness for Christ. Do excel at school (Sunday school and public school). Do separate yourself from evil influences. Do remember the Sabbath and keep it holy. Do keep quiet in church. And do act good.

I do not, by the way, summarily dismiss these do's and don'ts. Many of them have sound scriptural support, make common sense, and are spiritually helpful. All of these rules and regulations were enforced by my parents, who had my best interests at heart. I have come to appreciate some of the protections they provided.

ADVANTAGES—AND HIDDEN DANGERS

My background had some definite advantages. My mind was filled with God's truth that I treasure to this day. It kept me away from dangers to which others succumbed and by which they have now been destroyed. Loving people whose lives deeply touched mine became good role models. I learned early that Christians are called to be different and that it takes conviction and courage to follow Christ. I enjoyed an excellent reputation and commendable external behavior. And I acquired an in-depth understanding of religion, including the good, bad, and ugly, without which I would have been unable to write this book.

However, my religious roots also had some hidden dangers. It was easy for my Christianity to become like a favorite suit that I stepped into rather than an inner, cultivated relationship with a living God. Often I equated "Church-ianity" with Christianity; and religiosity with spiritual reality. Religious activities became the focus of my life rather than personal devotion to God. Though my external behavior was excellent, I was gripped by hidden sins of the heart.

I memorized Scripture voraciously. I won contests and found such success to be sweet and handsomely rewarded in Churchdom. I was praised and even won valuable prizes. However, it was easy, and natural, for my faith to be cerebral, intellectual, and academic rather than experiential. Even back then I noticed the paradox that the winners of Bible contests were seldom those who applied God's Word to their lives. Rather those honored as winners had quick memories, a competitive spirit, encouragement (and often help) from parents; they (and I) had tasted the sweet satisfaction of ecclesiastical success. Unfortunately, the distance between the head and the heart is often not bridged, and the difference between profession and possession is often not recognized.

CLOAKED COMPLIANCE

Some people with a background like mine tend to buck the system at every turn. I was not one of those. I fit nicely into the ecclesiastical world that reared me. Though energetic, I was a compliant child by nature. I wanted to make my good parents proud of me. I generally did not challenge the rules. Though competitive, I was sensitive and eager to please. Early on in life I discovered that playing by the rules works! And I played well! Moreover, I was temperamentally disciplined and intellectually able to memorize quickly, excellent attributes for a budding churchman who wants to appear religious to other churchgoers.

One of the most notable characteristics of a "good Christian boy" was a good reputation. I enjoyed that too. By the end of high school, I had generally subdued a fiery temper and had gained a reputation for patience and unselfishness. I had learned how to effectively manage the exterior of my life and hide the more sordid aspects. By graduation day, most of my besetting sins had gone underground.

Compliance, self-discipline, good external behavior, and eagerness to please are traits with built-in advantages. They are regularly affirmed by almost everyone. However, there is also a danger built into these traits. Subtly and unknowingly, self-righteousness slips in. Eventually the "good news" is acknowledged and accepted, but seems no longer necessary for daily living.

My public image was untarnished, but image does not always reflect the real you. For me, my reputation was solid, but on the sly I stole. I treated the opposite sex with respect, yet I battled lust. I appeared to be a patient person, but my hidden fiery temper waited to ignite. The net result: I was righteous on the outside, but rebellious on the inside. I was genuinely compassionate, but I could also be cruel. Hidden sins of the heart dominated me. Though I appeared to be separated from the world, I desperately wanted to be a part of it.

SAVING GRACE

Nevertheless, in spite of these inconsistencies, I retained a tenderness for Jesus. I also loved God's Word, and was loved by godly people I knew. My interest in the person of Jesus grew as I absorbed biblical truth. He consistently defied stereotypes, lived authentically, compassionately, and courageously, angering some and delighting others. He was different from many spiritual leaders that I had observed. He manifested qualities that I found most delightful in people that I liked. So, though I often felt inwardly torn, struggling with two selves, one reaching for Christ, the other reacting against His church, I never rejected Jesus as I questioned some in His church. Moreover, always drawn by its earthy ring of truth, the Bible had become a constant source of answers, strength, and encouragement. I have never seriously questioned its authority. So, though I often wrestled with disillusionment and doubts, amid my confusion the

Scripture provided a solid foundation on which to stand.

And, I never lost my love for the dear people of my past, many of whom had very tender hearts toward God and love for people. So though I often felt alone, as if no one could understand my struggles, I was supported by people who simply displayed Christlike love. Most of all, my parents modeled a Christian faith that was honest, humble, prayerful, and undeniably real.

COLLEGE DEGREE AND DISILLUSIONMENT

As a freshman at Wheaton College, I gladly signed "the pledge" for it was several degrees less restrictive than my background. I devoted myself to academics and also participated in various Christian activities, determined to add sacrificial service to my practice of Christianity. Among my Christian ministries were tutoring students in a Chicago housing project and, in Chicago's skid row, speaking with men about Christ and offering them meals. For two and one-half years, I ministered in downtown Chicago each Sunday morning in flophouses and street corners. Though my service there was not effective in terms of seeing transformed lives, it did much for me. I gained a heart for the needy and a gratefulness for the protections of my past. The experience jolted me out of a shell of separatistic living. Of course, I always made sure that I was back in time for Sunday evening church! Nevertheless, even sacrificial service did not provide the answers I was seeking.

I cherish my years at Wheaton, and a degree, with honors, from Wheaton College was a crowning achievement in this good Christian boy's résumé. But within I felt increasingly disillusioned, like many around me. I could no longer deny the reality of the gulf between the Christianity preached and the Christianity practiced. I recognized that some of the do's and don'ts of my youth did not stand up to biblical scrutiny. Moreover, I was increasingly troubled with the pick-and-choose nature of so much Christian teaching. Certain themes were emphasized ad nauseam while others were neglected as if they did not appear in Scripture. Conservative politics typically were equated with Christianity; however, in my reading of Scripture, it was impossible to box Jesus along such simplistic ideological lines. Though I continued to practice daily devotions, took long prayer walks on the streets of Wheaton, and still had a tenderness to things spiritual, I was growing increasingly cynical over the numerous flaws that I observed in Christianity, both my own and others.

MISSIONARY EXPERIENCE

The next step in my life was a surprise. In 1974 I was asked to serve as a short-term volunteer in Swaziland. *What could be a more glorious accomplishment than a stint in "Darkest Africa"?* I thought. The Swaziland Ministry of Education employed me, and I taught at a highly regarded mission school for Africans under the direction of The Evangelical Alliance Mission. For three years I taught history and biology at Franson Christian High School in Mhlosheni, Swaziland. I was surrounded by the kind of people I had idolized for years, those who occupied one of the highest rungs on our ecclesiastical ladder.

Stepping outside my culture forced me to see life differently. I had to live each day with my eyes (physical, emotional, intellectual, and spiritual) wide open. Though I initially experienced euphoria, I found that my questions did not subside; instead, they increased. I tried to glorify poverty as an essential ingredient of spiritual maturity. But upon looking deeper I discovered that poor people were materialistic also, just like me. The African church, though different in form, was not a lot different in substance from the United States. I thought it would have been better. From the perspective of two dissimilar cultures, I saw that much was amiss with the church. But I did not know what. I felt more and more that I did not fit in the church as I knew it.

I almost could have mouthed the words of the apostle Paul (Philippians 3:4–6): "If anyone else has a mind to put confidence in the flesh, I far more: circumcised the eighth day [churched from birth], of the nation of Israel [born into a Christian home in "Christian America"], of the tribe of Benjamin [conservative, evangelical, fundamental], a Hebrew of Hebrews [a Christian's Christian]." As Paul was a Pharisee, I also was learned, disciplined, and devout. Like Paul I was zealous, having volunteered for Christian service at home and abroad. Paul wrote, "As to the righteousness which is in the Law, [I am] found blameless"; as far as people could see, I too lived an exemplary life.

QUESTIONS AND CONCERNS

My evangelical résumé was impressive, yet I was haunted by unanswered questions about myself and other followers of Christ.

Maybe you, too, have asked similar questions. Questions like:

- Why do good spiritual roots sometimes produce flawed fruit? I had to admit that good backgrounds do not guarantee godliness.

- Why are people who strive so hard to be right at times so wrong? It struck me that something about rightness is wrong! The pursuit of righteousness frequently degenerates into patronizing self-righteousness.

- Why do people who know the truth sometimes miss the way? Why doesn't orthodox doctrine consistently produce a love relationship with Christ and compassion for others? Sometimes I observed the opposite: apathy towards God and cruelty towards people.

- Why is there a difference between the public and the private persona of some of the Christians I knew, including myself? I began to wonder if piety was little more than a public show.

- Why does tradition seem to dominate church ministry? I noted that when church tradition clashed with what appeared to be the teaching of the Bible, tradition usually won. Tradition ruled the ecclesiastical roost, though few if any seemed to notice it!

- Why do rules and regulations proliferate in a faith that promises freedom? Is freedom really that dangerous? I also saw that the gospel, which was supposed to be the greatest liberating force in the world, was often cherished by some of the most uptight and downcast people I knew, and I was sometimes among them.

- Why do those who so staunchly insist on the separated life often fail to resemble the behavior and burden of Christ? As far as I could tell, separatism was not resulting in greater holiness or helping us reach the world for Christ.

- Why do some who appear spiritually well turn out to be sick? What does authentic spiritual health look like? I began to conclude that my criteria for evaluating spiritual health were badly flawed.

We will address those questions in this book (especially in chapters 4–11). Those questions at one point had become almost insurmountable in my mind. I wondered: *Is there any hope for Christian authenticity and true righteousness?* I gladly discovered the answer is yes, and the Pharisees, no less, will show the way!

Chapter Two
A COMMON CARICATURE

Political cartoonists have mastered the art of the caricature, which is a drawing that exaggerates an unflattering
trait. In the 1996 presidential elections, for example, Republican
Bob Dole had deep, dark, baggy eyes showing his age. Ross Perot
had squinty eyes and big ears that made him look inquisitive and a
little clownish. President Bill Clinton had a bulbous nose that suggested a drinker and party-goer. Like all good caricatures, these
were generalizations, inaccurate and unfair to the individuals.

Caricatures are a convenient way to marginalize and demor-
alize those we want to ignore. Ever since creatures started drawing
pictures with stick figures and words, caricatures have been common. Christians are familiar with caricatures, or at least we should
be, for we are both the objects of caricaturing and regular con-
tributors to the art. The mischaracterization of Christians that
dominates popular culture is a case in point. We are often pictured as a monolithic group of right-wing fanatics who seek to
impose our will and values, even forcibly, on the culture. We are
popularly pigeonholed as hate-mongers and bigots, narrow-
minded and ignorant, the radical right and the wrong kind of
neighbors. We are sometimes clumped together with skinheads,
rednecks, white separatists, extreme Muslim fundamentalists,
and abortion clinic bombers. As a result of this perception, we
are often despised, stereotyped, and conveniently dismissed.

Caricaturing Christians began during the first centuries of
the church. Earlier followers of Christ were pictured as worthless people (because the early church attracted many poor and
despised), treasonous (because they did not worship the emper-

or), atheists (because some scorned the gods that made Rome great), haters of mankind and misfits (because they opted out of government service and avoided certain social events and entertainment), immoral and incestuous (because they called one another brother and sister, had "love feasts," and greeted one another with a "holy kiss"). Some critics even called them cannibals, saying they "ate Jesus' flesh" and "drank His blood" at the Lord's Supper.

A COSTLY CARICATURE

The caricature of Christianity that has emerged in popular secular culture is a gross distortion of reality, and we are furious. However, we conveniently forget that we too perpetuate caricatures. One such distortion is the perception of the Pharisees that dominates Christian thinking. Our partial and distorted knowledge of the Pharisees deludes us into thinking we understand them. I contend, however, that we would not recognize a real Pharisee if one bumped into us on the street, sat next to us in church, or stared at us in the mirror!

Furthermore, when we caricature the Pharisees, the consequences are spiritual and eternal. A distorted perspective of the Pharisees can lead to our misapplying the Scriptures and, far worse, to profound spiritual damage to the church and to each of us individually. If we create a false image of the Pharisees and fail to see how much we resemble them, we may rob ourselves of some of the most pertinent teaching in the Scriptures.

From years of personal experience and conversation with religious people, I am certain that most Christians have a seriously distorted view of the Pharisees. What we ignorantly presume to be accurate is, in fact, a caricature. W. E. Phipps astutely notes: "The caricature of the Pharisees by Christians is as absurd as that of Jesus in the Talmud. There he is alluded to as [an illegitimate son] and a sorcerer."[1]

A COMMON CARICATURE

Ask any devout Christian to play a word-association game with "Pharisee," and the responses will be overwhelmingly negative. The following words have been mentioned when I have asked people to suggest synonyms of Pharisaism: *hypocrites; against Jesus; self-righteous; prideful; legalists; nitpicky; and judgmental.* Others have replied with "I'm-right, you're-totally-wrong type of people"; "knew the Law but didn't practice it"; "rejected everybody"; "demanding"; and "the ones who killed Christ." I recall no word associations of a positive nature. (It is ironic that if we played the same game with a Jewish audience, probably all of the associations would be positive.)

Most Christians are undoubtedly aware of the names that Jesus and John the Baptist called the Pharisees, including: "blind" (Matthew 23:16–17, 19, 24, 26); "serpents" (Matthew 23:33); "brood of vipers" (Matthew 3:7; 12:34; 23:33); "son of hell" (Matthew 23:15); and, yes, "hypocrites" (Matthew 6:2, 5, 16; 15:7; 22:18; 23:13–15, 23, 25, 27–29; Luke 13:15). While this name-calling is unabashedly scriptural, much of it takes place in one chapter, (Matthew 23), where Jesus also castigates the religious leaders as "fools" (v. 17) and "whitewashed tombs" (v. 27). Actually, Jesus' name-calling took place on only a few occasions (when Jesus encountered traditions that twisted truth and tests designed to trap Him), and probably was addressed to some, not all, of the Pharisees. Perhaps because of the sharpness of Jesus' criticism in Matthew 23, many forget the other New Testament statements, implications, and examples that are positive.

As Bible teachers and preachers overlook Jewish writings and engage in selective readings of the Scripture through a prejudiced grid, many Christians develop a caricature rather than an accurate picture of the Pharisees. A caricature by definition is a distorted image that takes certain characteristics and exaggerates them to almost unrecognizable proportions. The result is a false freak. When we look at people as false freaks, we seldom, if ever, use them as mirrors to teach us about ourselves.

Recent Bible scholarship has recognized this wrongful caricature of the Pharisees and has sought to remedy it.[2] The good lives and positive characteristics and contributions of the Pharisees are duly noted. They deny in the strongest possible terms the strictly negative caricature that most Christians have. Moreover, they appeal persuasively for sound thinking and mutual understanding. However, this corrective action on the part of scholars has not made its way to the parishioner in the pew, nor into most of the popular pulpits and pages of the land. Pastors, even those who are sensitive to legalism, tend to miss the ubiquitous characteristics of Pharisaism among the faithful. Instead of zooming in for self-discovery, we resort to hyperbole and create distance.

If we desire to have as accurate a portrait of the Pharisees as possible, we cannot omit certain sources and exaggerate others. Nor can we overlook nuances and implications that tell a story about the Pharisees that may disagree with our preconceptions. I believe that both the Jewish and the Christian caricatures of the Pharisees are seriously flawed. The Jewish portrait is too puritanical and the Christian portrait too diabolical. One sees the goodness without the flaws. The other sees the flaws without the goodness. The net result is the same for both. Both are deluded! Both are denied a significant mirror into their souls. Both are led away from God rather than toward Him.

THE RISE OF THE PHARISEES

Who are these Pharisees? They emerged in Israel in response to religious, cultural, and political developments extending back to the Greek Empire and perhaps earlier. Appendix 1, "How the Pharisees Began," looks at the historical appearance of the Pharisees. They became prominent during the time of the Maccabees (ca. 160–60 B.C.), and their two greatest rabbis, Hillel and Shammai, appeared during the final decades before Christ's birth. Their respective schools dominated the religious scene in Israel for the next two centuries. Shammai was the conservative; Hillel the moderate. (See chapter 3 for specific teachings.)

By the time of Jesus, the Pharisees had become religious leaders in Israel. They controlled the synagogue and were represented on the Sanhedrin. They had as allies a growing group of eminent Bible scholars who were zealous for God's Law. After some bad experiences with politics, they specialized in their spiritual pursuits. Though the "hard core" Pharisees were apparently few in number,[3] their influence was considerable. Even Herod, who despised their views, was forced to respect their influence with the masses, and he was usually careful not to offend them.

STRIKING SIMILARITIES

Looking at the roots of the Pharisees historically, one can cite striking similarities to the Protestant Reformation with hints of the fundamental-evangelical movements of today. As the clergy and the religious culture of Judaism moved increasingly in a secular direction, a group of pious laymen ("pietists") rose up to reclaim the identity of the Jews as people of God's Word. They were determined to get "back to the Bible." These scriptural purists had a major hand in establishing a new rallying center for their religion, the "house of study," known to us as the synagogue. There the Jews could meticulously study and apply the Bible to every aspect of life. They were the chief proponents of a strong Bible-based education (forerunners of our emphasis on Christian education). The Pharisees asserted the responsibility of every Jew, not just the priests and scribes, to know and practice the Law. They were, one may say, among the first to assert the doctrine of the "priesthood of all believers."

They also protested ("Protestants") the corruption of religion and resisted the "humanism" of their day, Hellenism. (See Appendix 1.) In the ensuing "culture war," they clung to the "faith once delivered to the saints" with tenacity. They sought to purify a religion gone ritualistic and meaningless and live holy lives (Holiness Movement). They piously practiced their faith and were sometimes persecuted for it. Conservatives of any faith today would be duly impressed with roots like these.

COMMENDABLE CHARACTERISTICS OF THE PHARISEES

The righteous roots of the Pharisees are not, however, their only claim to religious fame. They built their lives on the solid foundation of God's Word. The Pharisees, as we will see, believed in right doctrine, sought to "rightly divide the word of truth," and were determined to live righteous lives based on the Bible. These traits we would heartily applaud.

Right Doctrine

If only a few statements were changed, most of us would readily sign the Pharisees' doctrinal statement! Though we tend to leap over it, Jesus affirmed the Pharisees' basic theological orthodoxy when He said, "The scribes and Pharisees have seated themselves in the chair of Moses; therefore all that they tell you, *do and observe*" (Matthew 23:2–3a, italics added).

Characteristically, we immediately move on to the next line in which Jesus warns against the disjunction between the preaching and the practice of the Pharisees. Nevertheless, the Pharisees, though most were not priests, tenaciously taught the orthodox tenets of Judaism. Moreover, Jesus agreed with the Pharisees' understanding of the central importance of the *Shema* and the love-thy-neighbor command (Matthew 22:34–40; Luke

10:25–28). As Merrill C. Tenney notes, "He (Jesus) was more nearly in accord with them theologically than with any other religious sect in Judaism."[4]

The apostle Paul likewise sided with the Pharisees theologically in Acts 23:6–10 when making his defense before the Sanhedrin. Yet we tend to not recognize the basic theological orthodoxy of the Pharisees. Why?

Perhaps we are blind to their beliefs because we are already biased against them. Perhaps we do this because we are familiar only with the negative warnings of Jesus (Matthew 16:6, 11–12).[5] Armed with these shreds of evidence, we draw wrong conclusions. We clump together the Pharisees and Sadducees when both would chafe at being in each other's theological company. Though the Pharisees had a number of fatal flaws, their doctrine was not the chief among them.

Right Bible Interpretation

From the outset of their movement, the Pharisees were people of the Book. Josephus writes, they "are supposed to excel others in the accurate knowledge of the laws of their country."[6] (For more on Josephus and other primary sources of study of the Pharisees, see Appendix 2.) They revered, studied, memorized, and sought to interpret the Scripture accurately. They made it their life pursuit to apply the teaching of the Scripture to every detail of life. The Pharisees had a very high view of God's Word and sought to obey its every command. They had a well-developed liturgy based on the reading and application of the Bible. The Pharisees' minds and lives were bathed in the Holy Scriptures.

The Pharisees, moreover, did not bypass the application of the Bible. Though they acknowledged the unchangeable nature of God's Word, they saw the Torah as a dynamic and evolving body of truth. With exemplary zeal, they pursued making the Scriptures applicable to changing cultural situations. The Pharisees earnestly desired the inculcation of God's Word into people's lives. With the best of motives, they endeavored to bring every sphere of life under the authority of God's Word and His moral will. They established traditions to codify their understanding of how the Law should be applied to life settings and circumstances. They built fences around the Law to help people to keep from breaking it. They wanted their fellow Jews to walk with God, not just talk about Him. Their goal was to bring every facet of life into subjection to God's truth. And they desired to bring this zeal for obedience to the masses, not just to an elite few.

Interestingly, the Pharisees' attitudes toward the Scripture match those of conservative Christians today. We, as they did, hold a high view of Scripture and pride ourselves on our fidelity to the Word. On all levels of the church, from the cradle role to the senior citizens, we encourage and honor Bible study. So did they. We favor the broad dissemination of the Scriptures so that the common person can understand them. So did they. We, like the Pharisees, seek to apply the Bible to every facet of life. We, like the Pharisees of old, believe and teach that the Bible is to be trusted and obeyed. And like the Pharisees, we Protestants pride ourselves on our ability to apply God's truth to changing cultural settings. The Pharisees in the Bible resemble our biblical aspirations and actions!

Righteous Lifestyle

The Pharisees were not only doctrinally orthodox and biblically learned, they also sought to live out their faith. They zealously pursued righteousness and were recognized as more religious than others.[7] Jesus provides perspective on the Pharisees when He says, "For I say to you that unless your righteousness surpasses that of the scribes and Pharisees, you will not enter the kingdom of heaven" (Matthew 5:20). Anyone in a first-century Jewish audience who heard Jesus speak these words would have felt helpless to achieve such a standard, for the Pharisees were cultural icons of righteousness. By almost every criterion that we employ today, the Pharisees were extremely righteous.

The Pharisees sought to live *pure lives*. According to Josephus, they tried "to do all things whereby (they) might please God."[8] The Pharisees' top priority was to promote biblical purity in Israel. They believed that God's commands regarding priestly purity should be practiced by all Jews.

The Pharisees devoted themselves to *pure worship*. They considered the Judaism of the temple rituals, presided over by the priests, Levites, and the ruling elite, as corrupt and designed a synagogue worship service that revolved around prayer, public reading, and exposition of the Scriptures (Luke 4:16f), and the "Jewish Education" of the children.[9] Through the synagogue, the Pharisees were able to influence a major portion of the worship life of Israel. Though the synagogue did not supplant the temple until it was destroyed in A.D. 70, it was the primary meeting place for those interested in a more biblical and less ritualistic faith.

The Pharisees modeled this righteous lifestyle in five other areas. The *prayer life* of the Pharisees was exemplary. They prayed publicly (Matthew 6:5–6), regularly, ritually, and respectfully. They not only prayed but often fasted as they prayed (Matthew 6:16; Luke 18:12). Second, they lived consecrated, *separated lives*. The very name *Pharisee*, according to the most common derivation, means "separated one."[10] They hated sin and actively pursued holiness. Third, they valued *fellowship*. Josephus records, "Pharisees are affectionate to each other and cultivate harmonious relations with the community."[11] They organized into small groups for the purpose of mutual edification and accountability, popular concepts today. They ate at each other's tables and studied the Scriptures. Fourth, they were *good givers*. The Pharisees left no conceivable source of income outside their determination to give God His due (Luke 18:12). Finally, they were *active evangelists*. Jesus said that they would travel over land and sea for a single proselyte (Matthew 23:15).

A NOBLE SOCIAL AGENDA

Sincere religion has social ramifications. Therefore we shouldn't be surprised that the Pharisees' social lives reflected their deep concern for piety.

The Pharisees were a solidly middle-class movement. They represented not just the religious but also the economic and social heart and soul of Israel. They were honest and hardworking people. Many were small businessmen who lived simple and comfortable lives. They were champions of human equality who were less interested in politics and economics than religion (though this is not to say that they were not politically active or economically motivated). Everywhere in the literature about the Pharisees, it is noted that the masses sided with them.

As political conservatives, the Pharisees maintained a political presence and a prophetic voice, though they did not actively resist Roman rule. They practiced civil disobedience only when necessary. They were wisely tolerant and able to compromise with Gentile government as long as their religious mission was not infringed.

The Pharisees, moreover, championed *"traditional values."*

They saw themselves as standing firm for the old ways against the encroachments of new, more secular lifestyles. Their ethical and moral standards were legendary, and, as could be assumed, they derived their cues from the Word of God, their plumb line in a pagan world. The Pharisees did not succumb to the superstition of the Canaanites, the moral looseness of the Egyptians, or the violence of the Romans. The Pharisees were respectful toward the elderly[13] and insisted on the integrity of the family.

Furthermore, the Pharisees were socially concerned. They were not hard-hearted, as many assume. In fact, the Sadducees were known to be more severe than the Pharisees. Hillel, one of the greatest leaders of the Pharisees, was exalted for his compassion. Gamaliel, another leading Pharisee, advocated tolerance and restraint (Acts 5:34–39). "The Pharisees, indeed, possessed an admirable reverence for humanity, and along with that reverence, a high regard for tolerance and a great love of peace," writes D. A. Hagner. "Hillel's famous saying recorded in the Mishnah, was 'Be of the disciples of Aaron, loving peace and pursuing peace, loving mankind and bringing them to the Law.'"[14] With their high view of human beings and strong belief in equality, the Pharisees would have made fine neighbors.

COMMENDABLE INDIVIDUAL PHARISEES

Because of our religious prejudice, we tend to overlook admirable Pharisees, mentioned or implied in the New Testament. Let me highlight ten individuals or groups of Pharisees that every balanced Christian should know.

Hidden away in the Gospel text are at least three Pharisees who had the kindness and courage to invite Jesus to their houses for dinner (Luke 7:36–50; 11:37–54; 14:1–24). *Extending hospitality* in that culture was a significant step. It implied the offering of acceptance and the extension of friendship. A good Pharisee would be very careful not to mix socially with those who had differing dietary scruples. The dialogue recorded in the Scriptures indicates that there was mutual respect. Moreover, these Pharisees who invited Jesus and His followers over for a meal would likely to have known of Jesus' track record on ceremonial issues. Thus they were risk-takers. Though each of these occasions resulted in a somewhat ugly confrontation (over a sinful woman, neglected ceremonial washings, and a Sabbath healing), it must not be lost on the Gospel reader that some Pharisees tried to reach out to Jesus and better understand Him.

In Luke 5:17–26 (cf. Mark 2:1–12; Matthew 9:1–8), we read of some Pharisees who came to hear Jesus out of curiosity and questioned His claims concerning forgiveness because of their sincerely held beliefs. However, the Scriptures record that they left glorifying God and saying, "We have seen remarkable things today." Some of the Pharisees were *genuinely touched* by the life and ministry of Jesus. They had spiritual sensitivity and a desire to learn.

Furthermore, a single verse in Luke 13:31 tells of some *life-saving Pharisees* who came to Jesus when He was under increasing danger of arrest and warned Him, "Go away. leave here, for Herod wants to kill You." It is easy to acquire the notion from the Gospel accounts that all of the Pharisees were intent on assassinating Jesus. A fair reading of the Gospels reveals that this is obviously not true.

Two well-known names in the Gospels are Pharisees: Nicodemus and Joseph of Arimathea. John's Gospel identifies Nicodemus as a high-ranking, perhaps the leading, Pharisee (John 3:1, 10). Doubtless he was a man of power and influence. Nicodemus seems to have been a genuine seeker of truth (John 3:1–4). Eventually he spoke out on Jesus' behalf and was criticized for it (John 7:45–52). After the crucifixion, Nicodemus requested the body of the Lord and spent considerable money buying spices for Jesus' burial (John 19:39). We tend to overlook that Nicodemus was a high-ranking Pharisee.

Nicodemus's associate in caring for the body of Jesus after His crucifixion was Joseph of Arimathea (Luke 23:50–55; John 19:38–42), likely a Pharisee. He was a man of means who was likewise a member of the Sanhedrin. Joseph was a devout man who put his faith into action, a man who had religious, political, and economic clout. But he was willing, for his love for Jesus, to sacrifice it all—another Pharisee who followed Jesus.

Sandwiched in the text of the Gospel of John is another reference to *Pharisees who stood up for Jesus*. We read in chapter 9 that Jesus' Sabbath healing of the man born blind not only divided the man from his parents and the synagogue but also divided the Pharisees. Verse 16 records, "Therefore some of the Pharisees were saying, 'This man is not from God, because He does not keep the Sabbath.' But others were saying, 'How can a man who is a sinner perform such signs?' And there was a division among them." The Pharisees obviously were not the monolithic group opposed to Jesus that we commonly assume.

Certain Pharisees were also in the forefront of protecting the apostles. The book of Acts (5:33–42) mentions Gamaliel, a high-ranking Pharisee, who argued effectively for tolerance in the face of a hostile group of his peers. His calming words were instrumental in diverting the homicidal intentions of the Sanhedrin against Peter and the apostles. Some years later, another group of Pharisees (Acts 23:1–10) helped to save the life of the apostle Paul.

Acts also records some *Pharisees who became believers* in Jesus Christ (15:5). Admittedly they found it difficult not to encumber their newfound faith with remnants from Judaism. Nevertheless, they are mentioned with those who believed—early members of the Christian church.

Finally, and most significantly, the apostle Paul was a Pharisee of the highest order (Acts 22:3–5; 26:4–8; Philippians 3:4–6). He was educated under Rabbi Gamaliel, grandson of Hillel. And before he met Christ, Paul's Pharisaic background was considered something of great gain. Paul does say that his former Pharisaism was inadequate, but not inherently bad. Rather he views it as a code of religious honor and a high human achievement.

A GOOD MOVEMENT WITH MANY GOOD PEOPLE

Who were the Pharisees? It should now be clear: The Pharisees were good people, like us. They emerged in reaction to Hellenism, the secular humanism of their day. In response to the pressures of cultural assimilation, they became the "separated ones." Resisting the liberal drift of the priests and Levites, they insisted on orthodox theology. Instead of falling headlong into cultural compromise and professional religion, they organized a lay-led, grassroots movement that returned Judaism to "traditional values." In response to the official religious leaders' focus on temple rituals, they emphasized scriptural study and application. In response to creeping paganism, they increased their vigilance to be pure.

The Pharisees of yesterday may have more in common with the Christian church and parachurch activists today than meets the eye. They sought to be pure like the Puritans and pious like the Pietists. They studied the Bible as we do in small Bible study groups. There they gathered regularly to converse about the

Word, "experience God," and to keep one another "accountable," as we do in the modern small groups movement. They were members of good Scripture-believing and preaching synagogues. Their disciplined lives might well have been attractive to the Navigators. Their evangelistic zeal could have made them prime recruits for Campus Crusade. Their mission-mindedness would have positioned them to be top candidates for various mission boards. Their stewardship would remind us of a faithful Southern Baptist. And their scrupulous separation from the world and things worldly would parallel that of the Independent Baptists. Their longing for experiences with God and His power would resonate with a good Charismatic. And their orientation toward holiness would be attractive to the Nazarenes.

Yes, the Pharisees were good people; they were "extremely righteous." This perspective shouts from the Jewish writings, is implied in the New Testament, and is corroborated by modern biblical scholarship. Pharisee-like people are our friendly neighbors and workmates, our upstanding citizens and civic leaders, and our church board members and pastors. Indeed, the Pharisees are us!

The Pharisees were well-meaning religious people. However, it was their essential goodness and godliness that was part of the problem they had with Jesus, and He with them. The Pharisees received such "harsh" treatment from Jesus not because they were so far from the truth but because they were so close. Realistically, it is often those we love the most to whom we speak most directly, yes, even harshly. Yet, as is often the case, those who are furthest from the kingdom of God are those closest to it, who cannot see the forest for the trees.

As Christians, who are increasingly the object of hurtful (do I dare mention hateful) caricatures, we should be particularly sensitive to misrepresentation. Thus, we must not maintain our caricature of the Pharisees. The parallels between the Pharisees of Jesus' day and evangelical Christians today are striking. We must look anew at this group of religious people and learn truths God has intended for our good.

Chapter Three
OUR BEST FRIENDS, THE PHARISEES

E very weeknight, comedian David Letterman unveils his "Top Ten List," a clever listing that pokes fun at a current topic. The Top Ten List has become a favorite among those watching his successful late-night TV show. The list is humorous, yet many of the items have a real ring of truth.

As we consider the role of the Pharisees, then and now, let's also take a Top Ten approach. I trust that the following Top Ten List will have a ring of truth, like Letterman's list—and a far more profound pull on our religious hearts. As we look at this listing of why we need an accurate portrait of the Pharisees, we will discover how these "enemies" of ours can actually become our friends. And we will understand better why knowing about the Pharisees can help us grow in our relationship with Christ and with our heavenly Father.

Here are the Top Ten Reasons why we need an accurate portrait of the Pharisees.

REASON #10:
THE PHARISEES ARE ALIVE AND WELL TODAY!

The Pharisees are alive and well and living in the most unlikely places: our seminaries, our churches—even our own homes! We may take pains to distance ourselves from these best-known and most-despised biblical bad guys. Nevertheless, the Pharisees are much more like us than most of us believe.

In truth, the groups that existed in Israel around the time of

Christ are prototypical of the religious landscape in every age. There will always be conservatives, liberals, and moderates. Today, as in Jesus' days on earth, we can find supernaturalists and naturalists. Today, as then, we can spot separatists and conformists. Further, the religious continuum now, as in Jesus' time, includes zealots and peace lovers, those who insist on strict orthodoxy and those who push the theological envelope.

I recognize the dangers of stereotypes. However, stereotypes tend to develop from things typical. It is foolish not to draw legitimate historical parallels, and learn from them. Solomon taught us that there is "nothing new under the sun." None of us is exceptional; each shares traits with all humanity. Human behavior tends to run in familiar patterns. The Pharisees were one of five identifiable groups that made up the social and religious landscape of Jesus' day. As shown in the chart below, they spanned the political and religious spectrum.

The most accommodating to the Roman rule were *the Herodians;* the most unaccommodating *the Zealots,* who were the radical rightists of their day. The isolationists, who wanted little to do with society, were *the Essenes.* They opted out of the culture to pursue the holy life to which they believed God had called them. *The Sadducees* were often the foes of the Pharisees and their fellow members on the Sanhedrin, the Jewish ruling body. They rejected

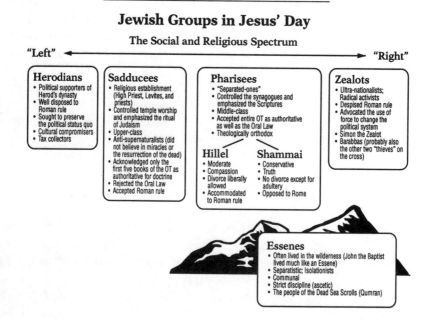

Jewish Groups in Jesus' Day

The Social and Religious Spectrum

"Left" ←——————————————————————→ "Right"

Herodians
- Political supporters of Herod's dynasty
- Well disposed to Roman rule
- Sought to preserve the political status quo
- Cultural compromisers
- Tax collectors

Sadducees
- Religious establishment (High Priest, Levites, and priests)
- Controlled temple worship and emphasized the ritual of Judaism
- Upper-class
- Anti-supernaturalists (did not believe in miracles or the resurrection of the dead)
- Acknowledged only the first five books of the OT as authoritative for doctrine
- Rejected the Oral Law
- Accepted Roman rule

Pharisees
- "Separated-ones"
- Controlled the synagogues and emphasized the Scriptures
- Middle-class
- Accepted entire OT as authoritative as well as the Oral Law
- Theologically orthodox

Hillel
- Moderate
- Compassion
- Divorce liberally allowed
- Accommodated to Roman rule

Shammai
- Conservative
- Truth
- No divorce except for adultery
- Opposed to Rome

Zealots
- Ultra-nationalists; Radical activists
- Despised Roman rule
- Advocated the use of force to change the political system
- Simon the Zealot
- Barabbas (probably also the other two "thieves" on the cross)

Essenes
- Often lived in the wilderness (John the Baptist lived much like an Essene)
- Separatistic; Isolationists
- Communal
- Strict discipline (ascetic)
- The people of the Dead Sea Scrolls (Qumran)

the oral traditions and did not believe in the resurrection of the body. This placed them at odds with the Pharisees, who defended the elders' traditions and espoused a bodily resurrection.

Glancing at the chart, we can see *the Pharisees* were not unanimous in their beliefs. They divided into two camps named for two great rabbis, Hillel and Shammai. While Shammai interpreted the law stringently, Hillel rejected what he saw as strict, inhuman applications of the law. Shammai fixated on the truth of God's Law. Hillel took the Law seriously, but he would bend it in the direction of compassion.

All five groups find parallels in today's religious groups. The Herodians can be seen in those seeking to embrace the culture; the Zealots in fringe groups (especially cults) that achieve notoriety; the Essenes in separatist or monastic groups; and the Sadducees in some liberal-leaning Christian groups.

Within the two Pharisaic camps, the Hillelite Pharisee is in many ways like the evangelical of today; the Shammaite Pharisee resembles the fundamentalist. Indeed, the Pharisees, more than any other group at the time of Jesus, are like us who are conservative Christians. They accepted the whole counsel of Scripture, not a pared-down and politically correct version of it as did the Sadducees. They walked the high middle ground between the extreme separatism of the Essenes and the capitulation of the Herodians. And they avoided the fanaticism and violence of the Zealots. They were prototypical of sincere, Bible-believing, Bible-practicing people of every age. They were the ones who were most serious about their faith without going off the deep end of fanaticism to either the left or the right.

REASON #9:
THE PHARISEES WIN THE
"BEST SUPPORTING ACTORS" OF THE GOSPELS

Movie ads always give the stars top billing. But the supporting players are equally important, as shown by the excitement at Academy Awards time when the best supporting actor and actress receive Oscars and the applause of their colleagues. If an advertisement for the Gospels were created, which actors would receive top billing? Obviously Jesus is the marquee attraction. The second billing, the principal antagonist and candidate for best supporting actor? None other than the Pharisees.

Why would God so prominently place the Pharisees at the

center of His holy Word, the four Gospels? Obviously God intended the reader to glean a lot from the Pharisees, or He wouldn't have devoted so much ink to them. But most of us, myself included, never consider the reasons for the Pharisees' prominence.

The Pharisees are the most important supporting actors in the great drama of salvation. They are mentioned in more than one hundred verses in the New Testament; yet Christians often ignore them except for an occasional sneer. To ignore—or misunderstand—the Pharisees is like watching a play without conflict, a drama devoid of some of its most important actors.

REASON #8:
UNDERSTANDING THE PHARISEES HELPS US
TO ACCURATELY HANDLE THE SCRIPTURES

A major evangelical film on the life of Jesus largely lives up to its claim to "present the Gospel of Luke with meticulous historical and scriptural accuracy." The actor portraying Jesus speaks only words from Scripture. However, a stunning error is tucked into the narrative: In the parable of the good Samaritan, the biblical context is ignored and a Sunday school–like setting is inserted into the text. The basic message of the parable, as told primarily to a group of children' is "be nice to everyone because everyone is your neighbor." That message contradicts the real intent of this scathing portion of Scripture. In reality, Jesus was teaching religious adults, not children, a powerful lesson about self-righteousness.

The parable was designed to pierce the heart of a self-justifying expert in the Law, as well as in the hearts of all religious people. But in the film—and in many Bible commentaries—it is changed. Why? I believe many are blinded to this Scripture's meaning because of a difficulty in admitting that it is addressed to religious people—modern Pharisees like us. We run (I believe subconsciously) from seeing ourselves in the clear teachings of the text.

We do this with many portions of the Scripture that address the Pharisees. Paul instructs us to be "accurately handling the word of truth" (2 Timothy 2:15), yet when we have a distorted understanding of the Pharisees, we misread and misapply Bible texts. Exegetical accuracy demands that we do better.

Regularly we falsely interpret and strip of power many texts of Scripture that are intended for Pharisees, past and present. For example, the powerful parable of the prodigal son was told primarily to the Pharisees. However, in my church background, pastors waxed eloquent on the wayward life of the prodigal younger brother (for evangelistic purposes), while they neglected a major theme of the parable, the attitudes and actions of the elder brother. This misemphasis is preached to pew-sitters, few of whom are true prodigals and scores of whom are like the stay-at-home elder brother, faithful yet without grace to the wayward.

These two parables are among the best-known and best-loved portions of the entire Bible. And yet because of our flawed understanding of the Pharisees, we miss their personal power. We need to understand the Pharisees in order to do justice to God's holy Word—to rightly, not wrongly, divide the Word of Truth.

REASON #7:
MISGUIDED PEOPLE CAN BE MORALLY GOOD

My children have friends at school and in the neighborhood who are part of the Church of Jesus Christ of Latter day Saints; they are Mormons. On numerous occasions my children have asked me, "Daddy, are Mormons bad?" I am prone to an immediate, "Yes!" because of the Mormon's misguided theology and my desire to protect my children from getting caught in its tangled web. However, honesty demands another approach.

I know, as do my children, that Mormons stand for many good things, and that their lifestyle often is exemplary. They are generally moral and good people. They are family-oriented and are often model citizens. However, their theology is deeply skewed and their religion is subtly seductive.

So I answer, "No, they are not bad people, but what they believe is not true." If I do not do this, I not only mislead my children but also know that eventually my dishonesty will be discovered by my children, and I will have sown seeds of mistrust. But I have an additional reason for the answer I give. I do not desire to communicate subtly to them that Christians are the good people in the world and those who are not Christians are bad. If I do this, I not only lie to my children but also set them up for a real crisis of conscience later in their lives. The truth is that a good religion does not necessarily produce good people and a bad religion, or no religion, does not necessarily produce bad people. I learned this lesson primarily from the Pharisees.

The simple truth is that people can be good and be wrong. Early in my religious life I acquired the notion that those who believed Christ's truth were good and those who ignored or rejected it were bad. But life is not that simple. Sometimes those who hold to truth are scoundrels and those who affirm error are saintly. One can hold steadfastly to a system of half-truths and subtle distortions and still live a moral life. There is not a necessary connection between truth and apparent morality.

The Pharisees are the ones who most graphically illustrate that goodness and true godliness are not necessarily connected. The Pharisees were stellar examples of humanity. Without the empowerment of the Holy Spirit, how did they pull it off? By what power did they live such "righteous" lives? The power of religion! Religion has the ability to powerfully influence human behavior. I have come to see that religion can be a powerful force for "good."

REASON #6:
RELIGION THAT WORKS, WORKS

I live near one of the more spiritual cities in America: Boulder, Colorado. If you know anything about Boulder, you probably would protest my assertion. Boulder is known as a party town and a New Age center. It is facetiously called "The People's Republic of Boulder" for its left-leaning political philosophy. It is highly antagonistic to historic Christianity.

Nevertheless, it is highly spiritual. It is easy to find crystal shops, metaphysical bookstores, tarot card readers, channelers, Eastern religious centers, and yoga training in Boulder. People here are deeply religious, seeking a "Rocky Mountain high."

Religion has become increasingly attractive as education, legislation, materialism, and technology are tried and found wanting. Innately religious, people are searching for meaningful spiritual moorings. Unfortunately, their quest often leads in bizarre directions. Understanding Pharisaism will reveal the grip that religion can have on the human soul irrespective of its truth. In Pharisaism we see religion at its best, yet it falls far short of God's true mark. Perhaps God placed Pharisaism so prominently in the Bible to provide a clear picture of a religion that can produce righteous behavior but not righteous hearts, one that has a handle on much truth but subtly twists it.

One of the most prevalent enemies of authentic Christianity for the past nineteen-hundred years has been legalism. The Pharisees stand as a constant scriptural reminder that religion can and inevitably will be counterfeited. From the time of Jesus onward, the subtle perversions of Pharisaism have steadily made inroads into the Christian church. Traditions, separatism, self-righteousness, and performance girds are some of its manifestations in the church today.

REASON #5:
UNDERSTANDING THE PHARISEES
HELPS PASTORS SURVIVE

Can you imagine a scout signing a baseball player to a major-league contract who has never seen a curve ball? Can a candidate for political office be elected without meeting reporters, especially antagonistic ones? Would a doctor trained in orthopedics perform brain surgery? Of course not. There are certain prerequisites to survive in almost any occupation. For any pastor to effectively lead Christ's church, his survival training must include an accurate understanding of the Pharisees.

Every pastor will encounter Pharisaism. A pastor armed with theology, Greek and Hebrew exegesis, expositional skills, and pastoral theology classes yet unaware of the pervasiveness of Pharisaism courts disaster. Conversely, understanding the Pharisees will equip a pastor to encounter the subtle twists and, at times, unsuspected cruelty of people within the church. It will even help a minister to face the forces that lurk in his own soul— the scourge of self-righteousness and its cousin, contempt for others. A pastor naive to the presence, power, and practices of the Pharisees is prone to get "blown away" by what he finds in the church—and sometimes his own soul.

Searching the Scriptures, one will discover that the most implacable enemies of God are seldom the "worldly" people. The chief enemies of the righteous are most often the religious! In the Old Testament, the primary foes of the prophets were the false prophets. In the New Testament, Jesus' primary opponents were the Pharisees, Paul's were the Judaizers, and the early church constantly had to contend with false teachers. All were insiders, not outsiders. In the modern church, pastors sometimes meet well-meaning Christians with mountains of Bible knowledge coupled with molehills of knowing God. It can be devastating for a young pastor or budding church leader to face for the first time the diabolical power of religion.

Understanding the Pharisees provides substantial help in leading a congregation toward biblical change and cultural impact. When a pastor can identify Pharisaism in his own soul and the lives of his flock, and when he understands Pharisaism from the Scriptures, he can both love Pharisees and hate Pharisaism.

REASON #4:
THE PHARISEES SUGGEST A NEW EVANGELISTIC STRATEGY: FIND THE LOST AND LOSE THE FOUND

Understanding the Pharisees can alter our evangelistic strategy. We are to find the spiritually lost but also help the religious see they may not have found God. During His ministry, Jesus encountered many who thought they were spiritual heirs of Abraham who were, in fact, outside the kingdom. Jesus knew that He had to get these people to recognize their lost state as a precursor to getting them to acknowledge their real need for a savior. With those who understood their spiritual sickness, Jesus was the gracious Physician. But to those who were proud of their goodness, He was quick to put His finger on their sins and not let up until they either repented or rejected Him. Jesus worked hard to show religious people their eternal lostness.

At least three solid scriptural examples come to mind of Jesus' ministry of "losing people." When the religious Nicodemus, a leading Pharisee, came to Jesus to engage Him in a theological discussion, Jesus put His finger on what was lacking, namely spiritual rebirth (John 3:3). Nicodemus thought that he was in the kingdom of God, and Jesus had to hit hard to convince him that he was actually outside. In the parable of the good Samaritan (Luke 10:25–37), Jesus masterfully tried to convince a self-justifying theological Bible scholar that he fell infinitely short of God's standard to love the Lord with all his heart, soul, mind, and strength, and his neighbor as himself. In love, Jesus worked to "get him lost." The main point of the story of the rich young ruler (Matthew 19:16–26) is not that one must sell all to become a Christian. Rather, the Lord's intent was to get a good man "lost" by placing His divine finger on an area of selfish idolatry. Once again, Jesus sought to get him lost as a precursor to the gospel.

Jesus devoted many of His parables and teaching to "losing people." He knew that genuine brokenness must precede openness to the gospel. He also knew that Pharisaism, the dominant religious expression of His day, produced a false sense of eternal security. He was not content to allow those who are spiritually dead to believe that they are alive. Nor should we. Instead, we must pray that the Spirit will convict "concerning sin and righteousness and judgment" (John 16:8). Pastors can hardly do a greater disservice to people than to convince those bound for hell that they are en route to heaven.

REASON #3:
THE PHARISEES SHOW US HOW TO RESCUE
THE DE-CHURCHED AND DISILLUSIONED

One of the large and growing segments of the American religious landscape is the "de-churched." These people were once active church members; some of them were highly involved church leaders. They have now, however, become burned out, bummed out, and, in some cases, missing from the church. There are a lot of wounded ex-churchgoers playing golf, fishing, and sleeping in on Sunday mornings. Some of them have chosen a lifestyle that is hostile to Christianity and have thus abandoned the church. Others are disgusted with religion. Some still long for a more meaningful religious experience; others simply do not care anymore.

You and I probably also have encountered things in the church that are wrong: Mistreatment, cruelty, and hypocrisy abound inside the church. When one sees wrongdoing and has to face its destructive power, it is easy to give up on the institution. But two things can help us stay the course. First, realize that most of us are as the Pharisees. It is the height of self-righteousness for me to condemn others for the sins of my very own soul. Second, recognize that throughout the Bible God has pointedly exposed religion as endemic: False religion and Pharisaism will *always* be among us. We must deal with them, without dropping out, for the sake of our own souls.

My heart goes out to the cynical and the disillusioned because I could so easily join their ranks. I could distance myself from Christ due to my frustration with the church. But I believe that a good understanding of the biblical Pharisees helps to put some of the disillusionment in better focus. It will let us love the church and even its Pharisees, flaws and all.

REASON #2:
THE PHARISEES CAN HELP PARENTS OF "GOOD" KIDS RECOGNIZE PASSIVE REBELLION

Most instruction today to parents crusades against the overtly disobedient child but ignores what hides within the compliant child. That's like a doctor who sees the outward symptoms of wheezing and congestion and diagnoses the flu, when further tests would show the flulike symptoms were hiding pneumonia. A good parent wants to go beyond surface symptoms of disobedience to detect a child's deep inner character. Interestingly, understanding the Pharisees can help parents see and effectively treat spiritual pneumonia in their children.

To me the finest text of Scripture on parenting is the parable of the prodigal son (Luke 15). Here a father, whose sons are both wayward, demonstrates wise parenting. We are prone to identify only the younger son as "prodigal." We are quick to see blatant rebellion and label it as sin. But if our children don't break the rules and maintain an active presence in the church, we are satisfied. We think we have done our job. The parable reminds us that there is a more sinister sin of the heart than active rebellion, namely passive rebellion.

We tend not to see the sin of the child who stays close to home, works hard, plays by the rules, doesn't get into trouble or ask for money, doesn't party hearty, etc. We praise such a child. But are we aware of the subtle sins of the heart that often remain unseen—and thus are even more dangerous? We classify disgraceful conduct as sin. But what about gracelessness? We are appalled by steamy sex. But what about the even greater spiritual malady of stewing bitterness? The "far country" is obviously the place of "wine, women, and song." But is it not possible that hardworking folk in the "field" of life may be equally led astray? When someone sees God as a cream puff and lives a profligate life, we cringe. But are we equally appalled when one of our brethren views God as a slave driver and obeys only out of fear of reprisal? Is legalism any better than lawlessness?.

Though Christian homes may do far better than the average at preserving children from debauched lives, parents and Christian leaders may unwittingly contribute to deluded lives. Often the consequences of overt sin are so obviously painful that one eventually comes to his/her spiritual senses, repents, and crawls back home. However, there is sinister security in spiritual sins.

They are even reinforced at home and by the church. And this reinforcement may cause one never to come to his/her spiritual senses. As a parent forced to make the choice, I'd probably prefer a child who strayed and eventually came to his spiritual senses over one who always did the right thing but never knew a right relationship with God.

Understanding the Pharisees can help enormously in Christian parenting, particularly in recognizing passive rebellion in our children.

REASON #1:
THE PHARISEES ARE US!

The number one reason to accurately understand the Pharisees is because of their personal relevance. The Pharisees provide one of the best mirrors the Bible offers for us to see our religious selves as we really are. Yes, the Pharisees are us!

When the Pharisees are the chief antagonists in the scene with Jesus, we normally take the perspective of detached observers. We do not feel that we can identify with them. The power of the text increases tenfold, however, when we see ourselves in the Pharisees, who were Jesus' bitterest foes but also those whom He dearly loved. If we correctly understand the assault that Jesus waged on their traditions, how He shattered their grids, how He shredded their fences, how He exposed their hidden insincerity, it is easy to see how the Pharisees grew to despise Him. We probably would do likewise if Jesus visited our churches today. More often than we would like to admit, our religious sensibilities and reactions are akin to the Pharisees.

The primary reason we need a correct understanding of the Pharisees is for our own spiritual development. Spiritual growth starts with a sense of desperate need deep in our souls. By God's Spirit we discover that we are not who we thought we were. We are spiritually bankrupt and we desperately need God's help.

The Pharisees are spiritual mirrors divinely given to us to reflect the condition of our hearts. What would we look like physically if we had no mirrors? We would be oblivious to our disheveled appearance. Eventually we would become convinced, simply out of ignorance of reality, that we looked good when, in fact, we do not. We need to look at the spiritual mirror of the Pharisees and see ourselves.

When I first saw myself as a Pharisee, I was appalled. I

started to recognize that the secret sins I had successfully hidden from others were no less evil than the blatant sins of my peers. Almost instinctively I did the right thing, but I was not growing in righteousness. Though my behavior was excellent, I would have been horrified for someone to tape-record my mind. I had trivialized the heart of the Christian message and become self-righteous, like the Pharisees.

Later, I read G. K. Chesterton and grasped a key truth: "No man's really any good till he knows how bad he is, or might be; . . . till he's squeezed out of his soul the last drop of the oil of the Pharisees."[1]

Those Top Ten Reasons for having an accurate portrait of the Pharisees may surprise you, but they show how much God can teach us through the stories of the Pharisees. Let's begin now to paint a fuller portrait of these seemingly righteous people. In the process we will learn what it means to be truly righteous—how to live rightly before God and our fellow man.

Chapter Four

WHEN RIGHTNESS
LEADS TO WRONGNESS

S everal years ago a Christian leader sat in a college president's office gathering his thoughts just prior to walking out and giving the commencement address. A member of the college board of directors was also in the office and fumbled to make conversation with the guest. Finally he blurted out a question.

"If Satan wanted to blow you out of the water, how would he do it?"

The speaker paused, taken back by such a question. "Well, I don't know how he would do it," he finally began, "but I know how he could never do it."

"Satan will never get me on an issue of personal relationships or morality. He just can't. I'm too strong there. I have paid all my dues in my marriage and my family. I've made a science out of it. I've written about it. I have a great marriage. So he may get me through pride, maybe through some arrogance, he may get me in a hundred other ways, but that's one way he will never get me."

Some time later, the leader fell into sin in a moral area.

This leader believed in, preached, and wrote about the depravity of the human heart. How could he come to think he was immune from certain kinds of sin? *He must be out of touch with himself*, I thought. *How could he be so blind to the potential for evil that resided within him?*

I have since realized the answer to that question: He became blind to the potential for evil the same way we are to ours! Too often, until we are forced by our failures to admit the evil within, we are blind to its reality or try to cover it up. Oh, yes, we may believe and defend the theological concept of depravity. Yet we do not always take it serious on a personal level. More than we would like to admit, there is a Hitler in each of us! Religion, however, tends to obscure this truth. As a result, self-righteousness has a perfect setting in which to flourish.

WHY IS OUR SELF-RIGHTEOUSNESS UNSEEN?

Those who follow Christ commonly affirm the total depravity of human beings and the imputed righteousness of Christ the Savior. Yet in practice we Christians deny those truths; we tend toward self-righteousness. In the early church, the apostle Paul labored to prevent law-keeping from destroying the gospel. But when salvation by grace seemed settled (Acts 15), sanctification by law-keeping was born (Galatians 3:3). And it has been maturing ever since.

Pharisaism's fatal flaw is self-righteousness. It lurks just beneath the surface of our evangelical souls. But we do not see it! Why? Perhaps we live such good lives that we look for sin in all the wrong places! We tune in to the external symbols of goodness but miss the internal symptoms of evil. The Lord Jesus does not want us, however, to live our lives in the pseudo-security of human righteousness. While on earth, He loved people too much to permit them to continue on their merry religious ways blinded to their true spiritual condition. Instead He regularly engaged in the ministry of enabling religious people to find freedom and true life.

The Holy Spirit is just as ready today as Jesus was years ago to open our eyes to self-righteousness. However, we have blind spots. We are blinded by society, by morality, by religion, and by knowledge.

First, we are *blinded by society*. Because we involve ourselves in good causes more than most people in our culture, we Christians can legitimately claim that our social concern is superior to that of many. This may blind us to the subtle seeds of self-righteousness sprouting in our souls. Pharisees, being generally good people, often are highly esteemed in society (Luke 16:15). When we compare favorably to our peers, we think we are doing well. It is easy to neglect a far more significant measurement, namely, the life of Jesus.

Second, we are *blinded by morality*. Basically Christians are dutiful keepers of the law, who display commendable morality. Those who live morally good lives, however, can be blinded to believe they actually meet a holy God's requirements. If righteousness is defined in terms of overt behaviors, it is possible, even probable, for religious people to convince themselves that they have indeed kept the Law. Nevertheless, Jesus points out that the Pharisees "kept" the Law only because they had effectively superficialized it. We are no different in our law-keeping.

Third, we are *blinded by religion*. If religion can be defined by what we believe and how we behave, then it is possible to convince ourselves that we are a success in religious terms. The Pharisee of whom Jesus spoke in Luke 18:11–12 thought himself righteous because he was religious; that is, he did religious things and avoided irreligious behaviors. His religious system convinced him that every sin had a solution and his religious activity pleased God. But his religion, though it worked to produce good external behavior, did not transform his heart. Religion can blind us to personal depravity.

Fourth, we are *blinded by knowledge*. Biblical knowledge can mask the awareness of our depravity. Knowing the Scriptures impresses people and leaves them with the notion (often false) that we must be walking closely to God. One of the dangers of having great skill with the Bible is the thinking that because we know His Word we know God. The connection is simply not that direct. Few in history had a better grasp of God's Word than the Pharisees. However, they were oblivious to God incarnate who lived among them. The apostle James even tells us that knowing without doing leads to self-deception (1:22). Even though we may understand that knowing about God is not the same as knowing God, it is easy to blur that distinction.

Society, morality, religion, and knowledge conspire to keep us from seeing our self-righteousness. How then can we see? By looking for certain telltale signs.

WARNING LIGHTS OF SELF-RIGHTEOUSNESS

Where do we look for symptoms of self-righteousness? Unfortunately, it does not come with a warning label; self-righteousness is not easily detected. If asked, hardly a single Christian (or any person, for that matter) would admit to being self-righteous. Our theology abhors self-righteousness. Even our secular culture shuns self-righteousness. We are sufficiently sophisticated and self-controlled to cover up most self-righteousness. And our minds are seldom as creative as when justifying ourselves.

So what subtle clues expose the hidden condition of our hearts? Certain stirrings in our psyche, like warning lights on a car's instrument panel, can help us to identify our self-righteous attitudes. In fact, through several encounters with the Pharisees, Jesus has pointed out the flashing warning lights that indicate self-righteous attitudes in our lives.

Warning Light #1:
A Contemptuous View Of Others

Do I compare myself with others and look down on those who do not live as I do? Of course, all the time! This tendency to compare my righteousness with others is endemic to humanity. Any level of contempt for others is a telltale sign of hidden self-righteousness.

Jesus told the parable of the Pharisee and the tax collectors to some who were self-righteous and viewed others with contempt (Luke 18:9). This contempt is a warning light of self-righteousness. How do we regard sinners who do not measure up and saints who have blown it? Do we subconsciously gloat over their misdeeds and glory in their shame? Do we subtly believe that we are incapable of their level of depravity and they are unlikely to achieve our level of goodness? Are we arrogant about our own avoidances and achievements?

For me the answer is yes, and then some. I rarely verbalize these thoughts, or even acknowledge them to myself. But they are there. They surface in my secret reflections and in what I mutter under my breath. They come out in unguarded conversations about people not present. They pop out in my prayers as I lament the evils of the culture more than personal and corporate sin. They slip out in my conversation about failing parishioners and fallen fellow pastors. Is the contempt light flashing on your dash too? Warning! A critical, contemptuous spirit emanates from a self-righteous heart.

Warning Light #2:
A Shallow Sense Of Forgiveness

How deep and well-developed is my personal sense of God's

forgiveness? This subjective sense is another telltale symptom of my level of self-righteousness. Our personal awareness of God's forgiveness will profoundly impact our level of self-righteousness. Our response to sinners, particularly those who wrong us, is an excellent gauge to measure potentially self-righteous hearts.

One day Jesus accepted an offer to dine at a Pharisee's house (Luke 7:36–50). An uninvited local sinner dropped in and made a scene by washing and anointing Jesus' feet. The host, appalled at the unfolding events, muttered under his breath that Jesus could not be a holy man or He would know the magnitude of this woman's sin. Jesus, knowing the Pharisee's thoughts, told a story about a creditor and two debtors. Since neither debtor could pay, the creditor forgave both debts, one large and the other relatively small. Jesus then asked, "Which of the two will love the creditor more?"

"The one whom he forgave," answered the Pharisee Simon. Jesus praised Simon's understanding of forgiveness but then exposed his blindness to its personal application. His final words to Simon are, "He who is forgiven little, loves little" (v. 47). There is a close connection between our personal sense of God's forgiveness and the depth of our love for Him—and, may I add, our level of self-righteousness.

We tend not to see the depths of our depravity. Our goodness, our affluence, our ability to control many facets of our lives, our propensity to rationalize, blame-shift, and justify ourselves, our focus on particular sins rather than sin itself—all contribute to a superficial awareness of our critical need for God's forgiveness. We simply do not believe that there is a Hitler in us until we are forced out of our comfort zones, fall flat on our faces, lose control, or commit some major public transgression. Since good religious people are generally better than the norm in society, we are less likely to see the depths of our depravity. Our love for Christ may well be shallow.

Perhaps an even more telling gauge of our self-righteousness is the stance from which we offer our forgiveness to those who have wronged us. Is our forgiveness offered from a pedestal? When sinned against, it is easy to occupy a superior position, extending forgiveness like a benevolent dictator to those who demonstrate their sincere repentance. Our stance is top down; our demeanor is paternalistic; our attitude is self-righteous. In Matthew 6:1–18, Jesus contrasted true piety with people-pleasing religiosity. Speaking about prayer, Jesus delivered a stern warning about forgiveness. Forgiveness, He said, is a natural and necessary fruit of our having been forgiven by God. We must forgive those who sin against us, not like benevolent dictators from the top down but rather as fellow sinners from the bottom up. Is the forgiveness light flashing on your dash?

Warning Light #3:
A Wrong Sense Of Grace and Fairness

How do I respond to working hard and being ignored when the less-deserving are rewarded and promoted? Fairness is a sense learned early in life; in fact, fairness is one of the most well-developed senses of a child. One phrase I hear frequently as a father is, "That isn't fair!" Something deep within children recoils against perceived unfairness, particularly from parents. Why is this so? Why do children (and adults) react so strongly when it seems that they are not getting what they deserve or that they are being treated less desirably than another? We all have an innate sense of self-interest and fairness that we seek to protect at all costs. We demand at least equal treatment.

But grace and fairness do not mix well. Grace by definition is unfair. It extends favor to the undeserving. Mark well what happened in the soul of a goody-two-shoes-son when a prodigal younger brother returned and dear old dad graciously threw a party (Luke 15:11–32). He felt resentful. All the tightly guarded venom of his soul spewed out on his father. He could not bring himself to rejoice with those who rejoice.[1] His father's grace to his wayward brother brought to the surface the poison of the elder's self-righteousness.

A similar complaint was heard when those who expended little time and effort received the same wage as those who had worked longer and sacrificed more: "It isn't fair!" Jesus told a parable about grace couched in the activities of the daily workplace of His culture (Matthew 20:1–16). Some farm workers who worked for one hour were paid the same as those who had worked for the entire day. The full-day workers cried "unfair!"

Take careful note when your heart cries unfair. God may be giving an opportunity for a sneak peek into the self-righteousness of your heart. One reason you and I so strongly react to perceived unfairness is that we cherish a too-lofty view of ourselves. We conveniently forget, "There is none righteous, not even one; there is none who understands, there is none who seeks for God; all have turned aside, together they have become useless; there is none who does good, there is not even one" (Romans 3:10–12). We forget that we were self-indulgent children of wrath upon whom a gracious God piled priceless gifts; we were spiritual trash whom God turned into trophies (Ephesians 2:1–10). Fairness without grace would have condemned us all to hell. Is the fairness light flashing on your dash?

Warning Light #4:
An Unhealthy View Of Failure

How do I respond to failure or being exposed as a sinner? In the parable of the mistreated son (Matthew 21:33–46), Jesus implicated the Pharisees in His looming execution. Jesus depicted the Pharisees as those who were planning to kill the son of the vineyard owner and as those who had rejected the chief cornerstone. The parable was a stern warning designed to produce repentance. But the Pharisees, rather than taking the rebuke as a warning and turning to God, turned on the Lord and tried to arrest Him (vv. 45–46). His exposure of their heart produced not repentance but revenge; not cries for mercy but cries for murder.

What do we do when we are exposed, when we fail or are found out? Do we fall prostrate before God or do we attack the prophet?

A warning is in order, however, about our response to personal sin and failure: There can be an unhealthy brokenness and a false humility. We must not emphasize the depravity of man, as some do, to the extent that it denies the dignity of being created in God's image and denies the worth of being the object of Christ's sacrifice on the cross. That is a religious counterfeit of the genuine work of God. The Christian virtue of being "poor in spirit" displays a *genuine* humility and dependence on God, even in failure and sin. But being poor in spirit is sometimes debased into poor-spiritedness: "I'm just a failure; there is no hope for me and I'm going to quit." That's a poor caricature of what Christ had in mind. Some also emphasize our fallen nature but do not communicate adequately the positive resources that God has given to triumph, in effect elevating Romans 7 at the expense of Romans 8. Exposing depravity without accessing divine resources is a counterfeit. Morbid introspection, likewise, is a cheap substitute for true brokenness and often leads to depression. Is the failure light flashing on your dash? Warning!

Contempt, forgiveness, fairness, failure. Each of these is a telltale sign of self-righteousness, a warning light on the dashboard of our lives. Each can help us see self-righteousness within. However, religious people routinely ignore these subtle warnings. Jesus did not.

HOW JESUS ATTACKED SELF-RIGHTEOUSNESS

The Master was masterful at exposing hidden self-righteousness. With those who understood the gravity of their spiritual sickness, He was quick to extend grace and forgiveness (Matthew 9:9–13; Luke 19:1–10; John 4:1–42). But with those who thought that they were spiritually healthy (Matthew 9:12–13), Jesus goaded them in the direction of brokenness, the first principle and indispensable ingredient of true righteousness (Matthew 5:3). Jesus loved them far too much to let them remain oblivious to their diseased condition. Two well-known Gospel accounts demonstrate how Jesus confronts self-righteousness in religious people.

The Parable of the Good Samaritan

Perhaps the most potent passage providing insight into Jesus' methodology as He performed spiritual surgery on religious people is the parable of the good Samaritan (Luke 10:25–37). This beloved story is often misunderstood and misapplied. For unknown reasons, many expositors and commentators ignore the context when seeking to explain this immortal parable. Clearly the person Jesus addressed was educated in the Scriptures: a lawyer, the contemporary equivalent of a theologian. He was sufficiently well-versed in the Law to give good biblical answers to Jesus' questions. Moreover, he apparently had some interest, even if only intellectual, in the way of salvation, as evidenced by his question, "Teacher, what shall I do to inherit eternal life?" But this man was self-righteous and spiritually blind. And he was confident enough to stand toe-to-toe with God incarnate and seek to justify himself (v. 29). This self-justification is the key to the parable and the root sin that the loving Savior must expose in order to bring this man to repentance.

So how did Jesus confront the lawyer with his self-righteousness? Did He tell, as is often suggested, a nice Sunday school story about a nice Samaritan man who did a nice deed to a needy soul by the side of the road? No; for Jesus to have told a nice little Sunday school story to a theologically astute, self-justifying human being would have been the essence of lovelessness.

Jesus is not Mr. Rogers singing, "Won't you be my neighbor?" The lawyer who heard the parable needed spiritual heart surgery, not cookies and milk! The Divine Surgeon wielded His sharp scalpel with extraordinary skill.

Jesus had lifesaving heart surgery to perform. He made three incisions. Each cut deeper into the tissue of self-righteousness. Jesus first cut through the religious lawyer's skin by placing him in the story as the priest or Levite, with whom he could readily identify. No doubt the lawyer prided himself on the fact that he loved his neighbor as himself. In reality, however, he had narrowly defined "neighbor," and even within that narrow definition, he had failed. He, like many of us, elevated his perceived righteousness above what the facts warranted.

The first incision, then, is to position the lawyer as the uncaring priest and Levite in the parable. In His second incision, Jesus cuts through the spiritual sternum by showing in the actions of the Samaritan the actual standards of God. Loving one's neighbor involves eyes that see human need, not skin color, class, or country. Such love also requires a heart of compassion that pities his plight; hands that get dirty washing his wounds; a schedule that flexes in response to the neighbor's situation; resources that are released to meet his needs. Such love also prompted the Samaritan to relinquish personal comforts in order to provide proper care.

If one had perfect success in this pursuit, he may have the right to stand before God and defend his righteousness. Of course, that is not possible to do all the time. Therefore, to convince ourselves that we meet God's standards, we often externalize and rationalize His commands regarding service and sacrifice. In effect, we lower God's standards. We make God's demands less demanding and ignore imperatives that we know we cannot achieve. For instance, we may define the length of a quiet time (seven minutes) that qualifies us as having spent time with God. We quantify our giving (10 percent) to assure us that we meet God's standards. And when we succeed by these standards, we feel profoundly proud.

In the third incision, Jesus' laser knife cuts through to the heart tissue. Having already laid bare the lawyer's padded self-appraisal, Jesus cuts deep into the lawyer's pride, exposing his folly in despising and judging others. In making the hated Samaritan the hero of the story, Jesus pierces the Jewish lawyer to the core of his being. Samaritans were universally despised by the Jews for their half-breed ancestry, non-Law-keeping morality, and unorthodox theology. Nothing could be more offensive to a Jew than to consider a Samaritan better than a purebred, Law-keeping, good-living Jewish theologian. The listening lawyer must have winced as he perceived Jesus had compared him unfavorably with the despised Samaritan.

Perhaps in our day Jesus might have framed the story as the parable of the good homosexual New Ager. There are people in our world, like homosexual individuals or those who embrace New Age theology, who may well be more compassionate than the majority of people found in a Christian church on any given Sunday. Some homosexuals, for instance, give all they have to help friends who are dying of AIDS. It would be hard to find many evangelicals who match their compassion! We cannot justify the homosexual lifestyle, but if we try to work our way to God, we must recognize some pagans will surpass our good deeds.

The point of the parable, then, is an answer to the lawyer's original question about eternal life: There is no way to earn it. We must give up any attempts to justify ourselves in the sight of God. Instead, in humility we must receive the free gift of God's grace that we will never deserve.

Lest self-righteousness creep in our souls, each of us must accept these truths: My actual performance of righteousness is far lower than I think. God's standards of righteousness are far higher than I can even conceive, much less attain. And people whom I despise for their lack of rightness can actually be more righteous than I.

The Parable of the Pharisee and the Tax Collector

Sitting on my office credenza is a rugged clay sculpture illustrating the parable of the Pharisee and the tax collector. The sculpture has two busts facing opposite directions; they are mounted on ball bearings that turn easily. The Sculptor, Tracie Guthrie, has inscribed on the base the text of the parable (Luke 18:9–14).

One of the busts portrays a pious-looking Pharisee, eyes and nose elevated, hands folded, phylacteries and tassels prominent, who is singing his own praises to God. The text astutely notes he was praying to himself. He was telling God what he hadn't been doing, the vices from which he abstained, how he was unlike others. Then he recited the religious acts in which he did engage. The list, though short, is impressive. He thought himself to be a cut above the rest.

The second bust on the sculpture is that of a tax collector, his face downcast and his eyes fixed toward the ground. His hands are not folded like the Pharisee's; instead he is beating his breast, a gesture of extreme anguish. And his head is not covered but bare and disheveled. All his body language demonstrates humility and penitence. The text notes that his prayer was short, "God, be merciful to me, the sinner." Jesus said he went down to his house justified—the sinner not the saint. The one who was broken and knew he was in need of God's grace found it. The one who acknowledged the grip of sin on his soul and cried out for God's help walked away a free man, fully justified.

With this short and simple parable, Jesus once again struck at the subtle sin of self-righteousness. As the context explicitly tells us (v. 9), self-righteousness and contempt for others are under divine scrutiny. Jesus desired to turn the Pharisees' preconceived notions upside down. Repentant attitudes, not religious acts, are meritorious with God. A worthy track record does not count with God as much as humble acknowledgment of one's unworthiness. An awareness of our own unrighteousness is the first essential step toward justification. Truly the way up is down.

Jesus' Masterful Methods

Jesus' ways of dealing with the self-righteous and religious people are instructive. First, *Jesus seemed to specialize in using shock therapy with the religious*. He was fearless in putting His divine finger on the faults of the faithful. He did not sugarcoat His message or attempt to burrow His way into religious hearts by tiptoeing around sin and cultivating a "positive mental attitude." Instead He startled the religious by saying and doing things that must have seemed absurd, such as, "Blessed are the bankrupt; happy are the sad" (Matthew 5:3–4, author's paraphrase). What a way to start His most famous sermon! Jesus knew that religious, self-righteous people easily become spiritually deaf. He loved them enough to break through, often in shocking ways. (To compare good religious people unfavorably with a Samaritan and a tax gatherer was staggering.)

Second, *the master teacher reached out to the Pharisees through stories*. Several of the best-known parables were addressed to the Pharisees (Luke 10:25–37; 15:1–32; 18:9–14), a fact of which many Bible readers are unaware. Why did Jesus do this? Stories have a way of penetrating the soul where exhortation cannot. It is not incidental that a story told by the prophet Nathan to King David broke through David's deceit (1 Samuel 11–12). Similarly, Jesus often employed word pictures to hook his hearers and address their hearts. Stories entice us to step into the action, identify with the characters, and bond with the victims. They arouse our emotions as they engage our minds. And they can effectively lower the boom in ways that prevent us from escaping. Jesus thus often dealt with the self-righteous indirectly, not directly; emotionally, not intellectually; in story rather than sermon.

Third, *Jesus consistently raised rather than lowered God's standards*. We religious people tend to do the opposite. He who beckoned us to come to Him to find rest assured us that His yoke is easy, His burden is light (Matthew 11:28–30), and His empowering us is great. Yet He also seemed to make the commands of the Scripture more difficult, higher, broader, deeper. Superficially I would have expected compassionate Jesus to be so concerned about my self-esteem that He would want me to succeed, or at least to think I am succeeding, in the pursuit of righteousness. But Jesus constantly made the way *harder,* not easier, to follow Christ (Mark 8:34–38), do good (Matthew 19:16–26), invest time or money (Matthew 6:19–34), contain lust and anger (Matthew 5:21–30), seek greatness (Mark 10:35–45), offer forgiveness (Mark 11:25–26), and deny self and take up a cross (Mark 8:34), to mention just a few of the hard sayings of Jesus. Jesus is more concerned about my brokenness than my self-esteem, my humility than my self-confidence. The rest that Jesus promised and the yoke that He called "easy" are available only by depending on Him and not on our own efforts.

Finally, *Jesus attacked inward sins as often as (and sometimes more than) outward sins*. Sometimes He seemed more concerned with pride than paganism, greed than gluttony, arrogance than alcohol, covert sins than overt sins, attitudes than actions, hypocrisy than hedonism. Jesus knew that defilement was essentially a habit of the heart.

THE WAY OUT OF SELF-RIGHTEOUSNESS

Any cure for Pharisaism must begin with a growing awareness and admission of depravity and dependency. After all, the fundamental flaw of Pharisaism is a superficial understanding of one's personal depravity and a corresponding failure to depend fully on God's grace.

A program that has helped numerous people recover from alcoholism is Alcoholics Anonymous. One of the reasons that AA and its Twelve Steps of recovery have worked is that they have tapped the power of brokenness. The first and second steps say:

1. We admitted we were powerless over alcohol—that our lives had become unmanageable.
2. We came to believe that a power greater than ourselves could restore us to sanity.

The more spiritually alive and mature we are, the more we recognize how far short we fall of the glory of God. The closer we get to a mirror, the more clearly we perceive our imperfections. The mirror for Christians is Christ. Therefore, it should not surprise us that those who have known Him best have been most aware of their imperfections and most appreciative of His love and grace. The apostle Paul, the self-proclaimed "foremost" of sinners (1 Timothy 1:15), could never seem to get over the marvel of a salvation that would include him, one who had killed Stephen, an innocent man with the face of an angel (Acts 6:15). But it was this perspective that uniquely qualified Paul to bring the truth of the gospel to the world (1 Timothy 1:12–17).[2]

Most of us, however, have a superficial understanding of our depravity. We are subtly enticed by our culture toward the notion of our innate goodness. A national *self-esteem movement* rightly sees the goodness but overlooks the evil. How much more true to life the balance of dignity and depravity that the Bible affirms! A *victimization movement* searches for causes outside ourselves for the flaws in our character and behavior. How much healthier to take responsibility for our faults without denying the reality that others do evil things to us as well. A *self-love movement* contends that if we only loved ourselves, we could overcome most of the demons within. The Bible, however, simply assumes that we naturally love ourselves (Ephesians 5:28–29, 33) and calls us by God's enablement to love God and others, neither of which is natural. Finally, the ever-present *self-help movement* shouts compellingly from every bookstore and magazine rack, "You can do it! Marshal the goodness within and work hard enough at it, and nothing is impossible." This movement ignores the intoxicating pull of depravity and the necessity of God's help.

The church likewise plays into the strategy of the Evil One, who loves to blind us to our depravity and dependency. Religion, true and false, exerts an inexorable pull. Though we believe in salvation by grace, at times we try to sanctify ourselves by gut power. We who love grace easily slip into law. We multiply activities and projects that leave us feeling that we are truly working hard for the kingdom. We soft-peddle sin in order to help us feel good about ourselves.[3] Or perhaps, even worse, we rail on sin such that sinners are forced to go underground and look outside the church for the grace of God.

Sometimes the church even promotes a spiritual pilgrimage of works. Thus in England, one can read the revealing gravestone of John Berridge. For twenty-six years Berridge was a believer trying to please Christ with good works. His marker reads, in part:

> Here lie the earthly remains of John Berridge, late vicar of Everton . . .
>
> I was born in sin, February 1716.
> Remained ignorant of my fallen state till 1730.
> Lived proudly on faith and works for salvation till 1754.
> Was admitted to Everton Vicarage, 1755.
> Fled to Jesus alone for refuge, 1756.
> Fell asleep in Christ, January 22, 1793.[4]

So what is the antidote to the poison of self-righteousness? We must see ourselves as we really are. We must allow God's Word and His Spirit to do spiritual surgery on our hearts. We must recognize our human tendency to cover up, hide, and blame others for our sin, a diabolical trio of evils we have perfected since the Garden of Eden. To do this we must steadfastly resist enormous cultural and ecclesiastical pressures.

The best means to see ourselves as we really are is not through comparison with others nor morbid introspection, but by deliberately getting with God. And when we see ourselves truly, against the standard of Jesus, pride has no place!

Honesty with ourselves and with God should lead to honesty with others about ourselves. We cannot project a false image of spirituality. For us to tell only the successes of our lives and not the struggles and failures removes us from a significant means to relate to people and to reach them effectively. After all, most of us learn by our mistakes. Remember, the Bible tells us honest stories about God's people—the good, the bad, and the ugly!

SOME POSITIVE FRUITS OF
FACING SELF-RIGHTEOUSNESS

Granted, personal depravity is a negative, even depressing topic. Can anything positive and uplifting come out of all this? Is there an upside to being aware of my depravity, of seeing my self-righteousness? Yes! Facing self-righteousness produces at least five good fruits.

Fruit #1: Christ's righteousness. Understanding our lack of righteousness is the front door for receiving Christ's righteousness. Speaking to a Pharisee, Jesus said, "He who humbles himself will be exalted" (Luke 18:14). God is near to those who know they need His mercy and ask for His help. Those who comprehend the depth of their depravity also appreciate the height of God's love (Luke 7:47).

Fruit #2: Graciousness. Experiencing God's grace gives rise to the fruit of graciousness. Understanding God's grace motivates us to be gracious to others. We become people of compassion rather than contempt, with a love for grace that surpasses the law. We cease judging others without first having judged ourselves (Matthew 7:1–5). And we are qualified to gently perform the spiritual task of restoring fallen comrades (Galatians 6:1).

Fruit #3: Freedom. The security of Christ's unconditional love frees us from fear of people. Thus, you and I can tell the truth about ourselves and take risks for His sake. God knows all, and yet we have received His unconditional and costly love. Therefore, we can become comfortable with our humanity and free to admit our faults, for we have nothing to hide, nothing to prove, and no pretense to maintain. It is amazing how God's wisdom works. We think that by hiding the truth we are better able to help others. However, by telling the truth we are set free and often are better able to assist others. There is great freedom in not having to expend the energy to maintain a facade.

Fruit #4: Confidence. This may sound like a contradiction in terms: How can someone who is broken have confidence? Brokenness that leads us to God results in a sense of confidence, not groveling self-condemnation. The apostle Paul seems to find this spirit of confidence in Romans 8 after he has wrestled with the depths of his sin in Romans 7. Likewise a spirited stallion running in the wild without control has little purpose or benefit to anyone. But that stallion, broken and brought under control by a skillful trainer, runs with focused power, fresh confidence, and greater impact. In the same way, we never truly reach our fullest potential until we come under submission to our Creator.

Fruit #5: Security. When we face the worst about ourselves and receive God's acceptance, we find the source of our security. God does not reject us! He knows everything about us: our secret sins, our malevolent motives, our unexpressed thoughts. He knows it all and yet He loves us. That realization gives us great security. The One who knows us best loves us most. One of the great fears in human relationships is that if others really knew it all, they would reject us. Not so with God. As one preacher puts it: "When we see ourselves at our worst, we experience God at His best."[5]

We began this chapter with the story of a leader who learned the hard way the personal truth of Oswald Chambers's statement, "An unguarded strength is a double weakness." Thinking he was safe and secure, the leader neglected to be vigilant and fell in an area of perceived invincibility. Where we know we are weak, we tend to post a guard. But where we think we are strong, we take our security for granted. As evangelical Protestants, who most pride ourselves on the doctrine of justification by faith and the imputed righteousness of Christ, could it be we have failed to guard our greatest strength: having Christ's righteousness and not our own? Have we fallen prey to the subtle, yet pervasive religious sin of self righteousness? I think so. Self righteousness sometimes masquerades as extreme righteousness.

Chapter Five
WHEN BIBLE KNOWLEDGE BLINDS AND BINDS

A few years ago a large group of gay-rights activists were demonstrating in Washington, D.C., when a handful of outspoken Christian protesters confronted many of them. The Christians shouted derogatory and inflammatory slogans as a group of gays marching under the flag of the Metropolitan Community Church sang "Jesus Loves Me." Author Philip Yancey observed the encounter and later wrote in *Christianity Today:*

> The abrupt ironies in that scene of confrontation stayed with me long after I left Washington. On the one side were "righteous" Christians defending pure doctrine (not even the National Council of Churches has deemed the MCC worthy of membership). On the other were "sinners," many of whom openly admit to homosexual practice. Yet one side spewed out hate and the other sang of Jesus' love.[1]

How is it that those who know and honor the Bible sometimes fail to demonstrate the character it commends throughout? It is embarrassing to us and confusing to the world. Perhaps part of the problem is a confusion about of the role of the Bible in the spiritual life.

DOES BIBLE KNOWLEDGE MAKE ONE GODLY?

The Scriptures and Me

As noted in chapter 1, I was immersed in the Scriptures early in life. My church put a heavy emphasis upon mouthing the right doctrines, memorizing the right verses, and mastering Bible content. I read the Bible, memorized it, systematically dissected it, studied it, and sometimes applied it to my life.

In truth I cherish the biblical foundation I received. The truths of God's Word dominate my perspective on life, for which I am eternally grateful. The Bible has been my lifelong guide and an anchor that gives stability to my life amid various storms.

But during my college years, my belief in the magical nature of the Bible to transform lives and the obligation placed on God to accomplish it began to be shaken. Doubts arose that challenged my certainty that people with right theology and a good knowledge of the Bible must inevitably become godly. The first rumblings occurred as I observed people who studied, memorized, taught, and preached the Bible whose attitudes and actions seemed to be not better but increasingly bitter. When Bible people didn't resemble the God of the Bible, I began to wonder if "God's promise" that His Word "shall not return . . . void" (Isaiah 55:11 KJV) was really true. I awakened sadly to the prevalence of hypocrisy among Bible-oriented people.

I also was shaken as I started to gain some familiarity with church history. I learned that Bible knowledge did not provide a foolproof hedge against sin. It can and should help. However, often those who had substantial familiarity with the Bible missed its message and misunderstood God. Sometimes "God's people" were the perpetrators of extensive evil. Often theological error springs from pulpits, not pews; seminaries, not small groups.

In addition, I was convicted as I looked into my own soul. I recognized that the Bible was not transforming me. I had acquired much Bible knowledge and maintained a regular practice of Bible study, but somehow there was not a straight line correspondence between Bible study and Christlikeness in my life.

Finally, I encountered Bible passages that defied my simple stereotype of "put in Scripture, out comes spirituality." Rather, I noticed that "knowledge makes arrogant, but love edifies" (1 Corinthians 8:1–3) and that receiving the Word without responding to it results in self-deception (James 1:22). Jesus taught in the parable of the soils (Matthew 13:1–23) that the key to fruitfulness in life is the soil of the heart, not the seed of the Word. Germination depends not on the quality of the seed, which is perfect, but the condition of the heart, which can vary greatly. The New Testament warns us that Bible teachers can be off base.[2] And then, of course, I met my friends the Pharisees.

The Scriptures and the Pharisees

As I became increasingly familiar with them, I discovered that few knew the Word of God as well as the Pharisees. They made an art and a science of studying the Old Testament. They knew the middle verse and letter, had counted all the commands, and no doubt some had memorized all 613 of them. (In contrast, few people today can recite the Ten Commandments and the Beatitudes.) The Pharisees were insistent on the correct interpretation of the Scriptures. Moreover, the Pharisees were not content, as frequently we are, to simply know the content of God's Word. They desired to obey it as well. So they aided its application by devising religious rules. But for all their Bible knowledge about God, many of them did not know God and therefore did not recognize God incarnate. Why?

Their right doctrine had produced wretchedness instead of righteousness. Proper doctrine is essential, yet even today it can give a false sense of spiritual security and superiority without true spiritual reality. Bible knowledge can calcify rather than tenderize the heart. It can blind and bind.

How can that be? Bible instruction can easily be diverted from its God-intended purpose: love of God and fellow human beings. In its place is a new, lesser purpose: the Bible as an object of curiosity and fruitless spiritual debate (1 Timothy 1:3–11). The Bible can become an end in itself instead of the means to an end. Subtly almost everything of God can and will be counterfeited by the Evil One, resulting in a sinister combination of an external appearance of goodness with a hidden dark side. The ultimate danger of being people of the Book is that we can acquire a knowledge about God without actually coming to know God.

THE PHARISEES' DOCTRINAL STATEMENT

God well understands this human propensity to substitute knowledge for spiritual reality. So He gave us detailed revelation about the Pharisees. And when we look at their doctrine, we

learn again that the Pharisees are us. They adhered to the orthodox core of Judaism, and much of their belief system parallels
ours. Excluding certain statements about Jesus, nuances regarding salvation, and the omission of any mention of the Holy Spirit,
the Pharisees would sign our evangelical doctrinal statements.
Their doctrine was right on but some of their hearts were dead
wrong. Clearly, they demonstrate that right doctrine does not
guarantee right hearts. "Right doctrine" may even mask the
deeper realities of the heart.

No less than Jesus Himself affirmed the Pharisees' orthodoxy. He said, "The scribes and the Pharisees have seated
themselves in the chair of Moses; therefore all that they tell you,
do and observe" (Matthew 23:2–3a). Though Jesus acknowledges
that the Pharisees were usurpers of the place of the authoritative
teachers of Israel, He tentatively affirms their theology. The
priests and Levites were authorized by God at the time of Moses
to be the handlers of the Word of God. However, most of them
were Sadducean in belief, having rejected most of the Old Testament as a suitable source of doctrine and were influenced more
by the culture than by the Scriptures. In contrast, the Pharisees,
through the local synagogues, faithfully taught the Word of God.

The Pharisees described and defended the doctrine shared
by the majority of pious Jews. And the doctrinal affirmations of
the Pharisees are hauntingly reminiscent of Christian theology.
E. P. Sanders summarizes what they believed:

> The Pharisees believed that God was good, that he created the
> world, that he governed it, and that it would turn out as he
> wished. God chose Israel: he called Abraham, made with him a
> covenant, and laid on him a few obligations. He redeemed Israel
> from Egypt; and, having saved his people, gave them the law and
> charged them to observe it. God is perfectly reliable and will keep
> all his promises. Among these are that he will act in the future as
> he has acted in the past. . . . He can be relied on to punish disobe-
> dience and reward obedience. He is just; therefore, he never does
> the reverse. When it comes to punishment, however, his justice is
> moderated by mercy and by his promises. He does not punish as
> he might, or who could live? He does not retract his commitment
> to his people. He holds out his arms to the disobedient, urging
> them to repent and return.[3]

The above summary would have little trouble passing an evangelical orthodoxy test.

WHAT'S RIGHT WITH RIGHT DOCTRINE?

Even with proper doctrine, dangers exist, as we shall see. But let's first recognize that a solid doctrinal foundation aids spiritual growth and maturity in several ways. Here are three.

First, *faith is only as good as its object.* Many adults believe, "It doesn't matter what you believe as long as you are sincere." That conclusion is false. Some people sincerely cherish mistaken beliefs and have, or will have, to suffer the consequences. The reliability of what we believe matters much more than what we believe. Doctrine is a statement of the *truths* that undergird our faith. Doctrine defines our authority, the character and works of God, the nature and destiny of human beings, and how we are to relate to God and our fellow human beings. We who follow Christ must get our facts right (1 Timothy 4:16). If we do not, we may well become religious clones of our culture, worship false gods of our own making, and cherish false notions of ourselves.

The Pharisees knew—as we should know—that truth is essential and must be protected. When we feel passionately about God but know powerfully little about Him, we are at the mercy of the shifting sands of the culture and our own emotional state at the moment.

Second, *a right understanding of doctrine helps us to distinguish truth from error.* Counterfeits are best identified by those who are most familiar with the genuine article. Without a standard of truth, we are unable to detect small but significant departures from the truth. A solid understanding of Bible doctrine helps us to sort out truth from error.

The Pharisees were able to wend their way through a maze of competing theologies because they insisted that orthodox doctrine based on the Scriptures be protected.[4] Such discernment is desperately needed in our relativistic, complex, and subtly deceptive culture. We must know where and when to stand (Galatians 1:8–9). Without a solid grasp of core beliefs, Christians are ripe for theological deception or superstition. Without a clear understanding of the "fundamentals" of the faith, believers are easy pickings for cults and defenseless against slick and charismatic wolves in sheep's clothing.

Third, *right doctrine anchors us during troubled times.* An anchor secures a ship to solid ground, steadying it in a storm and protecting it from the raging seas. Right doctrine provides a spiritual anchor that connects us with truth, helps us keep our spiritual balance, and enables us to withstand storms. While the culture was shifting toward Hellenism, the Pharisees regarded the Word of God as their anchor. When many of the priests and Levites "went liberal," following cultural trends, the Pharisees clung to the Scriptures.

Theological ignorance is not bliss! Without a clear understanding of the essentials, we tend to move toward the extremes or we compromise the essentials. One of the most difficult assignments in our culture is to find the right biblical balance, avoiding both extremism and compromise. Doctrinal truth is never safe; it is continually being assaulted by slightly skewed notions. And it must constantly be restated in the language of the culture. Doctrine can be an invaluable anchor that connects us to God's character and promises. It allows us to build our lives on rock rather than sand.

WHAT'S WRONG WITH RIGHT DOCTRINE?

Clearly, proper doctrine can give us a solid foundation, the ability to discern truth and error, and stability in tough times. Right doctrine, however, has a potential dark side. We can misuse doctrine and strip it of its power to help us serve God and His Son and love our neighbors. There are dangers associated with a correct understanding of doctrine that most of us do not consider. Let me cite several outcomes of misused doctrine.

1. Doctrine As a Grid Through Which We Filter Out Truth

The Pharisees rejected Jesus largely because He did not fit their theological scheme. They had a well-developed messianic grid that clashed with the person and work of Jesus. They expected a king; Jesus came as a servant. They anticipated freedom from Rome; Jesus purchased freedom from sin. They looked for a crown; He looked toward a cross. They presumed that the Messiah would nicely fit into their religious system; Jesus violated this system regularly. So, rather than reexamine the Old Testament Scriptures in light of the life and instruction of Jesus, the Pharisees stuck with their grids and missed the truths He taught.

On numerous occasions Jesus challenged the theological grids of the Pharisees. When He claimed to forgive sins, the scribes' definition of deity was challenged (Matthew 9:1–6). When Jesus restored sight to two blind men and speech to a demon-possessed man in Matthew 9:27–34, the Pharisees' faulty logic made them conclude that Jesus employed Satan's power to cast out the demons (see also Matthew 12:22–37). When Jesus received the praise of the people during His Triumphal Entry, the Pharisees' rigid messianic grid forced them to reject His kingship (Luke 19:37–40). When Jesus declared His divinity in terms the Pharisees could not dismiss in John 8, they called Him derogatory names—"Born of fornication," "Samaritan," and "Demon" (vv. 41, 48)—and picked up stones to kill Him. To do otherwise would have shattered their deeply cherished theological system.

And when Jesus achieved the ultimate theological victory—His death and resurrection—the religious leaders of Judaism chose to fabricate lies and pay hush money rather than rethink their systematic theology (Matthew 28:11–15).

An excellent study in twisting the truth to support "right doctrine" is found in John 9. The narrative begins with a blind man and a theological question from the disciples, "Who sinned that this man was born blind?" The theological grid of that day promulgated a direct connection between sin and sickness. Jesus proclaimed such an exclusive connection to be erroneous, because it lacks essential puzzle pieces. For in this case, the man's blindness was part of God's design to display Jesus' glory.

When the Pharisees were asked to explain the phenomenon, they noted that the day of the healing was the Sabbath and concluded, consistent with their theological grid, that the miracle-worker must be a fraud (vv. 13–16). If God was in a miracle, He would perform it according to the Pharisees' fences.

When the former blind man was called in again by the Pharisees to testify about the miracle, they attempted to browbeat him into calling Jesus a sinner (vv. 24–25). When he calmly and comically resisted their suggestions, the Pharisees reviled him (vv. 28–29), rebuked him (v. 34), and removed him from the synagogue (v. 34).

"Right doctrine" sometimes becomes an entrenched theological system that blinds us to the truth. When ideas do not fit our grid, we generally dismiss or distort them. In the Christian world, theological systems abound and have considerable pull on our way of viewing truth. Calvinism, Arminianism, Dispensationalism, Covenantalism, Catholicism, and Pentecostalism are some theological systems that we have adopted, often by default. Perhaps we are not so steeped in our theology that we would kill for it as the Pharisees did, but we seem just as intent on sticking to our systems even straight in the face of truth. Depending on the place we choose on the Calvinist-Arminian continuum, we may select our favorite Scripture passages and ignore others. Some so fear the "social gospel" that they excise any reference to social action in the Bible and focus on evangelism instead (and others do the exact opposite). Many Christians do not want to face the problems that exposure to the other side may cause to our theological certainty. Indeed, some may resort to name-calling, labeling those who differ *heretic, heterodox* or *neo-orthodox,* even *liberal.* Some commentators write about theological opponents but do not speak to them. How might we respond if we had among us Jesus, God in human flesh, and He did not fit our fine doctrinal grid? Would we not be just as compelled as the Pharisees to put God in a box?

2. Doctrine Acquired from Teachers Rather Than by Personal Study of God's Word

Often we accept specific doctrines because of our association with trusted teachers. This reliance on experts is common and necessary within religious circles; to ignore the insights of gifted teachers is foolish and arrogant. However, to place blind trust in others to think for us spiritually is unwise. Unthinking acceptance is dangerous. We should personally study and wrestle with the Scriptures.

The Pharisees and their followers apparently followed their experts in doctrinal matters. Authority was a key issue to the Pharisees who so sought to "get it right."[5] It was simply unacceptable among the Pharisees for one to be an "independent thinker" as Jesus was. Thus the Jews were asking themselves, "How has this man (Jesus) become learned, never having been educated?" (John 7:15). Every theological tenet had to be traced back to a renowned theologian. Perhaps the people were taught to fear thinking for themselves.

What about us? Most of us tend to rely on others to think for us. We gravitate toward those who seem to have the answers that we lack and to systems that make everything fit neatly for us. In other words, we depend on grids and gurus to help us make sense out of a confusing world. But what happens when the grids through which we view life are distorted? What happens when the gurus to whom we have attached ourselves are mistaken? What happens to our faith when our trusted teachers mislead us or fall? I have personally known several pastors who have had "successful" ministries yet were found to be sinning morally. Only one book is our authority and only one Teacher belongs on a pedestal.

3. A Spiritual Smugness and False Sense of Security

Spiritual smugness is the exact opposite of what God seeks. No doubt the Pharisees, like the teachers at Ephesus that Timothy had to confront, were confident of their every assertion and sure of themselves (1 Timothy 1:7). They aspired to teach the Scriptures and knew they had an excellent grasp of their material. They had no lack of confidence in their content or their ability to teach. However, Paul tells us that their teaching was fruitless and their motivation selfish. Sometimes those of us who treasure right doctrine think we possess an inside track on the truth of God. God informs us, however, that supposed knowledge, lacking in a pure love of God, is a sure route to spiritual arrogance (1 Corinthians 8:1–3). There is something about being cocksure of possessing the truth that breeds spiritual cockiness. Sometimes good theology subtly breeds conceit, the greatest cancer of spiritual health.

4. A Weak Disciple

Right doctrine does not necessarily make good disciples (though obviously bad doctrine is disastrous for disciple-making). Indeed, one can accurately profess the faith without actually possessing it. Johnny and Julie can give the "right" answers to baptismal or confirmation questions but not have a heart commitment to Christ. One can hold to orthodox theology, as the Pharisees did (Matthew 23:2–3a), while not practicing what is preached (vv. 3b–4). We can memorize all the "right answers" and even impress our peers without ever having struggled to make the faith our own. Good disciples combine truth with grace, faith, and obedience. The essential mark of a disciple of Christ's is not so much right doctrine as rightly motivated love.

DEVELOPING A BALANCED VIEW OF DOCTRINE

In spite of all these pitfalls, we know right doctrine is essential. How do we develop a balance, so that we can confidently affirm certain doctrinal truths, defending them with vigor and yet maintain humility and love? We must begin with a nonnegotiable core of beliefs that are explicitly taught in the Bible, commonly held by God's people throughout church history, and equally valid in all cultures of the world. We must be sure that our doctrinal basics are truly biblical and biblically balanced. Then we should stick to the basics, fight for the basics, and be willing to die for the basics.

Maintaining doctrinal integrity, balance, and tolerance is not easy. some suggestions are discussed in "Balanced and Right Doctrine" (see "The Right Way"). In summary, they are:

1. We need to be able to discern between nonnegotiables and negotiables. (A wise and godly person will be able to tell the difference.)

2. We must be constant learners, showing humility about what we know, and knowing we have more to learn as servants of God. We should not resort to ungodly methods to promote our theology, such as ridicule, name-calling, deception, coercion, or manipulation. (And yet we, like the Pharisees, frequently do these things.)

3. We must have a settled conviction that truth is powerful and questions are not to be feared. Questions and challenges make us think, and thinking makes us grow.

BIBLE STUDENTS EXTRAORDINAIRE

When the apostle Paul wrote, "as to the Law, a Pharisee" (Philippians 3:5), he was affirming his extensive knowledge of the Scriptures, a Pharisaic trademark. The Pharisees were doctrinally orthodox, primarily because they loved God's Word and seriously studied it. Jesus affirmed their dedication to the Word of God when He said to the Pharisees, "You search the Scriptures because you think that in them you have eternal life; it is these that bear witness of Me" (John 5:39). The historian Josephus, the Mishnah, and the New Testament all affirm the Pharisees' excellent knowledge of Scripture.

THE RIGHT WAY

Balanced and Right Doctrine

The Pharisees were exemplary in their pursuit of doctrinal truth. We, too, would be wise to develop a die-for core of beliefs. How do we determine right doctrine and show balance in how we handle that doctrine before God and our fellow man?

First, we develop doctrinal basics that are true to the Scriptures. Doctrine that is based on the Bible is doctrine to fight for, even to die for.

Second, we discern between nonnegotiables and negotiables. "In essentials, unity; in nonessentials, liberty; in all things, charity" is often-quoted and good advice. Those who wish to avoid Pharisaism must develop godly discernment.

Third, we must be constant learners, not theological know-it-alls. Humility, flexibility, and a willingness to change are theological virtues.

Fourth, we should not resort to ungodly methods, as the Pharisees did, to promote our theology. Ridicule, name-calling, stereotyping, slander, impugning motives, and power plays are all telltale signs that something is amiss. So are sarcasm, deception, coercion, manipulation, and use of force. Flaw-finding is simple and takes little spiritual insight. The Pharisees were intent of surfacing flaws and used whatever means were available to discredit Jesus. Sometimes we too find flaws and discredit people and movements. Would it not be better for the making of disciples to encourage freedom but teach discernment?

Fifth, we must have a settled conviction that truth is powerful and questions are not to be feared. I remember leading a small group Bible study on the book of Romans, early in my ministry as a pastor. When one of the women in the group invited her husband to join us, the dynamics quickly changed. A doctor of internal medicine, he had been educated in Catholic parochial schools and was bright, outspoken, and full of tough questions. Before he joined the group, we would blithely recite the right answers by rote to the questions in the workbook. But when he arrived, few of our previous answers were acceptable to him. He would goad us until we had to think for a change. When we left our grid and guru-given answers and began to think again, we grew; and, not incidentally, the doctor became convinced of Christ's identity.

As John Stott notes, the Pharisees and scribes took Bible study very seriously:

The scribes, for example, whose task it was to copy and teach the sacred text, subjected it to the closest scrutiny. They weighed its every syllable. They went so far as to count up the number of words, even letters, of each book. And they gave themselves [to] all this labour, not only for the sake of accurate copying but because they foolishly imagined that eternal life consisted in such accurate knowledge.[6]

The Pharisees argued about the relative priority of God's commandments and how they could best be summarized (Matthew 22:34–36). Every word of the Old Testament was important and worthy of study.[7] In keeping with Psalm 19:10, the Pharisees valued the Scriptures more than gold.

Though the Pharisees knew the words of the Bible, many did not understand the message of the Bible or recognize its Messiah. They knew the letter of the Word; however, some did not understand or incarnate its spirit. Their foreheads were filled with Scripture (literally), yet they neglected to notice the calcifying process that was taking place in their hearts. They lost sight of the fact that the Word of God is a means, not an end in itself. It had become to some academic rather than practical. The Pharisees teach us that Bible study can be a dangerous profession. It can blind the eyes, puff up the head, and harden the heart!

As later chapters will explore in greater detail, the Pharisees saw themselves as guardians of tradition (chapter 7) and builders of fences (chapter 8). Their goal in these areas was not to preserve the status quo but to make certain that God's law was protected and God's will communicated. They were practical people who sought to balance the unchangeable commandments of God with the changing cultural realities of the Jewish people. So they enshrined certain practices, derived from Scripture, of course, and defined in concrete terms what obedience looked like.[8]

"HAVE YOU NOT READ?"

It is ironic that Jesus commonly corrected the biblically astute Pharisees by pointing out their insufficient Bible knowledge. Frequently, He asked the Pharisees, "Have you not read?" (See Matthew 12:3, 5; 19:4; 21:16, 42; 22:31.) This was akin to an itinerant country preacher asking an erudite and well-respected seminary professor, "Do you mean to tell me that you never read this in the Bible?"

By examining the texts where Jesus chastised the Pharisees for not knowing the Scriptures, we can discover for ourselves a helpful list of the dangers we face as we grow in Bible knowledge.

A Teaching Encounter in Matthew 12

Jesus poked holes in the Pharisees' airtight system three times in Matthew 12:1–14. At issue was the Sabbath and what is "lawful." Jesus and His disciples were being criticized for threshing grain, a clear violation of Pharisaic Sabbath traditions. Jesus responded by pointing out some Old Testament holes in the Pharisees' understanding of Scripture (vv. 3–4, 5, 7).

Jesus countered the Pharisees' accusations with an appeal to Scripture. In verses 3–4 Jesus answered the Pharisees with the words, "Have you not read?" He cited an example of David's "breaking the law" (1 Samuel 21:1–6) to meet a physical need by eating the sacred bread despite the prohibition of Leviticus 24:5–9. Again in verse 5, Jesus asked, "Have you not read?" as He noted the practice of the priests' weekly "breaking the Sabbath" to carry out their God-ordained duties (Numbers 28:9–10). Priests obviously were exempt from the Sabbath law to work so that others could worship. Then in verse 7, Jesus again chided the Pharisees with the words, "But if you had known what this means" and then quoted Hosea 6:6.

What principles regarding the Scriptures was Jesus trying to teach in this passage? First, *the Pharisees did not distinguish between the Word of God (written Torah) and human traditions (oral Torah)*. They put tradition and truth on the same level, as we unknowingly do also. Second, *the Pharisees woodenly inter-*

preted God's Word in such a way that subtle distinctions, nuances, and balances that God intended were missed. Perhaps they, like us, focused on the prescriptions and prohibitions of the Bible but neglected the descriptions. Though it is right to give the greater weight to imperatives over examples, examples do serve to round out the truth of God's Word. Third, in their attempt to vigorously apply the Law to life, *the Pharisees missed God's priorities*, for God places compassion above ritual (Hosea 6:6; Matthew 9:13; 12:7; 23:23).

A Teaching Encounter in Matthew 19

With the words "Have you not read?" Jesus sidestepped the Pharisees' trick question regarding divorce and revisited God's original intention for marriage (Matthew 19:4). Jesus was being asked to choose sides between the two great Pharisaic rabbis, Hillel (the moderate) and Shammai (the hard-liner), on the issue of divorce. Hillel taught that divorce was permissible for a variety of "indecencies," including an improperly cooked meal. Shammai limited divorce to the single ground of gross sexual sin. The Pharisees, however, knew the Scripture well enough to counter Jesus' appeal to Genesis with instructions from Deuteronomy. "Why," they asked, "does Moses in Deuteronomy 24:1–4 allow divorce?" This time Jesus went beneath the words of Scripture to the hard heart of the matter.

What was Jesus teaching about the Scriptures in this confrontation? First, *the Pharisees evaluated truth by their favorite current interpretation rather than by going back to the original source*. Second, the Pharisees were quick to pick up on the details of Scripture while *missing the foundational principles* (see also Matthew 23:23). Third, *the Pharisees looked for loopholes in the Law to justify their sin* rather than the heart of the Law to draw them to God—just as we sometimes do.

Two Encounters in Matthew 21

In Matthew 21, Jesus twice confronted and corrected the Pharisees, pointing out their ignorance of the Scriptures. Jesus' first "Have you never read?" was spoken after He had cleansed the temple a second time (Matthew 21:12–17). People, particularly children, had begun to praise Him. The indignant religious leaders asked if Jesus heard the messianic praise coming from children, assuming He would stop it. Jesus encouraged the children's adulation, however, and asserted that it was entirely consistent with Psalm 8:2. The Psalm obviously refers to God, and Jesus applied it to Himself.

The Pharisees with all their Bible knowledge sometimes missed the obvious. The biblically learned may become so locked into a system that they cannot see what children can. Sometimes Bible scholars stumble over truths that are apparent to the simple. (The opposite, of course, also occurs. The simple, because of their prejudices, refuse to accept what can clearly be shown to be true by scholars.)

In Kimberley, South Africa, I twice was able to visit the world's largest man-made hole, left by diamond hunters. Here Cecil Rhodes, who would fund the famous Rhodes Scholarships, began to make his fortune. As miners dug they found diamonds, and soon the area was crawling with prospectors digging as deeply as they could. I was told that the biggest diamonds, however, were found on or near the ground surface. I liken the Bible to the mine in Kimberley. As deeply as we care to dig into God's Word, we can mine spiritual treasure. The source is inexhaustible. However, the most valuable "diamonds" of God's Word, contrary to what some of us preachers would have people believe, are on the surface, not deeply mined. The most important treasures of Scripture can be grasped by children. The little treasures may require more extensive tools in order to extract.

The second time in Matthew 21 Jesus asked those who so prided themselves on their Bible knowledge "Did you never read in the Scriptures?" (v. 42) is after He told the parable of the landowner (vv. 33–46). The Pharisees apparently understood the parable and affirmed that the evil vine-growers deserved severe punishment. However, they missed the fact that they were the evil vine-growers. So Jesus made it plain for them. *You* are the ones who are rejecting the "chief cornerstone." The kingdom will be taken from *you*. The Pharisees caught His drift and wanted to seize Him. What's my point? Even when the Pharisees clearly understood the warnings of the Word, they refused to see themselves in them. They understood theoretically but not personally and *neglected to apply Scripture to themselves*. So do we.

KEEPING GOD'S PRIORITIES CENTRAL

Jesus chided the Pharisees for their insufficient Bible knowledge on yet another occasion that Matthew records (9:13), after they had complained about Jesus' enjoying table fellowship with sinners (vv. 9–11). Defending His actions, Jesus said, "But go and learn what this means," a phrase that was a common rabbinical formula to instruct students to get back to the basics. Then, quoting from Hosea 6:6, He told the Pharisees they had bypassed a principle that was dear to the heart of God: "I desire compassion, and not sacrifice." It is important when we study the Bible to *keep God's priorities central.*

Bible knowledge should incline us toward and not divert us from doing what God desires. Jesus also pointed out a problem with the Pharisees' missing God's priorities in Matthew 23:23. They scrupulously tithed (a biblical mandate) but neglected justice, mercy, and faithfulness (a believer's mission). Thus, they had a warped sense of biblical proportion. They gave inordinate weight to lesser matters. They majored on minors.

MISSING THE BIBLE'S FOCUS

Finally, Bible students can miss the Bible's focus, Jesus Christ, in their studies. Jesus declared to the Pharisees, "You search the Scriptures because you think that in them you have eternal life; it is these that bear witness of Me" (John 5:39). They had missed the central requirement and focus of the Scriptures, Jesus Himself! John Stott comments, "The quarrel Jesus had with the Jews was not over their *view* of Scripture, but over their *use* of it. They, too, accepted its divine *provenance* (although God's Word was not 'abiding' in them, v. 38). But they misunderstood its purpose."[9] The Bible is designed to bring us to Christ.

THE GOOD AND THE BAD OF BIBLE KNOWLEDGE

The Pharisees' surpassing love and excellent knowledge of the Bible served them well, enabling them to detect and defend against counterfeits, and to communicate their faith to others. The Pharisees truly desired to honor God's covenants and keep His commandments. But beneath the surface of their Bible knowledge were some significant dangers.

With their thorough knowledge of the Old Testament, the Pharisees had deluded themselves, thinking they knew more about God than they actually did. Though they knew the Bible, many did not know its Author. And confident of their mastery of God's truth, they became unteachable, a great danger spiritually.

In the milieu of extensive knowledge of God, they lost touch with essential elements of His character.

The Pharisees' Bible knowledge became a source of pride rather than humility. Charles Swindoll asserts, "Knowledge can be dangerous when it isn't balanced by love and grace. Such knowledge results in arrogance, which leads to an intolerant spirit . . . an exclusive mindset."[10] Their pride prompted the Pharisees to look askance at young upstarts like Jesus, pigeonhole others, and generally associate with like-minded people.

Additionally, the Pharisees focused on the letter of the Law but missed the spirit of the Law; they knew the words of God but not the God of the Word. They selected which portions of the Bible they liked best and skipped others. They engaged in eisegesis (reading one's own opinions into the text of Scripture) rather than exegesis (reading God's truth out of the text of Scripture). And Jesus tells us they did not practice what they preached (Matthew 23:3). Their knowledge was sometimes theoretical, not personal and practical. Often they got caught up in minutia and missed the big picture. John White in *The Fight* wrote, "Knowledge, especially biblical knowledge has the same effect as wine when it goes to your head. You become dizzily exalted. But Bible study should be conducted not with a view to *knowing about* Christ but to *knowing him* personally."[11]

WAYS TO MISAPPLY THE SCRIPTURES

Well-meaning Bible students can even allow application of Scripture to go awry, as the Pharisees illustrate. First, if application proceeds from twisted theology, twisted hearts may result. Thus it was when the Pharisees' theology of defilement (stemming from faulty views of holiness and purity) resulted in unbiblical separatism. Second, if Scripture is selectively applied, our selections may well miss God's priorities. For example, the Pharisees chose to apply passages referring to religious acts while neglecting social obligations (Matthew 9:13; 12:7; 15:3–6; 23:23–24). They gravitated to Moses' permission to write a certificate of divorce (Deuteronomy 24:1–4) but ignored God's original intent for marriage (Genesis 1:27; 2:24; Matthew 19:3–12). And they overlooked several scriptural holes in their Sabbath fences that Jesus was quick to point out (Matthew 12:1–14). Third, profession of truth does not always coincide with the practice of truth (as Jesus points out in Matthew 23:3–4). Fourth, if the dutiful application of truth is wrongly motivated, unrighteousness will result. One can apply the Scriptures to life by the power of self-discipline, of personality, or of positive reinforcement, all of this devoid of God's Spirit. One can live the Christian life by the power of the Holy Spirit or by the power of the human spirit. In many ways they look alike. Finally, the process of applying truth can easily spawn legalism.

So what went wrong with the Pharisees? Why did their disciplined study of the Scriptures not magically yield the godliness that we might expect? How could they so accurately define God without finding Him? Much the same ways that we do, distorting and misapplying Scripture.

Neither we ourselves nor the Pharisees intend such distortions. Indeed we, like the Pharisees, typically have a high commitment to the Bible as the Word of God. Unfortunately, slight twists in the use of the Bible set us up for considerable spiritual damage and deceit. Extreme righteousness can become extremely wrong!

Chapter Six
WHEN A PRIVATE RELATIONSHIP BECOMES A PUBLIC SHOW

Ringling Brothers, Barnum and Bailey advertise as "The Greatest Show on Earth." Their circus is full of death-defying acts, magnificent pageantry and beauty, hilarious entertainment, and extraordinary talent. However, it is highly doubtful that it truly deserves the "Greatest Show" accolade. Instead, a strong case can be made that religion more fittingly deserves the title "The Greatest Show." Religion has far more fans, who pay far more money and who are far more serious than circus promoters could ever hope for. No athletic contest, no entertainment spectacle, no political gathering compares to the show that religion regularly parades.

The religious show is practiced all the time, every day, in every part of the world. The big productions take place on Friday among Muslims, Saturday among Jews, and Sunday among Christians.

Human beings are inescapably religious. We have a deep-seated sense of the spiritual, a longing for the supernatural, and a deep desire to connect with the divine. Religious faith and acts are universal among cultures. Even in our modern, post-God world, people feel compelled to acknowledge their devotion to God through acts of religious piety. Sadly, however, piety can easily degenerate into a public show.

Most religions prescribe similar behaviors by which one

demonstrates his or her faith. These typically include giving, prayer, and some form of self-renunciation, often fasting. Perhaps these three are common among world religions because they cover the three directions of true piety: outward in love towards one's fellow human beings, particularly those in need; upward in prayer to God; and inward in some form of self-denial to both stimulate and prove one's devotion.[1] Such acts of piety can be good, but because they can be observed, they can also become public shows that counterfeit true spirituality. In the Pharisees we can see true and false piety in action.

PHARISAIC PIETY
True and False Piety

Our friends the Pharisees were specialists in piety, deeply serious about their devotion to God. Their piety was regular, actual, and sacrificial.

Unfortunately, Pharisaism has become almost synonymous with false piety. While none would deny the presence of hypocrisy among the ranks of the Pharisees, their false piety was probably no more pronounced than ours. They were not universally hypocritical any more than we are. The Pharisees openly acknowledged some hypocrisy among themselves and soundly condemned it. The Talmud, for example, describes seven different types of Pharisees: "(1) The 'Shoulder' Pharisee wore his good deeds on his shoulder so everyone could see them. (2) The 'wait a little' Pharisee always found an excuse for putting off a good deed. (3) The 'bruised' Pharisee shut his eyes to avoid seeing a woman and knocked into walls, bruising himself. (4) The 'humpbacked' Pharisee always walked bent double, in false humility. (5) The 'ever reckoning' Pharisee was always counting up the numbers of his good deeds. (6) The 'fearful' Pharisee always quaked in fear of the wrath of God. (7) The 'God-loving' Pharisee was a copy of Abraham who lived in faith and charity."[2] The Pharisees' piety, like ours, was a mixture of false and true.

Recognizing False Piety

Nestled in the middle of the "Sermon on the Mount" is a hard-hitting exposé of false piety from the lips of Jesus (Matthew 6:1–18). Although the Pharisees are not mentioned by name in this chapter, it is certain that they are indicted. By not mentioning the Pharisees specifically, perhaps Jesus was suggesting that they were not the only ones who fall prey to false piety. The warnings here are for everyone who is serious about his or her devotion to God.

Let's set the context for Jesus' instruction on piety by looking first at Matthew 5. The Pharisees, suspicious of Jesus' neglect of their traditions, questioned His commitment to the Mosaic Law. Jesus assured them of His complete and unshakable commitment to the Law and said the problem lay with the Pharisees' interpretation of righteousness. The scribes and Pharisees had supplemented the Law with erroneous human additions; they had made it superficial, something humanly attainable without divine enablement.

Jesus strongly corrected their misguided and superficial theology with the words, "But I say to you" (vv. 22, 28, 32, 34, 39, 44). He deepened the Law's interpretation and corrected some misguided traditions of the Pharisees. He concluded the chapter with the words, "Therefore you are to be perfect, as your heavenly Father is perfect" (5:48).

At that point, any honest, self-aware person should have immediately asserted the impossibility of being perfect like the Father. If human perfection is God's requirement, then no one will make it. Precisely the point! If only the Pharisees had been willing to see their spiritual inadequacy, they would have been well on the way to true righteousness. For then they would have cast themselves on God's mercy alone and appealed for His grace. In any case, Jesus demolished the concept that human righteousness could be attained through the Law and hinted that another means was necessary.

Matthew 5 ends with "Be perfect" and chapter 6 commences with "Beware." Danger lurks nearby for the religious. Apparently the human compulsion to please God can easily go awry. Piety can easily deteriorate. Those who are serious about their religion run the risk of acquiring dangerous spiritual diseases. Religious practices are particularly prone to becoming fraudulent. A great temptation exists for religious people to parade their piety. Jesus pointed to three particular acts of righteousness—almsgiving, prayer, and fasting—and asked what motivated each.

We should also ask what motivates our acts. Who is the primary audience for our practice of righteousness? Do we do our deeds of devotion for people or for God? The answer to these questions makes an eternal difference. If God the Father is the audience, then He will duly reward our piety. However, if human praise and self-aggrandizement are our inner motives, then another kind of reward is forthcoming, temporary, and inconsequential.

THE PRACTICE OF PIETY

Righteousness is to be practiced. Jesus did not take the religious to task for acting on their faith. Such piety is assumed (notice the word *when* in Matthew 6:2, 5–7, 16). True religion will result in giving, praying, and self-denial. The pursuit of personal piety is not optional. Those wishing to avoid false piety are not to hold back in fear from the pursuit of piety. Nevertheless, piety is fraught with dangers.

Piety is perverted when the motive for pursuing it is to please the public rather than God. We can become religious exhibitionists, addicted to the praise of people. Or we can adopt the attitude that God needs to be manipulated in order to get what we want. In either case we use God to accomplish our ends. And it works; for all piety, both true and false, Jesus told us, is rewarded. This is good news to the religious, but not as good as we might have hoped. The reward of piety may be nothing more than the empty praise of people, devoid of divine and eternal reward.

The sad truth about religion is that false piety works! Piety can easily, subtly, and gradually become a means to human gain, socially, economically, and personally. Piety makes us appear spiritual. If one gives generously, speaks openly about his or her prayer life, as some do, or sacrifices conspicuously, human "Brownie points" are often awarded. We are duly impressed and confer honor and praise on the "faithful." Moreover, we are more likely to listen and defer to people who have an aura of spirituality. This many times opens up opportunities and affords privileges not given to "less spiritual" people. The appearance of piety can place one securely on a pedestal.

John Stott in *Christ the Controversialist* remarks,

> The same Pharisaic spirit still haunts every child of Adam today. It is easy to be critical of Christ's contemporaries and miss the repetition of their vainglory in ourselves. Yet deeply ingrained in our fallen nature is this thirst for the praise of men. It seems to be a devilish perversion of our basic psychological need to be wanted

and to be loved. We hunger for applause, fish for compliments, thrive on flattery. It is the plaudits of men we want; we are not content with God's approval now or with His "Well done, good and faithful servant" on the last day. Yet as Calvin put it: "What is more foolish, nay, what is more brutish, than to prefer the paltry approval of men to the judgment of God?"[3]

PIETY IN GIVING

When Jesus spoke to the Pharisees about money, He had their attention. They believed in giving to God and to the poor. They were intent on fulfilling the letter of the Law, even to exceed it. The Pharisees gave to support the temple and the synagogue. The religious community also provided relief to the underprivileged. R. T. France comments, "Almsgiving was a religious duty, not a philanthropic option, in Judaism and by the first century A.D. poor relief based on such almsgiving was impressively well-organized."[4]

The Pharisees were scrupulous tithers. They not only tithed the required portion of their possessions and property but also the portions not required, like their herb leaves (Matthew 23:23; Luke 11:42). The Pharisee in Jesus' parable of the Pharisee and the tax collector correctly affirmed, "I pay tithes of all that I get" (Luke 18:12). No God-fearing and self-respecting Pharisee would hedge on giving, as is so common today. Moreover, some Pharisees did honor secret as opposed to ostentatious giving.[5]

So when Jesus addressed Pharisaic almsgiving in Matthew 6:1–4, He was speaking about people who believed in and practiced giving. Thus Jesus was not addressing the issue of whether they (or we) should give to the poor, but how and from what motive. He immediately warned against trumpet blowing to advertise one's giving. Some Pharisees must have drawn attention to their acts of charity.[6] The statement "do not sound a trumpet before you" probably is metaphorical, akin to our common idiom, "Don't toot your own horn." Their motive was to gain some earthly interest on their charitable contributions, knowing, as we do, that a reputation as a giver is an effective means to gain the praise of people.

Jesus immediately labeled self-serving stewardship "hypocrisy." This strong word was often employed by Jesus when referring to the Pharisees. It means "to pretend" or "to play act."[7] The Pharisees did not act as if they were giving money and then retracting it. They really gave; they were dedicated to God and serious about doing His will. Their hypocrisy stemmed from the fact that they thought since they were acting in God's interest they were justified in advertising a bit. William Hendriksen summarizes their hypocrisy: "They were hypocrites because while they *pretended to give*, they really *intended to receive*, namely honor from men."[8]

Jesus' teaching revealed that those who seek human praise for their giving will be fully rewarded. They will get precisely what they have worked for (but not what they had hoped for). Jesus was wise enough to realize how human relations work. People are regularly recognized for their philanthropy. Those who seek human acclaim through the money they give to charitable causes will likely be applauded. When they are praised they should be pleased, He explained, for they have accomplished their mission; they have been paid in full.

Jesus proceeded to recommend an alternative path for proper piety. He introduced His better way with the word *but* (v. 3). When giving to the poor, "Do not let your left hand know what your right hand is doing." In this figurative language, Jesus "does not imply that we must not keep track of giving or that we be irresponsible in stewardship of finances or refuse to disclose how we spend our money for the sake of demonstrating financial accountability."[9] Jesus' point is that we should not publicly advertise our giving, nor should we be absorbed by our own giving.

Two wrong motives are in view. One is the intent to impress people. The other is the intent to impress ourselves ("What a good boy/girl am I!"). The antidote to both of these wrong motives is to give so sincerely and freely that I forget myself and seek only to please God through serving others. Those who give in this way will be rewarded by God. Nothing escapes His notice and nothing motivated by love for Him will be forgotten.[10]

Looking at Jesus' warnings, we should evaluate our own motives with three questions:

1. Are there ways that we "sound trumpets" or "toot our own horn" to advertise our giving?

2. Are we in danger of drawing inaccurate conclusions about ourselves and others by our level of giving?

3. Do we give for the praise of people?

In many subtle ways, the answer is yes. Let me illustrate.

In some church traditions much public ado is made over giving. Money is purposely and publicly extracted from congregants. I have vivid memories from my youth of collection baskets attached to poles. I feared some usher's placing the plate in my face and holding it there until I anted up. In some churches money is paraded to the altar. Multiple offerings are taken. Even announcements of giving amounts are broadcast and posted. Thankfully, in most churches giving is much more private, using envelopes, offering plates, and money boxes.

Still, we may practice more subtle, culturally correct methods of announcing our giving. Many churches use pledge cards to set their annual budget and conduct capital campaigns and "faith promise" to increase giving for missions. Though such giving can honor God when pledged in faith, the motive also can be mixed. For obvious reasons, some people give more when they sign their name on the dotted line. Meanwhile, many are motivated to give at year-end to save on income tax. Others give knowing the church treasurer and others will see our amounts. Our giving should be motivated not by IRS deductions, human reactions, or even personal self-esteem, but by passion for God and compassion for people.

Unquestionably, giving is a major issue in the church. Money is not only needed to keep the institution running but also can be a means to power and praise of individuals in the church and parachurch. The church through the years has devised ways to identify and reward those who have a larger financial stake in the institution. Churches and religious institutions commonly name buildings, wings, chairs, pews, and so on in the name of those who have given substantial sums. Moreover, church fund-raising programs often have a component by which they identify the bigger givers in the congregation and make special appeals to them. Lest I leave the subject of giving with a misunderstanding, however, let me add that some of the people whose spirituality most impresses me are the few to whom God has given much who live simply and quietly spread their wealth among many in need. Materialism is not a matter of money but of attitude.

Perhaps the most sinister financial practice of all is to evaluate our own godliness by the level of our financial contributions. Jesus' statement to not "let your left hand know what your right hand is doing" deals primarily with this danger of self-evaluation.

For not only is ostentation wrong, but so also is conceit, which can readily grow if we evaluate ourselves by the percentage of our giving. We can take much spiritual pride in giving, telling ourselves, *After all, I have been a tither for most of my Christian life* (there I go "tooting my own horn"). When I am ahead in my giving, I can sometimes feel smug. Conversely, when I am behind, I feel as if I am not in good standing with God.

Without question, God wants us to give. This giving must first be an expression of our love for Him, the One who owns all and has graciously given to us all we have. Our stewardship must not be self-conscious nor self-seeking. Conceit is perhaps the primary personal danger of having money to give (1 Timothy 6:17). And financial favoritism was (and is) a common enough problem in the church that God had to sternly warn us about it (James 2:1–13). It must be enough for us to know that God knows what we give.

THE PIETY OF PRAYING

The most common act of piety is prayer. It is universal among the religious. Perhaps it can be said that prayer is the highest act of piety, for it puts one in touch with God Himself. A parent loves few things more in life than to spend time in meaningful conversation with a beloved child. Prayer enables us to do this with our heavenly Father. Prayer is the believer's lifeline to God. Prayer is our source of power.

The Pharisees, as one might expect, were devoted to prayer. The first chapter of the first division of the Mishnah ("Berakoth") addresses why, where, when, how, and what to pray. Faithful Jews were required to pray the eighteen benedictions thrice daily, recite the *Shema* twice, and utter blessings before, during, and after meals. The Jews had times set apart for prayer, like our daily private prayer and prayer meetings. Hendriksen notes,

> Thus, there were morning, afternoon, and evening prayers (Ps. 55:17; Dan. 6:10; Acts 3:1). According to Josephus . . . sacrifices, including prayers, were offered in the temple "twice a day, in the early morning and at the ninth hour." There was also a sunset service.[11]

Many Pharisees, contrary to common Christian caricature, did not honor pretentious displays of public piety nor the mechanical, rote recitation of prayers.[12] Silent, private prayer was encouraged among the Pharisees. Moreover, they cited both biblical and rabbinical cautions against making long-winded prayers. And they believed, as Jesus taught, the futility of asking for God's forgiveness and then refusing to extend the same to others.[13]

The Heart of the Matter

However, Jesus, ever One to get to the heart of the matter, found serious fault with the prayer life of some of the Pharisees. He dealt with the subject of prayer in Matthew 6:5–15. In this section, which contains the immortal Lord's Prayer (vv. 9–13), Jesus once again assumed that people who are serious about their faith will pray. Three times Jesus said, "When you pray" (vv. 5–7), and when introducing the Lord's Prayer says, "Pray, then, in this way" (v. 9).

Jesus first criticized ostentatious prayer (v. 5). His listeners were cautioned to avoid the practice of the hypocrites who prayed at the most opportune times and places for maximum public exposure. The practice condemned here has nothing to do with the posture of prayer. It was typical for the Jews to pray standing up.[14] The fact that the setting is a public place—synagogue or street corner—is not the crux of the problem either. Hendriksen comments, "Scripture nowhere condemns public prayer (II Chron. 6:14–42; Neh. 9; Acts 4:24–31), nor individual prayer offered in a public place."[15] In the weekly worship in the synagogue, someone from the congregation may be asked to pray publicly, standing in front of the scrolls. Jesus probably participated in this activity, for we know that He attended the synagogue and worshipped there (Mark 6:1–2). Thus, there is nothing wrong with public prayer when it is sincerely offered to God with the right motives.

Prayer said for its impact on the audience is another matter altogether. Though most Pharisees probably did not deliberately position themselves in a public place to pray, apparently some did. Why the publicity? Perhaps some of it was because people then, as today, were simply asked to pray on the spot and had to say something. Maybe the one praying volunteered for the job because he had a way with pious words. Some may have prayed publicly because knowingly or unknowingly they sought to be admired for their prayer life. More likely, however, Pharisees prayed publicly because they thought what they were doing was pleasing to God.

As with the almsgiving, so also with prayer. The motive determines the reward. Pray to be heard, and people will respond favorably. They will appreciate your prayers, perhaps imitate your prayers, and accord you holy status because of your prayers. If this is the goal, the reward is forthcoming and paid in full. God, however, entirely neglects such "prayer."

Jesus offered an alternative. Instead of seeking publicity, find a solitary place (not an easy assignment for people at Jesus' time, many of whom lived in one-room houses). Pray to God, not peers. Seek communion with the Father, not human applause. Those who do will be rewarded by God. The main emphasis of Jesus' counsel is not the place but the motive and attitude. Secrecy is not as important as sincerity. Jesus was not forbidding public prayer. If He were, His disciples surely did not obey Him, for we read of numerous prayer meetings in the book of Acts. Moreover, Jesus' command does not require the building of prayer closets nor prayer rooms!

Wrong Motives, Wrong Methods

Prayer is perverted not only by wrong motivation but also wrong methods. Gentiles, believers in false religions, also pray, noted Jesus (Matthew 6:7). They are sincere, sometimes dead serious about connecting with the divine. (Consider the prophets of Baal cutting themselves at one encounter in 1 Kings 18:25–29.) But their method is to heap up words, hoping to badger God into giving the desired request. Their error is in believing that the essence of prayer is in the art. Their focus is on the right words and phrases meaninglessly, almost unconsciously, repeated at length in the hope that God would hear and grant their requests. Their prayer was like so much babble. The Jews, by the way, were not free from this problem. Charles Swindoll writes, "It was actually believed that whoever was longest in prayer was heard more readily by God. And the more flowery, the better. One well-known prayer had no less than sixteen adjectives preceding the name of God!"[16]

Once again, let's be careful to not misunderstand Jesus' intent. Repetition is not in and of itself wrong. Jesus, we are told, repeated Himself in prayer (Matthew 26:44). Nor is a set form of prayer wrong. For in Matthew 6:9–13, the most-quoted prayer in Christendom is taught by none other than Jesus. Nor is it wrong to use many words when praying. Jesus prayed all night (Luke

6:12), and the Bible does record several lengthy prayers. More-over, Jesus recommended persistence in prayer (see Matthew 7:7–11; Luke 18:1–8).

What is condemned is threefold. First, thoughtless, mechanical, vain prayer is exposed as useless. God prefers the spontaneous expression of our hearts to the rote piling up of pious words. Second, excessive verbiage is not necessary when talking with God. Apparently this was a scribal and Pharisaic trait (see Matthew 23:14; Mark 12:40; Luke 20:47). The prayer Jesus gave, as well as numerous examples in the Bible, demonstrated that prayer doesn't have to be wordy to be effective (note the "arrow prayers" in the book of Ruth and how specifically they are answered). Third, God is not One who demands that we get the formula right. The words we choose are not important, for He already is clued in to our needs and only wants to hear our requests so He may help us.

Once again Jesus did not condemn without offering corrections. Thus He taught the model prayer (vv. 9–13). This prayer is brief. Like the Gettysburg Address, it does not seem overly impressive at first. Obviously, wordiness is not what God wants; communion is. The Lord's Prayer is relational, not promotional. It is to and for God, not one's peers. It is designed to encourage intimacy, not publicity. And when talking to Daddy ("Abba"), one does not need to twist His arm.

The Lord's Prayer immediately exalts God to His rightful place. It acknowledges His supremacy and sovereignty. It longs for the honoring of His name, the coming of His kingdom, and the doing of His will. It places our simple yet profound physical and spiritual needs at His feet. Such a vertical perspective flies in the face of pursuing one's own agenda and seeking the applause of people. It shows us that forgiveness is foundational to prayer.

Modern Prayers

"Mirror, Mirror on the wall, who's the Phar-i-see of all?" Let's see how we compare to the Pharisees of old. The Pharisees indisputably believed in and practiced prayer. Many of us, though we say we believe in prayer, do not practice what we profess. I seriously doubt that the hypocrisy of the Pharisees was any greater than our hypocrisy in prayer today. Few Christians today could say they practice prayer as diligently as the Pharisees did. In this respect at least, we would be wise to emulate the Pharisees.

Certainly we are prone to the same Pharisaic prayer faults that Jesus here delineates. Listen to public prayers sometime and ask the simple question, "To whom was that prayer really addressed?" Some without a doubt are for the ears of humans, not God. We pastors are some of the greatest culprits. We use prayer to sermonize and summarize, to point fingers and make points, to announce and denounce, to scold and enfold, to give the latest church statistics and to "give an invitation." We multiply theological jargon, throw in some trite phrases, and quote Scripture back to God. This is seen as particularly pious. Our prayers sometimes even preach mini-sermons to God! People commonly use terminology, tone, volume, and inflections in public prayer that are never used elsewhere. God is not impressed with our language; He observes our hearts.

There are numerous other ways that we publicize our prayer lives today. Prayer before meals, especially in public places, can become a badge of piety that we proudly wear. Our prayer postures sometimes draw attention to ourselves, whether it be the raised hands of the charismatics, the bended knees of the Catholics, the bowed heads of the evangelicals, or the physical prostration of the super-spiritual.

Prayer can additionally become an acceptable alternative for authentic godliness. At times there is little correspondence between the fervency of our prayer and the faithfulness of our lives. Why? Perhaps prayer is a placebo, giving us the sense of spiritual health without any actual benefit. Sometimes prayer is used as an escape from reality and responsibility. Of course, the opposite takes place as well, probably more often. A person devotes him or herself to ministry to such an extent that prayer is neglected. Somehow we justify this lack of communion with the Father by our level of commotion for the Father.

On the matter of meaningless repetition, we are also caught red-faced, for we are no less prone to meaningless repetition and multiplied words than the Gentiles and Pharisees of Jesus' day. See "Pray It Again" for the many ways we repeat ourselves, and the solution to such babbling.

THE RIGHT WAY

Pray It Again

Like the Gentiles and Pharisees of Jesus' day (Matthew 6:7), our prayers often include meaningless repetition. For instance, we have our canned prayers. "Now I lay me down to sleep" is a classic bedtime prayer. "God is great and God is good, let us thank Him for our food" is a favorite at mealtime. The Lord's Prayer is the prayer of choice at church time. And "Bless so-and-so" is our formula for anytime.

Next we have the repetitive phrases that we meaninglessly deposit into our prayers. "Let's have a word of prayer" is our favorite introduction. "Dear Father" is our favorite title. "God bless," "Be with," "Watch over," and "Help so-and so" are favorite requests. As we insert them at key points, time after time, they lose meaning.

"Bind Satan" is a common catchphrase. "If it be Thy will" is our favorite out. "ACTS" is our favorite prayer formula. "Yes, Jesus" and "Praise Jesus" are our favorite responses. And "In Jesus' name, Amen" is our required ending.

What is the answer to vague, repetitive prayers? Short prayer provides a check on Gentile babbling. Short prayer helps to focus the mind and heart as well as remove the aura of super-spirituality. Of course, there are times when one must pour out the pain or praise of a heart too full. This may take hours or days. Yet short prayers often are very powerful.

So what is the antidote to perverted prayer? Jesus provided some clues. First, if we actually took seriously the call of Christ to pray, we might experience fewer problems with the perversions of prayer. Perhaps prayer becomes public to hide the lack of private prayer. I know this is sometimes true in my life. The first solution, then, is to pray often and regularly, so we are comfortable talking with God.

Second, we must constantly check our motives in prayer,

particularly, but not exclusively, when we pray in public. Often we should ask ourselves the question, "For whose ears am I praying? Who is my audience?" Sincere prayer is singular in its focus on God.

Third, secret prayer is a hedge against the hypocrisy of public prayer. One's public prayer life should never supersede one's private time with God. However, I can cite seasons in my life when the total time devoted to participation in prayer meetings has exceeded the time I spent alone with God. And I doubt I am the exception.

The most straightforward and liberating words I have read on prayer come from Charles Swindoll in *Strengthening Your Grip*. He notes that the Bible is devoid of people who are dissatisfied and perpetually guilty about their prayer lives. Then he asks a profound question: Why are we Christians, past and present, deeply dissatisfied with our own prayer lives? Why do we so often feel guilty about our prayer lives? His answer is that perhaps we have bought into a model of prayer that is derived from tradition, not Scripture. A great barrier "keeps us from entering into authentic prayer," Swindoll writes. "That barrier is the traditional wrappings that have been placed around prayer." He continues:

> At the risk of sounding heretical, I'm convinced that for centuries Christians have forced prayer into a role it was never designed to play. I would suggest we have made it difficult, hard, even painful. The caricature that has emerged through years of traditional (not biblical) modeling is now a guilt-giving discipline, not an anxiety-relieving practice. It is self-imposed. It doesn't come from God.[17]

Prayer is a simple act of sincere communication between a dependent child and his or her heavenly Father. When we turn it into a public spectacle or a means to badger God to get what we want, or a speech contest, or a means to get from God what we are unwilling to give to others, we run the risk of falling into the same traps that the Pharisees did two thousand years ago.

THE PIETY OF FASTING

Religious people feel that it is important, even necessary, to demonstrate their piety by various forms of self-denial. Through the ages the most common form of self-denial has been to abstain voluntarily from food and drink in order to devote one-self more fully to God, to placate God's wrath, or to obtain His favor. Fasting is prominent in Hinduism, Islam, Judaism, and Christianity, among other religions, and has served ritualistic, ascetic, religious, mystical, even political purposes. It is required for Moslems during Ramadan, Jews on Yom Kippur, and Roman Catholics during Lent and Advent. Mahatma Gandhi is the best known of many individuals who have used fasting for political purposes.

Since fasting is an almost universal practice among the religious, one might expect that the Pharisees, highly religious people that they were, would be among the world's most prolific fasters. Indeed they were. The Pharisees' devotion to fasting was derived from the direct teaching of the Old Testament, the oral traditions, and numerous regulations designed by the sincere to help faithful Jews walk with God. It would be wrong, however, to assume that the Pharisees encouraged empty displays of piety. Israel Abrahams, a reader in Talmudic at the University of Cambridge, writes, "He who fasts, and makes a display of himself to others, to boast his fasting, is punished for this."[18]

The Old Testament commends fasting both in precept and example. God commanded that the Jews fast on the Day of Atonement. This fasting is implied by the prohibition of any work. The purpose of this fast was to express humiliation as the people confessed their sin. Such a connection between fasting and confessing sin is common in the Old Testament.[19] Fasting was also often combined with prayer.[20] It was a natural manifestation of bereavement and heavyheartedness. When judgment seemed inevitable, people characteristically fasted in a desperate attempt to stay God's hand. (See Joel 1:14–15; 2:12–15; and Jonah 3:5–9.)

Fasting by the Pharisees

However, fasting grew exponentially as the Pharisees became more intent on pursuing their extreme righteousness. William Hendriksen comments,

> The law of God suggests only one fast in an entire year, namely, on the day of atonement. . . . In course of time, however, fasts began to multiply, so we read about their occurrence at other times also: from sunrise to sunset (Judg. 20:26; I Sam. 14:24; II Sam. 1:12;

3:35); for seven days (I Sam. 31:13); three weeks (Dan. 10:3); forty days (Exod. 34:2, 28; Deut. 9:9, 18; I Kings 19:8); in the fifth and seventh month (Zech. 7:3–5); and even in the fourth, fifth, seventh, and tenth month (Zech. 8:19). The climax was the observance of a fast "twice a week," the boast of the Pharisee (Luke 18:12).[21]

The Pharisees at the time of Jesus, never ones to be outdone in their acts of piety, fasted Monday and Thursday every week.

Thus Jesus' words on fasting (Matthew 6:16–18) would rivet their attention. He began with tacit approval of the practice of fasting. He said "when," not "if" you fast. He assumed, as mentioned later in the Gospels, that fasting was an appropriate spiritual activity (Matthew 9:15) and one that might be necessary when encountering certain kinds of situations (for example, Acts 13:1–3; 14:23).

A False Motive

However, the Pharisees' fasting had assumed an air of acting, for they let it be known to all that they were fasting by disfiguring their faces and neglecting their appearance. Perhaps they neglected to wash and shave. Maybe they put on ashes and dirt as an actor would put on makeup. Maybe they looked gaunt and groaned from the hunger pains. Whatever they did, it somehow went public. Ironically, by making themselves unrecognizable they sought recognition!

The motive behind this fasting was to make a public impression regarding the faster's piety. Jesus remarks that those who fast for people will be praised by people. People are duly impressed by those who go to great lengths to show their devotion to God. And this is reward enough! God, however, is not moved by this kind of piety and thus does nothing to reward it.

So Jesus offered an alternative. Fasting should be done secretly, without any visible change in one's normal appearance or hygiene. Genuine fasting, Jesus said, should be between the one who fasts and the One for whom one fasts. The temptation to leak to the public the fact that one is fasting is so great that special care should be taken to camouflage it (Matthew 6:17–18). Fasting done out of sincere devotion to God will be seen and rewarded by Him.

When We Fast

Fasting has its place in the life of the believer. When the heart is broken, the stomach often is uninterested in food. When one has sinned grievously, eating isn't the right thing to do. When one is heavily burdened about a pending decision, time spent alone with God is far more important than feeding one's face. When there is a need for extraordinary mental concentration, food sometimes seems to dull the mind. And when one is prone to the sin of gluttony, fasting may well be a good antidote.

However, though fasting is recommended, there are some serious scriptural qualifications. We have mentioned the tendency to fast for the publicity it accrues. In addition, fasting can be a ruse designed to cover up evil (even murder; see 1 Kings 21:9–12). When mixed with injustice and oppression, fasting is offensive to God (Isaiah 58; Zechariah 7). Moreover, fasting can wrongly be viewed as a superficial means to atone for one's sins or to merit God's favor (Jeremiah 14:10–12).

Fasting doesn't ultimately work to curb the influence of the flesh (Colossians 2:18–23). Perhaps this is why the apostle Paul, a man who knew deprivation, did not dwell on fasting in his letters. Ironically, early church history tells us that fasting quickly became twisted. Some taught that if one fasted, he or she sinned, while others specified the days that one must fast. In any case, fasting is not to be used as a means by which we evaluate the spirituality of ourselves or others.

In American evangelicalism there seems to be a growing interest in fasting. Perhaps Richard Foster gave the initial momentum when he wrote *Celebration of Discipline*. Well-known evangelical personalities have let it leak, or have specifically stated, that they fast (even for forty days). I have no doubt about the sincerity of these leaders. I do wonder, however, why such was publicized. Advertisements in our religious mail trumpet fasting and prayer. Occasionally I still hear people mention, "Giving up for Lent." It is hard to deny that fasting is a badge of the super righteous in our Christian culture.

TRUE PIETY NOT A PUBLIC SHOW

How can we acquire the true piety that Jesus recommended to His disciples, while avoiding the false piety He exposed? Matthew 6 offers several clear clues.

First, *true piety is difficult, not natural.* The practice of false piety is a real danger for religious people. Pointedly Jesus introduced the topic with the word "Beware!" There is a subtle, sinister, and seductive pull to piety. If we are not careful, we will naturally slip into false or superficial piety. The Bible well illustrates that acts of piety can easily become a substitute for authentic piety. (See, for instance, 1 Samuel 15:22; Psalm 51:16–17; Proverbs 15:8; Isaiah 1:11–17.)

Second, *true piety is practical, not mystical.* We must not let the fear of hypocrisy and publicity keep us from practicing our piety. Piety is to be active, not passive. In Matthew 5:16 Jesus told His disciples to let people see their good deeds, but in such a way that glory is diverted upward. We need not fear praying in public will necessarily pull us from God. The Scriptures regularly commend public and group prayer. It is probably imprudent to refuse to keep financial records so as to avoid the tendency to broadcast one's giving. One can keep records without gloating or trumpeting one's stewardship. And fasting and other acts of self-sacrifice for spiritual goals are good, provided they are done for God and not our peers.

Third, *true piety is often unnoticed, not publicized.* Public piety works! This is precisely why it is so dangerous. Religious practices result in substantial earthly and temporal rewards. Public piety brings "honor" to the pious (v. 2) and has its rewards (vv. 2, 5, 16). Being known for one's stewardship, prayer life, and self-denying devotion to God are sure routes to ecclesiastical success. There are few arenas in which it is easier to fool people, even oneself, than religion. True piety concerns itself with what is really going on inside and with the One who sees all (Hebrews 4:13).

Fourth, *true piety is vertical, not horizontal.* At the heart of piety is our motivation. Why and for whom do we do it? If we are honest, we will have to admit that we sometimes give either out of obligation or to please the treasurer, that often we pray for the ears of those who are listening, and it is hard to avoid dropping hints about our devotion to God. God earnestly desires a pure relationship with us alone. We must sincerely covet God's favor, not human praise.

Fifth, *true piety is simple and secret, not showy.* Jesus said that one of the best ways to check our natural tendency to make our piety public is to do it secretly and simply. Our stewardship should be unself-conscious and unpublicized. Our prayer life should be far superior in private than it is in public. And our acts of self-discipline for Christ's sake should be studiously hidden, even covered up. In truth, who we are in secret is who we really are.

Sixth, *true piety is social as well as spiritual.* We must not forget that there is a connection between our private piety and our public lives, but not the connection that we usually make. God's forgiveness of us is in some ways predicated on our forgiveness of others. Our lack of forgiveness of others is a certain indication that we have not internalized the forgiveness of God for us.

Above all, let us remember that true piety is a relationship with the heavenly Father. A stronger relationship with God should be the goal and motive for everything we do. We must not seek to fulfill some set of religious requirements or, worse yet, seek to please people. The heavenly Father has called us into relationship with Him. He longs for this relationship to be based on His grace, not our pious acts.

God wants us to see who He really is, infinitely superior to any person or group. God is not into my carefully prescribed acts of piety. He wants me. He wants you. And He seeks an extreme relationship of love and service with Him.

Chapter Seven
WHEN TRADITION TWISTS TRUTH

In the musical *Fiddler on the Roof,* the Russian Jew Tevye watches as change all around him seems to threaten his very life. In his village of Anatevka, tradition gives stability. "And how do we keep our balance?" he asks the audience. "That I can tell you in one word—*tradition!*"

In the Christian church, almost *everything* we do is based on humanly devised traditions. The days, times, and places we meet for worship are all traditions. The meetings we hold and ministries we offer are largely based on tradition, not Scripture. The way we dress, the structure of our service, our style of music, and the instruments used are dictated largely by tradition. We have theological traditions, denominational traditions, psychological traditions, sociological traditions, ethnic traditions, national traditions, even geographical traditions. Tevye in *Fiddler on the Roof* was correct when he said, "Without our traditions our lives would be as shaky as a fiddler on the roof."

Traditions are everywhere and influence almost everything we do. They have their benefits, but they must not be confused with God-given commands. Tradition should never have the same authority as Scripture. Yet often we fail to recognize our traditions as comfortable patterns, not God-ordained instructions. We elevate them to unshakable truths, just as the Pharisees did.

If you doubt the power of tradition, try to change one sometime. You will likely arouse considerable emotion and encounter strong opposition. Jesus certainly did! A significant portion of the antipathy He aroused was because of His violation of traditions.

Tradition has been defined as "the handing down of information, beliefs, and customs by word of mouth or by example from one generation to another without written instruction."[1] Traditions are familiar and habitual patterns of doing things passed on from those who have gone before us, patterns that we practice naturally, usually oblivious to their source. Many traditions are helpful. However, tradition poses one of the most serious potential threats to authentic maturity and ministry. As Pelikan puts it: "Tradition is the living faith of the dead; traditionalism is the dead faith of the living."[2]

WHAT'S "RITE" WITH TRADITION

Before we explore the dangers of tradition, let's elaborate on some of its benefits. We must acknowledge that traditions, first and foremost, are part of the fabric of our lives. Without traditions we would not know who we are (our identity), where we came from (our roots), what we believe (our mind-set), nor how to behave (our lifestyle). By traditions we order our lives. Traditions make life easier by taking the guesswork and anxiety out of most life decisions. We simply cannot live in a state of constant flux and ambiguity. Because of our traditions, we don't have to continually "reinvent the wheel," or try to fix what "ain't broke." Instead we can benefit from the past, from the "tried and true."

Traditions help us in three specific ways. First, *traditions exert an enormous pull on our emotions*. Because they connect us in profound ways with our past, traditions provide sameness, security, and stability to our present. The reason we tend to react immediately and strongly to those who violate our traditions is that traditions attach themselves more to our emotions than to our intellect. Traditions just "feel right." Try designing a wedding service without tradition and see what happens!

Second, *traditions enable us to function effectively in community*. They define our comfort zone and give us a sense of belonging. Traditions provide common memories, aid human bonding, and help us to perpetuate corporately that which is positive from the past.

Third, *tradition may be helpful in doing ministry*. In the musical *Fiddler on the Roof*, Tevye states, "Because of our traditions every one of us knows who he is and what God expects from him." Most of our religious attitudes and acts are based on long-standing traditions originated by good people zealously trying to live out their walk with God. Moreover, it is largely traditions that define us into particular denominational groupings. It is not by accident that worship services run in familiar grooves in various religious groups anywhere one may go in the world. Ministerial traditions help us to remember and reenact from the past things that are true, noble, beautiful, and useful.

The New Testament itself commends tradition, properly used and understood. (See "The Right Way," page 105.) And the Pharisees understood certain traditions were given by God and helpful to their faith.

JEWISH TRADITIONS

The word *Pharisee* is often rightly associated with tradition. Most Jews are proud of this association, for they believed their traditions were given by God Himself. The Pharisees believed that God gave Moses on Mount Sinai both the written Torah (Genesis through Deuteronomy) and the oral Torah (the "traditions of the elders"). The Written Torah was enshrined in the Holy Scriptures. The oral Torah, according to the Jews, was diligently passed on orally for many centuries until it was compiled and codified by Rabbi Judah the Prince about A.D. 200 in The Mishnah.

The oral Torah is divided into six sections containing laws and traditions about agriculture, festivals, women, civil and criminal law, sacred things, and ritual purity. The Mishnah states, "Tradition is a fence for Torah." Jews generally agreed, "When a man turns his back on tradition, he really severs himself from Judaism itself and from its national essence."[3] The Pharisees of Jesus' day and much of Judaism today revere their traditions. The traditions of the elders were held in equal esteem with the written Scriptures, and some would say even higher. Moreover, because the oral Torah dealt with specific behaviors, it tended to be observed with greater stringency than the more abstract written Torah.

Since the traditions were held in such high esteem, it is not surprising that the Pharisees of Jesus' day would insist on compliance. Donald Hagner writes, "For the Pharisees *the* measure of righteousness and thus loyalty to the Torah was obedience to this sacred tradition."[4] The Sadducees, on the other hand, rejected the oral Torah and regarded only the five books of Moses as authoritative for divine doctrine. This significant difference of opinion was at the root of much of the antipathy between these two groups. Jesus, though no friend of the Sadducees, took strong exception to the Pharisees' view of tradition. While He complied with a number of Pharisaic traditions like synagogue attendance and the public reading of Scripture, He refused to give equal weight to the traditions of the elders and the divine Word of God.

A CASE STUDY: HAND-WASHING

All traditions should be periodically examined. Though we cannot live without traditions, we must beware lest traditions dictate how we live. The hand-washing practices of the Pharisees provide the classic New Testament example of the negative impact of traditions. Since this practice is foreign to most of us, it is imperative that we understand its origins and how it worked in Jesus' day. We will focus our attention on Mark 7:1–23 (and to a lesser extent Matthew 15:1–20) to obtain a clearer understanding of the effects of traditions.

A formal delegation of Pharisees and scribes undertook an investigative trip to question Jesus about His violation of Pharisaic tradition. As anticipated, they caught Jesus' disciples eating bread without having washed their hands. Hand-washing was one of a trio of major marks of Jewish identity: circumcision, Sabbath observance, and dietary laws, including ritual cleansings. As the apostle Mark explains,

> The Pharisees and all the Jews do not eat unless they carefully wash their hands, thus observing the traditions of the elders; and when they come from the marketplace, they do not eat unless they cleanse themselves; and there are many other things which they have received in order to observe, such as the washing of cups and pitchers and copper pots. (7:3–4)

Ritual washings were matters of great religious significance. J. Neusner tells us that "approximately 67 percent of the whole (law), directly or indirectly concern table-fellowship."[5] Jesus had already run afoul of the Pharisees on the all-important issue of the Sabbath; now a second major mark of Judaism was being ignored by Jesus. The Pharisees now accused the teacher and His disciples with having "impure" (unwashed) hands.

THE RIGHT WAY

Good Traditions

Though in the Gospels, Jesus warned us about the dangers of traditions of the elders, as the apostle Paul did in Colossians 2:8, the New Testament also commends tradition. Jesus was the product of extensive Jewish tradition, including His circumcision, naming, and dedication (Luke 2:21–35). He observed the Feasts (Luke 2:41; Mark 14:12) and worshipped at the temple and synagogue (Luke 2:46–50; 4:15–30; Mark 6:1–6).

The apostle Paul praised the Corinthian believers for "hold[ing] firmly to the traditions" that he had taught them (1 Corinthians 11:2), while he admonished the wavering Thessalonians to "stand firm and hold to the traditions which you were taught" (2 Thessalonians 2:15; note also 3:6). The great apostle passed on various doctrinal and practical traditions to the churches among whom he ministered (1 Corinthians 11:23; 15:2–3). He does not suggest that anything is wrong with this practice. In fact, traditions often help to keep us on track theologically. The key, however, is that the traditions Paul passed on had their roots firmly planted in the truth of God, not the opinions, however helpful, of human beings.

Therefore, we should have a healthy respect for traditions. The word *tradition* is not a theological curse word, as many Protestants suspect. "The question, then, is not whether we have traditions, but whether our traditions conflict with the only absolute standard in these matters: Holy Scripture," writes J. I. Packer in *The Comfort of Conservativism*. We must never forget the human origins of traditions and resist the deep-seated urge to grant them divine status. Scripture, not tradition, is the final test of truth.

Hand-washing was not primarily for hygienic reasons. It was instead a means to religious purity. Defilement was encountered when an observant Jew knowingly or unknowingly came into contact with someone or something deemed unclean (Leviticus 11–15; Numbers 19). When this occurred ritual cleansing was required. The consecration requirements were even more stringent for priests, particularly as they carried out their religious duties (Exodus 29–30). Studying these scriptural washings required for the priests, the Pharisees applied them to all faithful Jews.

The Pharisees' traditions on hand-washing were plentiful and specific.[6] The actual washing procedure included even the positioning of the fingertips. As one may imagine, the rabbis disagreed about the exact procedure. Hillel and Shammai took different positions on the details. Nevertheless, they agreed that ritual cleansings were essential. If one failed to wash his hands in the prescribed manner, Barclay notes, Jewish leaders ruled him to be "unclean in the sight of God" and even "subject to the attacks of a demon called Shibta." Furthermore, "To omit so to wash the hands was to become liable to poverty and destruction. . . . A rabbi who once omitted the ceremony was buried in excommunication."[7]

WHAT'S WRONG WITH TRADITION?

The Pharisees' traditions developed naturally. They began innocently, usually by sincere people trying to please God. Generally, biblical proof texts were found to justify some religious practice. Once it became mainstream in a particular group, it would be labeled a tradition, and people were indoctrinated. Deviation from tradition then became grounds for judgment, censure, and even excommunication.

Like the Pharisees, we often have our lives governed by traditions. And like the Pharisees, we must beware that traditions have numerous potential perils, especially to our spiritual lives. Jesus was quick and blunt in pointing out these perils, highlighting five significant dangers of traditions in Mark 7:6–23 (cf. Matthew 15:3–20). Though He was talking with the Pharisees, His words alert us to the dangers we must confront too.

1. Tradition May Foster False Religion.

With uncompromising directness, Jesus attacked the Pharisees' traditions (Mark 7:6–8). "Rightly did Isaiah prophesy of you hypocrites," He began. This introduction is not generally thought to be a good way to win friends and influence people. The straight-forwardness of Jesus' approach thus signals us that the issue at hand was of great spiritual significance. His strong language was necessary.

The Pharisees' traditions were in reality ungodliness masked by the beauty and seeming rightness of religion. Jesus applied Isaiah's words to the nation to the practice of the Pharisees. The Old Testament text reads, "This people draw near with their words and honor Me with their lip service, but they remove their hearts far from Me, and their reverence for Me consists of tradition learned by rote" (Isaiah 29:13). About 700 B.C. when Isaiah prophesied, religion in Judah was strong, but so was injustice, immorality, and idolatry. The Jews of Isaiah's day comfortably combined external religion with internal unrighteousness. Isaiah 1:10–23 provides a snapshot of the multiplied sacrifices, offerings, incense, assemblies, feasts, and prayers, which were coupled with injustice, mercilessness, unrighteousness, and pride.

Jesus used a single word to describe this phenomenon, *hypocrisy*, calling the Pharisees *hypocrites* (v. 6). This is the first recorded instance of Jesus using the "H" word, which He will later use repeatedly to describe the Pharisees. Hypocrisy denotes the discrepancy between people's profession of faith and their actual possession of it; of the difference between the mouth and the heart. To make a show of devotion to God while giving preference to humanly concocted traditions that do not appreciably promote the ways of God renders one's worship worthless.

Humanly devised traditions, no matter how seemingly holy, contain the seeds of hypocrisy. Traditions look good, they grip the emotions, they govern our behavior, and they tend to acquire divine doctrinal status. However, traditions have an often unseen down side. Traditions stick because they work, because people *can* keep them. Often traditions are followed mechanically and mindlessly. Over time, the distinction between the truth of God and our traditions becomes blurred, and we tend to cling more tenaciously to our human traditions than to the Holy Scriptures.

Traditions are easier to obey than God's truth. Traditions often focus on actions while God focuses on attitudes that motivate actions. Traditions can be accomplished by gut-power while God's truth requires Spirit-power. Living God's truth requires a relationship with Him. When traditions become automatic, it is easy for the intimacy to be lost.

Do our own traditions foster false religion and contribute to hypocrisy? In many ways they do. Surely Sunday morning worship can include rousing music, celebrants with uplifted hands, and obvious emotion, yet not be connected to true heart devotion. Faithful church attenders may readily classify themselves as "evangelistic" and "missions-minded," but never speak to anyone outside the church about Jesus Christ. Some give generously to missions but neglect to practice missions where they live. We promote outreach in words but not in deeds. It is vintage hypocrisy for people to criticize the evangelistic methods of the church when they do no personal evangelism themselves. This is false religion.

Prayer is another area where traditions can foster false religion. Imagine that I, your pastor, invite you over for dinner. My wife prepares a sumptuous feast. All are summoned to the table and take their respective places. I then say, "The food's getting cold, so dig in," and begin chowing down. Not even one religious person would miss the fact that we didn't pray. Immediately, probably consciously, you would wonder what is wrong with me. Am I forgetful or unspiritual? Perhaps you would make a comment or ask why we didn't "say grace." Even if you were too polite to comment to me about my breech of tradition you would certainly have noticed, probably will talk about it to others, and undoubtedly will have some concerns about my spirituality.

Praying before we eat is a tradition, not a command of God. Yet if we dare to omit it, our spirituality will be called into question. Please do not misunderstand me. It is obviously right to regularly acknowledge the goodness and provision of God. Surely Christ set the example when He blessed the food before multiplying it (Mark 6:41). But did God anywhere tell us that we must always pray before eating? Is there some command that we are violating if we do not? I do not think so. (By the way, I personally believe it is advisable to pray before eating. This is a good tradition that can and should be infused with meaning.) Prayer before eating is only a tradition, one that we often piously practice without meaning, giving us the sense of spirituality.

How do we avoid fostering false religion by our traditions? We should raise traditions to a conscious level. We must name and claim them as traditions, not truth, and refuse to award traditions doctrinal status. We must not institutionalize forms devoid of meaning. It is essential that we remember who we are worshipping and how He wishes to be worshipped, "in spirit and truth" (John 4:24).

2. Tradition May Supplant Scripture.

Jesus' second point in confronting the Pharisees concerning their traditions was that sometimes tradition subtly supplants Scripture (Mark 7:9–13). This time, rather than citing Scripture, He points out a current Pharisaic tradition. The Pharisees believed vows to be sacred, particularly those that involved God and the temple. The Mishnah devotes a section to the issue of vows (Nedarim). One of the key words in vow-making according to the rabbis was "Corban," a verbal pledge of a future offering to God. Such an offering, once pledged to God, could not be given to others (though it could conveniently be used for one's own purposes). In Jesus' day, Jews made pledges (or declared them "Corban") to the temple that were to be transferred upon death. These vows allowed them full personal use of all their estate but denied access of the funds to care for the present needs of aged parents.

Apparently the religious powers-that-be saw this as an effective means to enhance law-keeping (and perhaps to raise money), so they made it into a binding tradition. Most adversely affected by this tradition were the families of those who made the Corban declaration.

Jesus, however, saw this tradition as a direct violation of Scripture. The fifth commandment (Exodus 20:12; Deuteronomy 5:16) required children to honor their parents. This honor involved caring for one's parents financially in their old age (1 Timothy 5:3–8). The Scriptures prescribe strong penalties for dishonoring one's parents.[8] However, this Corban tradition directly contravened the stated Word of God to honor one's parents. Thus the Scriptures had been subtly supplanted by human traditions.

Sometimes traditions, even those begun for good reasons, twist God's truth. Tradition must always be recognized as tradition and not be permitted to supplant Scripture. Scripture is and must always be kept supreme; tradition, subordinate. However, in actual practice this distinction often gets blurred. How does this happen? Usually it occurs over time, generally based on other "conflicting" proof texts of Scripture and often for some practical (and profitable) purpose. What is wrong with this tendency? It confuses the divine with the human. Tradition tends to become sacrosanct, stealing priority over Scripture. It reverses the priorities of God. Tradition can enshrine that which is at the heart self-centered rather than God-centered.

Could it be that some of our traditions likewise contradict God's commands? Consider the venerable institution of the Sunday school. Robert Raikes popularized this institution, which was started in 1769 by Hannah Ball. The original purpose of the Sunday school was both spiritual and social. It began to help poor children become literate and reach them with the gospel of Jesus Christ. Now more than 225 years later, the Sunday school in most churches is still going strong, even if its purpose has changed through time. Today many regard the Sunday school as the primary agency for the spiritual nurture of children. Ask most parents what they expect of the church and they would answer, "A strong Sunday school."

But wait. Did God issue any commands about the spiritual nurture of children? He did. In Deuteronomy 6, the best-known text in the Bible on transferring the faith to the next generation, God gave the job of theological education primarily to the parents, not to the community of faith. His reason for this choice is obvious. The transmission of the faith cannot be accomplished in a single hour per week, in a classroom setting, even with the most gifted and loving teachers. Surely the church can provide invaluable assistance, and the Sunday school has been powerfully used of God for evangelism and edification. However, God designed the family to carry the "lion's share" of the responsibility of Christian nurture, not the church.

Nevertheless, many Christian families today do little if anything intentionally to pass on the Christian faith to their children, confused, perhaps by tradition, that it's the church's responsibility. Is it not possible that this magnificent Sunday school tradition of ours subtly contradicts God's truth, as its presence and impact allow parents to dismiss their God-given responsibilities?

Another tradition by which pastors and churches confuse Christians and may cause them to ignore the Scriptures is the "altar call." This relatively recent tradition (1800s) is so ingrained in many people's spiritual psyche that they are distraught when an invitation is not given and comforted when it is. I see no inherent fault in the altar call. It is a method used of God to bring many people to Himself for salvation and sanctification. However, I wonder if this form of public evangelism does not assuage our consciences when we neglect private evangelism? God did not design public evangelism to be a substitute for personal evangelism. Nor should corporate edification be replaced by worship services designed primarily to save lost souls. Generally speaking, evangelism is supposed to take place "out there" rather than "in here," Monday through Saturday rather than solely on Sunday, and done by all, not just by the pastor.

How do we avoid falling prey to our traditions subtly supplanting the Scriptures? Once again, we must be alert enough to identify traditions as traditions. Most of us noncritically accept tradition as our guide. We must steadfastly refuse to let traditions become vested with divine authority. Though we call ourselves Protestants, we sometimes act as if we have forgotten the Reformation call, *sola Scriptura*—the Scriptures alone. All traditions must then be run through the grid of Scripture, not vice versa. Our traditions must be regarded as negotiable and subordinate to God's truth.

3. Tradition May Twist Theological Truth.

Jesus summoned the crowds at one point to address one of the most common and sinister sources of tradition, a distorted view of defilement (Mark 7:14–16, 21–23). With words packed with intensity, the Master implored His audience to "Listen up!" Then He made the truly revolutionary pronouncement that nothing outside a person could defile him or her. Defilement proceeds from the inside out, not the outside in. Defilement resides in the human heart.

That contradicted the Pharisees' view of defilement. They (and we also, at key points) believed that evil is external and environmental. One can and will become defiled by certain persons, places, and things. Thus "good" Jews would avoid contact with Gentiles or Samaritans (half-Jews) and with tax collectors and sinners. Similarly the Jews avoided walking through Samaria, considering it unclean as home to the mixed-race Samaritans. The list of defiling places and activities was extensive.

But one cannot avoid defilement by trying to steer clear of evil people, places, and things, Jesus explained. The only way to deal with defilement is to address the issues of the heart.

Tradition for the Pharisees had contributed to a misguided definition of impurity before God. In fact, the traditions may have increased defilement because they obscured the true source of spiritual dirt, namely, the depravity of the human heart. Similarly, modern traditions that attempt to clean up our external acts may blind us to the depravity of our hearts and the resulting need for internal cleansing. Traditions may give us a false sense of righteousness. They may deceive us into finding the wrong source of and solution for our sin and provide rationalizations for our depravity and alternatives to dependency. Real defilement of the variety that is enumerated in Mark 7:21–22 comes from within, not without.[9]

This does not mean that defilement is unimportant for the Christian. The New Testament also commends purity and condemns defilement.[10] But those who desire to have pure lives need to recognize that the source of sin is within themselves, not in the presence of others or activities.

Sometimes our traditions compromise our theology; they even encourage us to look toward wrong solutions to the sin problem. We Christians at times produce lists of rules that protect us from defilement. Though it may not be packaged as such, defilement is viewed as "out there in the world." Certain people are designated as defiling. Thus we were taught (wisely) to pick good friends and avoid bad people. Certain places are inherently compromising: wherever alcohol is served or pot smoked, wherever rock music is played and bodies move to the beat—wherever secular activities occur. And certain objects like face cards and a variety of magazines are dirty. While there is wisdom in many of these rules, they subtly communicate the antithesis of bedrock biblical theology, namely, that defilement is internal and not external.

Today many Christians are increasingly frightened of creeping secularism and doing whatever they can to protect themselves and their families. Home schooling and Christian schools are seen as safe havens and places for values instruction that is lacking in public schools. As a parent of five, I too seek to protect my children from evil; this is my duty as a father and, up to a point, is necessary for my children's maturation. However, I never want to be lulled into thinking that by limiting their access to certain people, places, and things I can lessen my children's defilement, for they carry defilement wherever they go. Their fallen hearts go with them.

As parents, we want our children to know that the fear of God—not the fear of culture—is the beginning of wisdom (Proverbs 1:7). We must be careful what message we really believe about defilement. Sometimes our traditions inculcate a diabolical lie.

How do we avoid falling prey to traditions that twist our theology? Again the Bible is to be our guide and our grid, not tradition. Though tradition may have the appearance of wisdom, beware lest it violate the thrust of God's truth. Evil must not be blamed on external sources. Our numerous traditions designed to keep us clean sometimes miss the heart of the matter—the human heart.

4. Tradition May Contribute to Spiritual Blindness.

Matthew reports that the statement about defilement aroused the ire of the Pharisees (Matthew 15:12–14). This confirms how traditions engage, and enrage, the emotions. The Pharisees felt as if Jesus had taken a cheap shot and they were duly offended. Perhaps the Pharisees were so upset with Jesus' words that they left the scene, for they are not again mentioned in this passage. Certainly Jesus' disciples did not understand the implications of Jesus' statements regarding defilement. In any case, they confronted Him.

Jesus then doubled the offense when He called the Pharisees unplanted plants and blind guides. The Pharisees thought they were wheat; Jesus saw them as weeds (Matthew 13:40–42). The Pharisees were convinced that they were guides to the blind (Romans 2:19); Jesus saw them as blind. Since God did not plant them, they would be "weeded" from His garden, Jesus said. And since they were blind, people followed them to their great peril.

These words could not have cut much more. The Pharisees took enormous pride in their roots. They were Abraham's children. They were planted by God. Moreover, they saw themselves as the spiritual guides of Israel whose task it was to lead the people toward the light. Jesus likened them, however, to weeds and blind guides. Ouch!

Jesus made it clear that Pharisaical traditions posed a much more serious problem than the disciples imagined. It was perilous to their spiritual health to hang around with those who equated tradition and truth. These were tough words from a troubled Master. It is more dangerous than we know to follow Pharisees, ancient or modern. Traditions, which are often a large part of the package of legalism, must be strongly confronted.

One of the surest tests of what we truly believe is revealed by how we emotionally react to various situations. Emotional reactions expose the inner workings of our souls. Which of our traditions enrage us? Do any of our traditions have a blinding effect?

Several years ago at the church that I now pastor, a controversy raged over the Sunday evening service. The proposal of some was to substitute small groups for the Sunday evening service, thinking that this would increase participation and enhance spiritual life. The suggestion of this contemporary tradition clashed with an older tradition, and emotions were aroused. The Sunday evening service was in the minds of some almost sacrosanct; an anchor amidst stormy seas; a link with conservatism and a hedge against liberalism. It was one of the meetings by which God's popularity and our spirituality could be measured. Others were just as insistent that small groups were the wave of the future, a necessary means of spiritual nurture.

I suspect that few involved in the debate knew the origins of the Sunday evening service. It began on the frontier as a means to reach the unsaved with the gospel. It was therefore called the "Sunday Evening Evangelistic Service." The hook used to entice "sinners" to the service was gas lamps, which were installed early on in the churches. These lights were a novelty and therefore attracted the curious. Once the gas lamps drew the people in, the preaching of the gospel drew them to Christ. So the Sunday evening service began as an innovative experiment designed to promote evangelism.[11] Now many years later, there are rarely unbelievers present on Sunday night. They are comfortably nestled in their "pews" in front of the ball game or *60 Minutes*.

Somewhere the Sunday evening service changed its focus from evangelism to edification. Of course, edification of believers is a worthy goal. And there is nothing wrong with holding Sunday evening services. Nor is there anything wrong with small groups. But Sunday evening services and small groups are both merely traditions, human methods to enhance ministry. If we forget this, we become blind and can misspend much emotional energy.[12]

How do we avoid falling prey to the emotional offense and spiritual blindness that traditions can produce? First, when our emotions rise over religious issues that we know are not biblical commands, it is time to take a time-out. We ought to listen to the other side. Then we should ask ourselves if our offense is justified or if God is trying to nudge us. Next, we must be sure that our lives are guided by God's Word, not human traditions. For to lead people into traditions as if they were the essence of Christianity is no different than a blind man leading a tour through the Grand Canyon.

At the same time, we must be prepared to cause offense if we seek to truly follow Jesus. I do not believe that we should try to be offensive; instead, we should seek to be as gracious and patient as possible. And surely we should never confront traditions with a haughty spirit. Few things are as offensive as arrogant youth seeking to replace crusty traditions with contemporary traditions. This is major-league hypocrisy (and very common today).

Finally, we must beware lest we attach ourselves to those who lead us with traditions. I believe that there are many whose major emphases are traditions rather than truth. People tend to follow them in droves simply because traditions connect us with meaningful events from the past. Beware!

5. Tradition May Stifle Effective Ministry.

According to Jesus, the hand-washing traditions of the Jews not only contradicted the truth of Scripture regarding defilement, they were no longer necessary (Mark 7:17–20). Jesus declared that the food laws of the Old Testament were henceforth superseded. The logical implication of Jesus' biology lesson is that no food, unwashed hands, pots, or pans are inherently defiling. One can eat anything—pork, shrimp, or ostrich!

The food laws of the Jews had a theological positive purpose: to set the Jews apart as God's chosen people (Leviticus 11:44–45). So why the change by Jesus? If the food laws for the Jews were allowed to continue while God was in the business of raising up a global family headed by the Lord Jesus Christ—one that included Jews, Samaritans, and Gentiles—there would be insurmountable division and disunity. The food laws would always be a reminder of the distinctiveness (and perhaps superiority) of the Jews. Food laws and the traditions that emanated from them would hopelessly stifle ministry among the lost people of the world.

This Jesus would not tolerate. So with one stroke of the pen, Mark drew the implication from Jesus' words that food laws were canceled (v. 19). This removed one of the greatest impediments to effective ministry that any Jewish evangelist, church planter, or pastor would ever have to face. It is not by accident, by the way, that the very next event recorded in Mark's Gospel

involved Jesus' reaching out to a Gentile woman (Mark 7:24–30).
If Jesus had been hung up by dietary concerns, He would have
avoided her.

One of the greatest dangers of tradition is that it can effectively block new Spirit-led ministries. In fact, tradition is a
potential giant killer of ministry, for traditions tend to be maintained long after they have lost their usefulness. Ironically, some
of our most cherished traditions began as avant-garde ministries
that someone had the courage and conviction to initiate.

Let me cite some examples of our traditions that potentially
stifle effective ministry. The style of music that we deem holy
greatly impacts ministry. If we believe that evil resides in the
beat, style, instrumentation, tempo, or the volume of music, we
will likely not be able to reach a particular subculture (that is,
unless they renounce their "ungodliness" and embrace our traditions). Consider the organ. This instrument was first used in a
North American church in 1703, not sooner because it was
opposed by those with Puritan roots. Finally in 1770 the first
Puritan church, probably real risk-takers, acquired one![13] By the
choices of music and instruments that we regard as acceptable,
we may narrow our ministry. And the ones whom we hurt are not
only those who are excluded but also those who are comforted.
For teaching that a particular kind of music is holy stifles our
understanding of spirituality.

Consider how our traditions regarding morning service
times affect ministry to those in the pews. Most churches have
worship services Sunday at 10:30 or 11:00 A.M. Leith Anderson
writes, "I have never milked a cow. . . . Most Americans have never milked a cow. Yet many churches still hold their Sunday
morning services at eleven o'clock, an hour originally chosen to
accommodate the milking schedule of dairy farmers."[14] Perhaps
ministry would be better served if church services were on Saturday evening at eight or Sunday morning at eight. Tradition, not
God, has set the time of our services. When society's work and
play schedules change, perhaps service times for worship services should change as well.

How do we avoid the tendency to let tradition stifle effective
ministry? Once again, we need to keep tradition and truth separate in our own minds. We will help both spiritual growth and
ministry when we differentiate between traditions and truth. It is
wise to distinguish between the two. Next, we need to keep

methodology fluid and changeable. The message of the Scriptures is primary and should not be changed. The methods, however, are negotiable and should be changed for effective ministry in changing cultures. Sometimes we do the opposite, compromising the message to fit our methods. To keep the priority of ministry over methods, we will have to develop the spiritual virtue of risk-taking. This does not come easy for most of us in light of the fact that traditions define our comfort zones.

BALANCING TRADITION AND TRUTH

Our mission as followers of Jesus Christ is to wisely balance God's truth and human tradition. How can we balance the two? First, we must recognize that traditions are all around us. They govern (usually unknowingly) much of our lives and determine to a large extent how we evaluate others. Thus, we must raise to a conscious level the effect that traditions have on our minds and lives. Second, we must never forget that by definition tradition is man-made. However, we tend to confuse tradition and truth because religious traditions are often traced back to scriptural proof texts. Thus, traditions tend to become sacrosanct over time. We must remind ourselves often of the roots of our traditions and regard them as negotiable.

Third, traditions tend to reinforce external religion, to focus largely on external acts rather than heart attitudes. Thus, we must beware of the false religion and heart hypocrisy that traditionalism can easily spawn. Let us remain grateful for traditions but beware of traditionalism. Fourth, what we see in traditions may not be what we get. Traditions have the appearance of wisdom, and because they "feel so right" they seem righteous. However, they may subtly twist truth and give a false sense of righteousness. Tradition can contribute to spiritual blindness and result in great spiritual evil. Thus, discernment is needed as we deal with the traditions of our lives.

Finally, tradition can be one of the greatest enemies of what God is trying to do. He is infinitely creative and continually moves in unexpected and delightful ways. However, it has been said that the seven last words of the church are, "We never did it that way before." When we cling tenaciously to tradition, we tend to stifle ministry. It takes courage to confront traditions and face almost certain opposition. Yet the alternative, to repress eternal ministry, may rob the church of God's initiative and blessing.

God has called us to be committed, not necessarily comfortable. When traditions based on God's truth enhance ministry, they are to be defended. But when they inhibit ministry, they must be reevaluated and revised, along with a searching heart check by all involved.

Chapter Eight

WHEN FENCES BECOME THE FOCUS

The motion picture *Chariots of Fire* told the compelling story of Eric Liddell, the "flying Scotsman." It won the Academy Award as best film of 1981. A stunning hit in Hollywood, it also captured an enthusiastic audience among Christians, for "Chariots" stood for solid Christian values. In the movie, Liddell won the gold medal in the 1924 Olympics in the 400-yard race, an event he was not supposed to run. He refused to participate in his featured event, the 100-yard dash, because some of the preliminary heats were held on Sunday, "the Lord's Day," and he was a strict Sabbatarian. Few people, secular or religious, failed to applaud Liddell's character, convictions, courage, and, of course, his success!

No doubt Liddell acted according to his conscience, and things worked out well. But was his stand normative for all sincere Christians? If Jesus had been Eric Liddell's coach, what would He have advised about running on the "Sabbath"? For thousands of years the Sabbath observance has stirred deep religious convictions. And it represents the heart and soul of a very significant Pharisaic practice called "fencing the Law."

The Pharisees ardently believed that God had told them to fence the Law. The Mishnah declares the Pharisees' mandate: "Moses received the Law from Sinai and committed it to Joshua, and Joshua to the elders, and the elders to the Prophets; and the Prophets committed it to the men of the Great Synagogue. They said three things: Be deliberate in judgment; raise up many disciples; *and make a fence around the Law.*"[1]

God had revealed His will so that people would, by trusting and obeying Him, become holy. Indeed, the Law, the highest expression of this will, was not only essential for the spiritual life of the individual but also the survival of the nation. It stated the irrevocable will of God for His people. It must be protected, communicated, and kept. However, God's unchanging Law is by nature somewhat ambiguous. It requires interpretation and application in changing cultural settings. Thus the great teachers of the Jews took up the task of explaining in specific terms the meaning and application of the Law to life. They felt duty-bound to protect the sacred and to keep people from transgression of God's commands caused by ignorance, indifference, or insolence. This highly valued process was known as "fencing the Law."

Fence-building was not an independent and random process. Rather, fences were carefully constructed by eminent Scripture scholars, duly recognized by the people, according to the mandate of Deuteronomy 17:8–11. These fences were not envisioned to become a rigid system of dry dogmas. Rather, they were intended to take the absolutes of God's Law and make them applicable to contemporary life.

THE FIRST FENCE

Fence-building goes back to the beginning of the human race. Eve built the first fence around God's commands when she added the words "or touch it" in Genesis 3:3. Perhaps she thought (mistakenly) that the best way to avoid forbidden fruit was to build protective barriers around God's commands. Apparently she felt that obedience would be aided by being stricter than God. The fencing process began with a simple addition to God's Law.

Given our human nature, the fences would have proliferated if others were involved: "Do not smell it; do not see it; do not go near it; rope off that part of the garden; build a wall around the forbidden tree." Perhaps someone would eventually decree that the tree should be cut down and uprooted! Since God's freedom was frightening, fences became the focus.

By her fence-building, Eve bypassed the heart protection that God offered through an open relationship with Him. We do the same today. Whenever God offers a command and sincere people, like us, seek to obey it, fences are constructed, often replacing a heart relationship with God. Fences have become so much a part of our religious scenery that we hardly see them.

THE NATURE OF FENCES

A fence, of course, is a boundary. According to *Merriam Webster's Collegiate Dictionary*, it is "a means of protection; a barrier intended to prevent escape or intrusion or to mark a boundary." In agriculture, fences are devices designed to keep animals from straying. Fences give us a sense of security, ownership, and control. In religious terms, fences are humanly devised interpretations, explanations, and applications of biblical commands. Their purposes are to (1) protect God's commandments and (2) keep people from transgressing those commands. By living within these fences we believe we can live safely before God. Those who make fences are usually well-intentioned Bible teachers. And religious people in general demand that their instructors define fences so as to standardize religious behavior and simplify obedience.

Fence-building differs in significant ways from traditions, the topic of the previous chapter. The following chart may help to highlight some of the differences:

Traditions Versus Fences

Traditions	Fences
Key Scripture: Matthew 15:1–20; Mark 7:1–23	**Key Scripture:** Matthew 12:1–14; Mark 2:23–3:6
Test Case: Hand-washing traditions	**Test Case:** Sabbath fences
Purpose of Traditions: To promote and enhance ministry	**Purpose of Fences:** To protect the Law and prevent disobedience
Source of Traditions: Ministries (usually based on proof texts from Scripture) that have worked in the past	**Source of Fences:** Scriptural commands that must be interpreted and practically applied
Positive Contributions of Traditions: Preserve effective ministry; provide stability and security; connect us with the past	**Positive Contributions of Fences:** Protect from sin; provide standards and strictures; restrain people from flirting with evil
Dangers of Traditions: May contribute to mindless religion; may subtly contradict God's truth; may contribute to spiritual blindness; tend to lose sight of their human origins; often resist change and perpetuate the status quo; the great potential enemy of ministry	**Dangers of Fences:** May not be consistent with the whole counsel of God's Word; may pervert God's priorities; may contradict common sense and practice; may divert attention from true intent of the Law; the great potential enemy of maturity

Nowhere were the fence-building activities of the Pharisees more pronounced and prolific than in the Sabbath regulations. The observance of the Sabbath was at the very heart of the Pharisaic system. The laws that grew up around the Sabbath were voluminous. Judging by the amount of space devoted to it in the Mishnah, it is the single most significant subject to the rabbis.[2] However, Jesus viewed God's Law and humanly devised fences differently than the Pharisees. Seven clashes between Jesus and the Pharisees over the Sabbath are recorded in the Gospels.[3] These, as one can imagine, raised their religious hackles. They could not comprehend why a reputed "holy man" would not fully comply with their "holy" fences. Conflict over the Sabbath precipitates one of the major turning points in the ministry of Jesus. Before the events recorded in Matthew 12, Jesus was something of an irritating novelty. Henceforth, He would be the object of intense scrutiny and eventually homicide.

HOW SABBATH FENCES DEVELOP

Conflict over the Sabbath began one Saturday in the springtime in Israel as Jesus and His disciples were going for a stroll. Jesus was discussing rest, an appropriate Sabbath subject, with His band of friends. They became hungry and started to glean some grain from the fields through which they were walking. This was a normal activity for poor people. But not on the Sabbath! Well-established Jewish fences prohibited such activities. And the Pharisees noticed it and said something.

Sabbath observance was one of the big three marks of Judaism along with circumcision and the food laws. Thus the Pharisees viewed Jesus' activity on the Sabbath as a major offense. God's Word was clear: The Sabbath was established by God in creation (Genesis 2:1–3); "Remember the Sabbath . . ." was the fourth, and longest, commandment (Exodus 20:8–11; Deuteronomy 5:12–15). Sabbath rest was a God-given sign for Israel, God's covenant people, which distinguished them from the surrounding nations (Exodus 31:12–17). Furthermore, violation of the Sabbath was decreed by God through Moses to be a capital offense (Numbers 15:32–36).

It was not clear, however, how to apply the Sabbath commands in contemporary society. What does "remember" mean? When does the "Sabbath" start and stop? How does one make a day "holy"? And trickiest of all, what is meant by "work"? The

Scriptures did not provide detailed instruction on the particulars of Sabbath observance, and to make it more difficult the two major schools of Pharisaism disagreed on many fine points. The Sabbath commands, like most of the 613 commands in the Old Testament, seemed to demand explanation and beg for practical application. After all, the faithful want to know where they stand with God. Thus began a major effort of the Pharisees and their rabbis to define the Sabbath and explain to the people of God what constituted proper and improper Sabbath conduct.

Perhaps, though this issue is not brought up in the text, Jesus and His disciples had walked too far that day. The rabbis had decreed that a stroll on the Sabbath must be limited to just over a half mile from one's residence. They did not arrive at this number arbitrarily. Instead by combing the Scriptures and ingeniously combining texts, they arrived at a safe distance to travel without "breaking God's Law."[4]

However, what constitutes one's residence? This matter is a little trickier. Are there any exceptions, any loopholes? Of course! And these were decreed with characteristic precision. One could redefine the boundaries of one's residence and thus increase a Sabbath day's journey. Or one could place various objects, like a rope, across the road and thus increase the size of one's "home." Moreover, the rabbis decreed that performing certain activities, like the boiling of an egg, made that place one's "dwelling." And one could connect many homes together, creating a kind of communal home that was very large indeed, conveniently increasing the acceptable Sabbath distance.

The specific offense for which Jesus and His disciples were interrogated, however, was not the distance traveled on the Sabbath but the "work" they engaged in. The rabbis ruled that thirty-nine activities were out-of-bounds for the Sabbath. At least four, and perhaps more, of these explicitly prohibited Sabbath activities were engaged in by the disciples.[5] And when the Pharisees saw Jesus' disciples "reaping grain" on the Sabbath, they voiced their concern. To them the activity of Jesus' disciples was "not lawful." He had transgressed the "Law."

POSITIVE CONTRIBUTIONS OF FENCES

Fences can be helpful. First and foremost, *they can protect and instruct the innocent and immature.* A parent would not think of allowing a child free access to a hot stove, a busy street, or a fragile glass object. As I write this book, I have an infant in my home. We have erected fences in strategic places to prevent him from falling down stairs, from getting too close to dangerous or expensive items, and from going into places where he is not allowed. Those fences are a great help to us. They minimize our fears and maximize our parental freedom, not to mention protect Seth's life and limbs. Fences are good and necessary for the protection of children. Religious fences protect the immature. Because of their lack of knowledge and experience, youth often need things spelled out in concrete terms so they can understand and comply.

Furthermore, *fences can have a positive psychological function.* People do not deal effectively with continual ambiguity and freedom. Knowing what to do and not to do gives us security; knowing where we stand gives us a sense of satisfaction, even control in a complex world. Personal fences made together with God and based on one's conscience and convictions are encouraged in the Scriptures (Romans 14–15). Fences can provide the boundaries we individually need to have balanced lives and to say no to compelling, yet unwise, temptations.

Fences also sometimes serve the function of instilling awe for the Law. Fear can be a God-given protection. Law-fences help to keep us from evil and promote social order. They are part of God's common grace. Many of our fences silently serve us by limiting our propensity for sin. They protect my areas of weakness. They highlight the potential dangers of seemingly harmless activities. The numerous fences of my childhood, which I generally did not violate out of fear, spared me from much trouble and lessened the scars of my life. During high school, for instance, I avoided mind-altering substances. My fear of punishment and loss of self-control protected me from addictions that could have hurt me and others.

Fences can additionally help shape positive habits that reinforce godly lifestyles. Many habits, such as communing regularly with God individually and corporately, can be helpful. Jesus Himself, though He violated some of the Pharisees' fences, complied with others. The Scriptures imply that He attended the synagogue, presumably regularly, though the Law did not specifically require this. Positive habits, however, always can be perverted. Devotion can degenerate into duty. Church attendance can become rote legalism.

Thus fences can serve a valuable function in our religious lives and communities. They are perhaps a needed accommodation to the fallenness of the flesh. However, fences often have significant spiritual dangers that Jesus was quick and careful to point out.

THE DANGERS OF FENCES

No one who ever lived was more concerned with righteousness than Jesus. Like the Pharisees, He wanted to protect people from the pain of sin. Nevertheless, Jesus had some significant problems with their fences. Jesus' interaction with the Pharisees in Matthew 12:1–14 highlights six dangers of humanly devised fences.

1. Inconsistent with God's Word

Our fences may not be consistent with the entirety of God's Word. In Matthew 12, Jesus first confronted the scripture-loving Pharisees with the fact that their Sabbath fences had Scriptural holes. Though their fences were built on scriptural proof texts, they sometimes did not square with the whole counsel of God's Word.

Jesus, the itinerant peasant preacher, must have stunned the biblically learned of the day when He said, "Have you not read what David did when he became hungry, he and his companions, how he entered the house of God, and they ate the consecrated bread, which was not lawful for him to eat nor for those with him, but for the priests alone?" (vv. 3–4). Jesus was referring to an event in Israel's history recorded in 1 Samuel 21:1–6. David, the anointed king of Israel, while he and his comrades were running from King Saul, entered the tabernacle at Nob, lied about their mission, and were given the consecrated bread to eat by Ahimelech, the high priest. This bread was given despite the restriction of Leviticus 24:5–9. Presumably the consecrated bread was eaten because no ordinary bread was available. It is likely that this event took place on the Sabbath since the consecrated bread had just been changed. (Each Sabbath twelve fresh loaves replaced the former ones.)

Clearly David violated the written Law but was not blamed as a law-breaker. Rules and regulations sometimes allow exceptions based on legitimate human needs and the status of the "law-breaker." Jesus warned the Pharisees to beware of building a case and calling it scriptural from incomplete data. Besides, the One who violated the Pharisees' Sabbath fence is none other than David's greater son!

In this area some of our fences are no less riddled with scriptural holes than the Pharisees'. What we present as solidly biblical is not if we examine all of the evidence. But we often do not recognize this. We consider our fences to be God-given and endow them with divine authority; we highlight and exaggerate certain texts but omit others. One of the great ironies of fence-building is that those who are most prolific at the art are the most convinced that they are people of the Book.

For example, we catalog and communicate the biblical texts that condemn alcohol consumption, and they are numerous but curiously fail to mention the verses, and they are not few, that allow, even commend drinking.[6] We are fully justified in pointing out the dangers and deceptiveness of alcohol as well as its devastating potential consequences.[7] However, we must be wary of the construction of elaborate defenses of abstinence, utilizing human fences as our method. While warning against alcohol is helpful and fully scriptural, some of our fences degenerate into significant Scripture twisting, skipping, and distorting. What does this teach people who have come to trust us when they encounter evidence in the Scriptures that contradicts our "airtight" biblical exegesis? Freedom always offers the potential for abuse, but it also provides the opportunity for true convictions and character to develop.

Various fences involving worship also are on precarious ground if we consider the whole counsel of God's Word. Dancing, for example, was a prohibited activity in my background. The temptations of sexual arousal motivated the construction of these fences, and I have grown to appreciate the protection that they provided. Some dancing in Scripture is associated with evil (see Exodus 32:19; Matthew 14:6).[8] However, an across-the-board ban on dancing is not supported by Scripture. God must believe that the body can rightly be used in celebration and worship. Moreover, we cite texts on reverence in worship but are silent about those that speak of noisy celebration with "clashing cymbals," no less (see 1 Chronicles 13:8; Psalm 150:5). Rigid fence-building can turn us into judgmental thinkers rather than Scripture-submitting, Spirit-led people. Jesus would likely get out His wire cutters and hack away at some of our fences just as He did two thousand years ago with the Pharisees.

2. May Ignore Special Ministries and Exceptions

Humanly devised fences may fail to recognize divinely ordained ministries and exceptions. At times, circumstances require that fences, made for man's protection, be broken. Jesus pointed out to the Pharisees that certain divinely ordained ministries may supersede humanly devised fences. Thus today's police officers become "law-breakers" when they run red lights in order to carry out their duties and protect people from harm.

Once again, Jesus' appeal was to Scripture, this time from the Pentateuch (Numbers 28:9–10). He said, "Or have you not read in the Law, that on the Sabbath the priests in the temple break the Sabbath and are innocent? But I say to you that something greater than the temple is here" (Matthew 12:5–6). Technically the priests broke the Law every Sabbath by performing their tasks, but no one regarded them as Sabbath-breakers. The nature of their work as God's worship leaders demanded that they violate Sabbath fences. There are, therefore, valid reasons to "violate" Sabbath fences. Moreover, God—who made the Sabbath—has every right to supersede Sabbath fences.

Some of our fences, like the Pharisees', illegitimately restrict service to God and ministry to people. They do so by fencing out what God allows or encourages. Consider corporate worship and what we ask of our choir or minister of music. We subjectively define what is "sacred" and "secular" music. Then we construct fences according to our age, subculture, upbringing, musical tastes, theology and view of God, denominational heritage, and so on. We learn to associate certain rhythms and instruments with certain people and movements and thus regard that kind of music as spiritually worthy or unworthy. We tell our minister what music to fence out of the worship repertoire.

God must be allowed to tell us what His music tastes are without foisting our fences on Him. In the preeminent God-inspired hymnal, the Psalms, we learn about the kinds of instruments He prefers (Psalm 150) and His tolerance of repetition (Psalm 136). This hymnbook makes clear that God is not partial to theological content and adverse to emotion, as some suggest. Psalm 95, a classic text on worship, directs us to rejoice in His greatness, revere Him for His goodness to us, and respond to His Word. We are not wise, or scriptural, to choose one facet of worship and deify it. I wonder how many opportunities for ministry have been lost because our humanly devised fences have locked out ministry to certain kinds of people?

3. Forgetting God's Priorities: People

Jesus admonished the Pharisees of His day (vv. 7–8) that humanly devised fences may misrepresent God's priorities. They sometimes substitute rituals for relationships, programs for ministry, and sacrifices for compassion. At times significant social concerns are drowned in a sea of religious trivialities. Fences sometimes defy the priorities of God. They may subordinate compassion, a high divine priority, to rituals that regulate external behavior.

Once again Jesus rebuked the Pharisees from the Scriptures. Here He quoted Hosea 6:6 (from the prophets) and highlighted God's priorities: "But if you had known what this means, 'I desire compassion, and not a sacrifice,' you would not have condemned the innocent. For the Son of Man is Lord of the Sabbath" (vv. 7–8). The Pharisees' Sabbath fences had evolved such that they restricted acts of mercy and even condemned those who engaged in them. God always put compassion above ritual, but they had turned God's priorities upside down.

Sometimes our fences likewise defy God's priorities. For instance, consider the "Daily Quiet Time." Also known as "devotions," they have become a required part of a good Christian's routine. Early in life, I concluded that if a day of devotions was missed, God was miffed. (Please note that I am entirely in favor of spending time alone with God. In fact, I believe that one of the great losses of the Christian church in America today is devotion to God.) Fences specified when such devotions should occur ("first thing in the morning") and how long they should last (at least "Seven Minutes with God"). Bible memorization was a necessity as was "inductive Bible study" when I was introduced to it. The ACTS prayer formula (adoration, confession, thanksgiving, and supplication) provided a helpful fence to organize my prayer life and to make sure I didn't leave anything essential out.

The result of these external fences for me, one who worked hard to be right, was the mechanical following of a regimen of devotions almost with a stopwatch and checklist in hand to be sure I "put in my time." When I did, I felt good. When I didn't, I felt guilty. Somehow I missed the point that my "Quiet Time" was not supposed to be an end in itself but a means to an end. I have come to learn that God wants my devotion and not my devotions; He wants my heart and not just my time. If our fences help us to get to God's goal, then they are helpful. But if they do not, they can be harmful.

Even the fences we place around Christian marriage at times may also reverse God's priorities. We have devised formulas for a maximum marriage and raised great expectations that often lead to frustration. What is strangely lost in this sea of dissatisfaction is simple commitment, servanthood, forgiveness, and grace, virtues extremely high on God's priority scale. "Intimacy" has become the holy grail and "faithfulness and love" are no longer enough. Husbands and wives seem more concerned about "deep relationships" than simple service to one another. And people are so concerned about the state of their psyche that they live miserably within themselves rather than for Christ and others.

4. Forgetting Who Is in Control

As a crowning blow to the Pharisees' fences, Jesus then declared Himself to be the Lord of the Sabbath. He had previously implied that He was David's greater son (vv. 3–4) and a priest greater than the temple (v. 6). Now He bluntly made a Messianic claim calling Himself the "Lord of the Sabbath" (v. 8). The Messiah has the prerogative to determine how the day He had a part in planning should be spent. It is the height of presumption for humans to tell God how to keep our fences. It should be the other way around. God should be telling us what He meant by the Sabbath and how it should be spent.

God retains the prerogative to interpret His commands and even to change them if He wishes. He does this, of course, consistently with His nature, promises, and plan. Human religious fences, however, sometimes fail to consider divine changes. It is wrong to instruct God in what He can and cannot do, particularly when He has spoken clearly on a matter. But this is precisely what we do with some of our fences. For example, God decreed food laws for a time (Deuteronomy 14:1–21) and then canceled their necessity (Mark 7:14–23; Acts 10; 1 Timothy 4:1–5). But some still insist on following food laws that God has specifically abolished. Moreover, Christians often are in the forefront of political action for so-called "blue laws" that prohibit shops from transacting business on Sundays. Rest is part of the rhythm of the universe that God created. However, the New Testament says that Sabbath observance is not binding in any legalistic form (Romans 14:1–12; Colossians 2:8–17). The norm of the New Testament is the exercise of responsible freedom in Christ, not reversion to the Law of Moses.

5. Not Always Logical or Consistently Applied

Fences at times do not follow common sense, nor are they applied consistently. They may even expose our fundamental inhumanity. In Matthew 13:9–13, the Pharisees put Jesus to the test with a disabled man present in the synagogue. According to rabbinical rulings, it was permissible to heal on the Sabbath, provided life was at stake.[9] If the healing could wait, however, a delay was expected to maintain the integrity of the Sabbath. A man with a withered hand was obviously not in a life-threatening situation. The fence was clear. Would Jesus comply with their fences or defy them?

Reasoning now from common practice and common sense, Jesus asked a simple question of the Pharisees: "What do you do when a sheep falls into a hole on the Sabbath?" The question was framed expecting that they do allow "working" to extricate the animal from a pit. By implication Jesus pointed out that the Pharisees valued animals more than human beings, economic interests more than social concerns. Sometimes Pharisaic fences not only contradicted Scripture; they also defied common sense and common practice.

Some of our fences likewise are downright inconsistent and silly. In the 1960s and 1970s, hair length was a major issue and considered an unmistakable symbol of rebellion. Regularly 1 Corinthians 11:14 was mentioned from the pulpit. ("Does not even nature itself teach you that if a man has long hair, it is a dishonor to him?") However, I do not recall ever seeing an artist's rendition of Jesus, or any contemporary of His, sporting a crew cut or flattop. The paintings always showed Jesus with long hair. And yet those who looked like Jesus were called hippies. No one ever tried to explain this oddity to me. Furthermore, when theaters were the only place where Hollywood movies were shown, it was possible to consistently ban the industry through fences. However, as the video cassette recorder emerged, and now the Internet, fence-making has become increasingly difficult to apply. Still we try with our rating systems.

THE RIGHT WAY

Keeping the Fences Up

Many rules and codes of living can be obeyed by human effort. We Christians can heed the fences we fashion without a right motive. But some of God's commands are not so easily kept. They often require divine enablement. Rather than human effort, they demand dependency on God.

Fences may direct us to God, but they will not make us holy. We must watch that fences do not become a substitute for a relationship with God. Keeping the fences up does not necessarily keep us close to God. The Scriptures teach that the growing Christian trusts and obeys God with the help of Christ's Spirit (John 15:4–5; 16: 7–8, 14).

Romans 14–15 and 1 Corinthians 8–10 tell us some of the principles and distinctions we are advised to make as we walk this road with and for Christ. Clearly the Christian life was intended to be upright, not uptight. Fences subtly teach us that God wants us to "play it safe" rather than walk by faith. Keeping up fences, like keeping up appearances, only works for a time. But living in God's power through the Spirit can sustain us and empower us day by day.

6. An Opposite Outcome: Bondage

Jesus returned the Sabbath to God's original intent and offered a divine interpretation when He declared, "So then, it is lawful to do good on the Sabbath" (v. 12b). And the parallel passage in Mark 2:27 records, "The Sabbath was made for man, and not man for the Sabbath." The Pharisees' fences had come full circle. What God originally intended as a gift to human beings had become, through the art of fence-building, a prison. The Sabbath, intended to provide time to help people see God better, had been made into that which obstructed their view.

Often fences miss the heart and intent of God, and they may distract from that which they were designed to protect. The Pharisees' Sabbath fences turned a God-designed day of rest, remembrance, reflection, rejoicing, and renewal into a day of petty, nitpicky rules and regulations. A blessing became a burden (see Isaiah 58:13–14). The Sabbath was designed by God to promote ministry, not to restrict it.

Jesus, as Mark 3:5 tells us, was angry at the hardness of heart to which the Pharisees' fences had contributed. Accusation, not compassion, motivated them. A desire to condemn, not a desire to learn, was behind their question. Jesus refused to be bound by such ungodly and irrational fences. He could have waited until Sunday, but He refused to do so! So He healed the man's hand right in front of the Pharisees, right in the synagogue, right on the Sabbath!

It is common for our human fences likewise to miss the original intent and spirit of God's commands and even to contradict them. For example, sexual fences are the subject of many popular Christian books for teens. Called divine standards, they sometimes propose various lengths of clothing, distances of separation, kinds of body contact, times and places where couples can be together, varieties of dating (now courting) behavior, and so on. God's desire for purity in mind and body is often lost in a maze of restrictions and requirements. The fences may be "obeyed" in behavior while purity is defied in attitude. The fences that I followed did protect me from behavioral evil and its consequences, for which I am most grateful. However, the fences failed to curb my curiosity or develop my discernment. Loophole thinking and practice rather than true righteousness often become uppermost in the minds of the "faithful."

Moreover, we have a plethora of separatistic fences bolstered by an array of biblical proof texts, including: "Do not be bound together with unbelievers" (2 Corinthians 6:14–18) and "Bad company corrupts good morals" (1 Corinthians 15:33). Such cautions were not designed by God to eliminate redemptive relationships with sinners (John 17:14–19; 1 Corinthians 5:9–13). Furthermore, church attendance fences like "not forsaking our own assembling together" (Hebrews 10:25) tend to make us content with mere attendance rather than true accountability, with warm bodies in a pew rather than warm words that stimulate love and good deeds (Hebrews 10:24). And we regularly judge people by noncompliance with our Sunday morning, Sunday evening, and Wednesday evening service fences.

Sometimes our fences become like prisons that militate against doing good. We may be called upon by God to intentionally violate fences in order to do good. We may have to trespass fences that keep us from doing evangelism where the "sinners" are. We may need to take a stand against ideological fences that limit reaching out to the poor and needy.

BALANCING FREEDOM AND FENCES

One of the strange ironies about human beings is that we both despise and delight in fences. On the one hand, we sing, "Don't Fence Me In," while on the other, we cannot build fences fast enough. We cry "Freedom!" and construct fences. Being without boundaries is frightening for societies and individuals. But it seems to produce downright paranoia for religious people. Of all the people in the world, perhaps we religious folk are the most fond of fences. They make us feel secure, they define for us what is and what is not acceptable, they motivate and protect us, and they help us keep score for ourselves and on others. However, sheep are not best tended with fences but by a relationship with a good shepherd. One of the marks of Christian maturity is the ability to find freedom in Christ and live a life of love. But how do we do this? Perhaps Jesus can offer us some clues.

The Need—and Challenge—of Finding Freedom

Jesus' interactions with the Pharisees demonstrated that freedom from fences was not easy. When fences were violated, sparks flew on both sides (Matthew 12:2, 10–14). Fence-breaking makes religious people profoundly angry. In Jesus' case the anger turned homicidal. Though Jesus had encountered opposition previously,[10] here for the first time the Pharisees turned toward plotting His assassination! I find it peculiar, yet true to life, that the breaking of fences prompted such a radical reaction from the Pharisees. We must recognize that at times a disciple of Christ must trespass human fences and risk misunderstanding, even anger, in order to follow Him and do good.

Apart from the specific dangers of fences that Jesus highlighted in His interaction with the Pharisees, fences tend to replace freedom in Christ with rigidity and legalism. They may subtly substitute human effort for divine enablement. Fences can become human attempts to avoid disobedience without genuine faith. Usually fences can be obeyed if one works at it. They are designed so that they can be kept and one can view himself or herself as compliant. Yet many of God's commands require supernatural help. They cannot be obeyed by one's effort. (See "The Right Way," page 131.)

Though fences may help the immature to find stability in the Christian life, they are of only minimal value in stimulating true maturity. Over the long haul, fences do not work. If they become the focus of our lives, they are perhaps more likely to lead to legalism than to true lordship. And when fences "work," they may superficially counterfeit the work of the Holy Spirit and make Him unnecessary. Moreover, fences, though security-producing, do not develop discernment. Robert C. Roberts comments,

> There's something comfortable about reducing Christianity to a list of dos and don'ts, whether your list comes from mindless fundamentalism or mindless liberalism: you always know where you stand, and this helps reduce anxiety. Dos-and-don'tism has the advantage that you don't need wisdom. You don't have to think subtly or make hard choices. You don't have to relate personally to a demanding and loving Lord.[11]

Finding the Balance

How can we live practically, balancing the freedom and fences of our lives? First, we should recognize the value of fences, particularly for the young and immature. None of us can live without boundaries, nor should we. Boundaries are good for us, they help us, they protect us. They provide structure and needed guidance for those who are not yet able to make responsible choices (yes, even young disciples of Christ). Also, they provide useful boundaries to check our propensity to sin. Second, we must learn to distinguish between human fences and divine commands. We must resist the urge to give fences the same authority as Scripture. They are not, contrary to popular opinion, the same and should not be confused. We must be constantly vigilant lest we add personal preferences to God's Word and pawn them off as scriptural. Third, we must seek to discern the heart of God in each of the commands we find in His Word. Often fences lead us in directions away from God's heart rather than toward it. A good way to get at the heart of God's commands is to seek to state them, particularly the negative ones, in positive terms. What good is God trying to protect? If the Pharisees had done this with the Sabbath commands, perhaps they would not have constructed some of the fences that they did.

Fourth, we must resist the strong temptation to universalize our personal fences. What is wise, protective behavior for me is not necessarily normative for others. We must not seek to pawn off our personal fences on others. Fifth, fences always present the danger of transferring our trust from God to human devices. Fences work! They can, and often do, help people to live what seems to be a godly lifestyle. They rein in our rebelliousness and help us establish good spiritual habits. If fences serve to increase our dependence on God and intimacy with Him, they are helpful. However, fences can easily become cosmetic substitutes for real righteousness. We must beware of appearing godly without looking inward.

Finally, we must seek to overcome the fear of freedom as we grow in Christ. One of the traits of those who live by the Spirit is that the necessity for law (and fences) diminishes (Galatians 5:22–25). We must be courageous enough to confront God's Word for ourselves. We must pursue a relationship with the Lord Jesus Christ, not seek a "righteousness of my own derived from the Law" (Philippians 3:9–10). We will likely have to become more comfortable with ambiguity. We will not substitute a system for sincere submission to God. When God, not fences, becomes the focus of our lives, we will find freedom and the path to Christlike maturity.

Chapter Nine
WHEN SEPARATISM LEADS US ASTRAY

One of the dirtiest words in our religious vocabulary is *worldliness* and its adjectival form, *worldy*. Worldliness by ecclesiastical definition is the antithesis of godliness. It evokes images of sinful people and seedy places, of dabbling in prohibited activities, of breaking faith, fences, and tradition. Those we label worldly have denied the faith, compromised their principles, and fallen under the spell of the Evil One. To be called worldly can subject one to censure and possible discipline in the church.

Religious individuals and institutions instinctively spot and label worldliness by asking questions. *With whom* do you associate? *Where* do you hang out? *What* do you do or not do? For the most part, the question *why* is irrelevant. It is simply assumed that those who associate with worldly people, in worldly places, doing worldly things must be worldly. The goal for a godly person is to be separate, not a part of the secular status quo. On this issue the Pharisees, ancient and modern, are firm.

Unfortunately, the separated life, just like traditions and well-meaning fences, can lead us away from godly service. In fact, separatism can stimulate sin! It also can inhibit ministry. We will see this in the lives of the Pharisees and our lives as well.

Interestingly, the word *Pharisee* derives from an Aramaic word meaning "separated ones."[1] The Pharisees took pains personally and were widely regarded publicly as those who had separated themselves from evil so as to serve God. They first separated themselves from the Hellenists (proponents of Greek culture) and the Romans. They distanced themselves from the defilement that resulted from contact with Gentiles and Samaritans. They further separated themselves from fellow citizens of Israel who did not keep the Law as they did. The heart and soul of Pharisaism was a sincere desire to be set apart from sin for God.

THE CALL TO SEPARATION

Today we too disdain worldliness and desire to be separate for godly (and biblical) reasons. Most who are schooled in the Bible can make a case against worldliness and for separatism. God chose Israel to be His special people, a holy nation, separate from the surrounding ungodly societies (Exodus 5–6). When God's hand of judgment was about to fall, God said to Moses and Aaron, "Separate yourselves from among this congregation" (Numbers 16:21). After centuries of compromised living, the people of Israel under Ezra promised to separate themselves from Gentile impurity (Ezra 6:21; 9:1–2; Nehemiah 10:28–31). Jesus pronounces those blessed who are spurned by the society for Christ's sake (Luke 6:22). And in Jesus' high priestly prayer (John 17), He states His desired discipleship goal of being in the world but not of it.

The epistles likewise seem to commend separatism. "Do not be deceived: 'Bad company corrupts good morals'" (1 Corinthians 15:33) and "'Therefore, come out from their midst and be separate,' says the Lord" (2 Corinthians 6:17) are two often-quoted Pauline proof texts for separatism. Second Corinthians 6:14–7:1, which contains the "unequally yoked" prohibition, is perhaps the Bible's preeminent separation text. And two apostles have issued these warnings, often cited: "Love not the world, neither the things that are in the world" (1 John 2:15, KJV) and "Abstain from every form [appearance] of evil" (1 Thessalonians 5:22).

However, all this talk about holy separation has some significant scriptural flaws. First, separation contradicts the spirit of the Old Testament. God's design for Israel was not to withdraw from all contact with pagans, but to serve God "as a light to the nations" (Isaiah 42:6–7; 49:6; Luke 2:32). Moreover, each of the passages quoted as substantiation for separatism, as I will explain later, does not mean what is commonly thought when the context is considered. And most tellingly, the false separatism of the Pharisees came into considerable conflict with the God-man Jesus. Jesus' words and deeds gave a stiff challenge to the prevailing notions of worldliness. Indeed, Jesus, the ultimate standard of righteousness, modeled and taught how to be *more*, not less, worldly.

A PROPER DEFINITION

The key to understanding Jesus and the Pharisees is in the definition of worldliness. The Bible defines worldliness for us in 1 John 2:15–16, "Do not love the world nor the things in the world. If anyone loves the world, the love of the Father is not in him. For all that is in the world, the lust of the flesh and the lust of the eyes and the boastful pride of life, is not from the Father, but is from the world." Worldliness, therefore, is the life pursuit of pleasure, possessions, and pride. It is living to satisfy the urges of my flesh, to satiate my lust for material things, and to stoke my ego. Worldly-mindedness has everything to do with ungodly lusts (Jude 18–19). Worldliness is, therefore, more a matter of life pursuit than of people, places, and performance.

Worldliness *is not* best defined by whom one hangs around with, where one goes, and what one does or does not do. Unfortunately, this misdefinition of worldliness has been unwittingly accepted by most religious people who truly care to follow God. (Remember, the premise of this book is that the Pharisees represent religious people who are serious about their faith, not those who are casual about their commitment to God.) In subtle and unseen ways sin at times is stimulated and ministry is undermined by our false definition of worldliness. Rather than approaching the godly goal of being "in the world but not of the world" (John 17:14–18), we have swung toward separatism on one hand or antinomianism—a disregard for God's commands—on the other. Sometimes our lifestyle and mind-set are not appreciably different than our secular counterparts (we are "of the world"). And yet, we do not relate well to unbelievers (we are not "in the world").

THE WORLDLINESS OF JESUS

Jesus, always the right model to follow, practiced a correct type of worldliness. True worldliness means we associate freely with the people of this world without compromising our integrity. Jesus is the perfect example of such worldliness. Matthew 9:9–13 offers a beautiful snapshot of Jesus' worldliness. From the text let's answer five questions:

1. Whom did Jesus associate with?

2. Where did He go?

3. What made Jesus so attractive and effective with worldly people?

4. How was Jesus received by the religious?

5. Why did Jesus do what He did?

Other supporting texts (Luke 7:36–50; 15:1–32; 19:1–10) will round out our understanding of Christlike worldliness. We will examine the rationale for and results of the worldly actions of Jesus. And we will seek to make appropriate applications for today for us who seek to follow in the footsteps of our Lord and not fall into the traps of the Pharisees. For the great need of our world is for people who are worldly like Jesus!

Meeting with Sinful People

A commonly cited statistic in evangelical circles today is that by the time one has been a Christian for about two years, all of his or her friends are Christians.[2] There's good news to this statistic: the new convert has detached him/herself from the former bonds of sin and bonded significantly with fellow believers. But there's also bad news: Christians have removed themselves from the lives of the very people they are trying to reach. Christ did not do this, but apparently the Pharisees did, and they expected the Master to do likewise.

Jesus fraternized with a broad spectrum of people. He built relationships with the "pious" and the pariahs, the rich and the poor, male and female, the learned and the common, the "churched" and those who wouldn't darken its door. He spent the majority of His time with His disciples, much time with crowds of people, and some time with individuals. He devoted Himself to fellow Jews, both friend and foe, but also interacted with Samaritans and Gentiles. Jesus spent most of His time with committed followers, some time with the religious, and much time with sinners. The time spent with sinners raised the hackles of the separatists.

Jesus' association with disreputable people was well known. He was called "a gluttonous man and a drunkard, a friend of tax collectors and sinners" (Matthew 11:19). Matthew 9 finds Jesus going to the home of Matthew, probably a customs agent, where He dines with other tax collectors and sinners. From the perspective of the Pharisees, this cast of characters was despised, regarded on the same level as robbers.[3] Customs and tax collecting jobs involved collusion with the hated Romans, getting rich at the expense of fellow Jews, and neglecting the Law, which would bring banishment from the synagogue. Thus Matthew and his friends were unpatriotic traitors, wealthy extortionists, immoral sinners, and spiritual untouchables.

Jesus was also called "a friend of . . . sinners." *Sinners* was a general term for local riffraff, people who did not keep the Law or the traditions of the elders. This category included the immoral, the irreligious, and the irresponsible. These people would not attend the synagogue, nor would they be admitted had they tried. Like the tax collectors, the "sinners" were cultural outcasts. Perhaps they could be likened on one extreme to modern pimps and prostitutes, drug dealers, Mafia members, or outlaw bikers.. And on the "less sinful" end of the spectrum, they compare to the hearty partyers, sex addicts, substance abusers, and dishonest businessmen and women.

The worldliness of Jesus involved significant and intentional contact with irreligious and sinful people. The combination of "tax collectors and sinners [or harlots]" is idiomatic in the Gospels for the "wrong kind of people" (Matthew 11:19; 21:31–32; Luke 15:1). Jesus often hung out with the wrong people—local customs collectors like Matthew, tax-collecting bigwigs like Zaccheus, the sinful alabaster-anointing woman in Luke 7:36–50, the many-times married Samaritess in John 4:1–42, and the adulteress in John 8:1–11. Jesus' mission was to "seek and to save that which was lost" (Luke 19:10). Thus, building redemptive relationships was at the heart of His game plan.

Of course, dangers exist in having significant contact with irreligious people. It is much safer to keep company with the saints and call out to the sinners to clean up their acts than to risk rejection and misunderstanding, as well as subject oneself to temptations. But should disciples abandon the lost and ignore the "go" of the Great Commission (Matthew 28:19)? No. Following Christ's example, for Christ's sake, Christians cannot abandon the "sinners" of society. We must not separate ourselves from them, run scared from them, or regard them sanctimoniously. Instead disciples must, like Jesus, seek to build redemptive relationships with them. Christlike worldliness includes having significant contact with sinful people.

GOING WHERE THE SINNERS ARE

In sports, one of the greatest assets is the so-called "home-field/court advantage." The home team enjoys cheering fans and feels comfortable in its own stadium or arena. They are well rested too, thanks to having their own bed and home cookin'. No wonder most teams have much better records when they play on home turf. Likewise, we in the church prefer—indeed often expect—sinners to come to us. We want to meet them on our turf, where we feel comfortable and can maintain the home-field advantage.

What about Jesus? He reached people where they lived, where they felt comfortable. He invaded their turf, giving them the "home-field advantage." He went to the lost rather than calling them to Him. Shouldn't we follow His example?

In Matthew 9:9–10, we find Jesus on the move, meeting people. First, Jesus is walking on the outskirts of Capernaum. Then He stops by a custom-collection booth. Finally, Jesus goes to Matthew's house. In the course of everyday life, Jesus is on a road, at a place of business, and at a dwelling place. He wasn't at the Temple or a synagogue. He goes where the people He wants to reach are, where they feel most comfortable.

When Jesus stopped by Matthew's place of business, not on business, eyebrows must have raised. But when he entered Matthew's house—with the company Matthew kept—there must have been a sense of scandal. Entering the confines of someone's house in Jesus' day did not mean what it means to us today. The offering of hospitality implied acceptance, friendship, and good will. People in Jesus' day carefully guarded their "guest lists." Reputations were on the line. People and places could be defiled. Offering and accepting hospitality sent clear cultural messages. When Jesus accepted the invitation to Matthew's party, He was unmistakably saying, "I accept these people." This offense the Pharisees could not take silently.

But there is a method to the Master's "madness." Giving away the "home-field advantage" more quickly breaks down barriers; deeper emotional ties tend to be established, and a sense of acceptance is communicated. Lost people feel much freer and cared for if we go to them. The courtesy of meeting on their turf can confound prejudices, break down barriers, and touch them deeply.

Of course, some caution is in order in visiting the spiritually lost. Wisdom is required. The careless exercise of freedom in Christ can negatively influence others (Romans 15; 1 Corinthians 8–10). And it is true that we can easily be impacted by peer pressure and place pressure. Thus, though the general thrust of the worldliness of Jesus is to take the gospel to the sinners, where they work, play, and stay, some cautions are necessary with this approach. One should never go to places where one's conscience is compromised, where the temptation is too great to bear, or where one thinks that he or she is immune from sin (1 Corinthians 10:12). The conscience can be educated, but it should never be violated. Those who struggle with substance abuse, for example, should not frequent bars or hang out with drug dealers.

There are times to invite nonbelievers to church, of course. Sadly, though, for many "sinners" the church is the last place they would go if they needed help. Author Philip Yancey told how a friend who works with the down-and-out in Chicago learned this truth.

> A prostitute came to him in desperation—homeless, her health failing, unable to buy food for her two-year-old son. As the woman described her plight, my friend asked if she had ever thought of going to a church for help. A look of shock and unfeigned incredulity crossed her face. "Church!" she cried. "Why would I ever go there? They'd make me feel worse than I already do!"[4]

Unfortunately, the church is not often known as a place of grace. Sinners are not generally going to come to us.

Christ's command to "go" has not been rescinded. Perhaps we as a church may need less church programming and more equipping and encouragement to be in the business of building redemptive relationships outside the confines of the church. We also can offer common courtesy to those we want to tell about Jesus. People seem both startled and softened when we show them the simple kindness of taking an interest in them on their stomping grounds.

DISPLAYING ATTRACTIVE ATTITUDES AND ACTIONS

When I meet Jesus one day in heaven, one question I plan to ask is, "What about you was so attractive to worldly people?" Why was Jesus on the guest list when secular parties were being planned? I'm not! On the contrary, people go to great lengths with all kinds of gesticulations to show their "spiritual" side when they find out (sometimes too late) that I am a pastor. What did Jesus have that caused the local sinners to seek out His company? As Yancey asks, "How did he, the only perfect person in history, manage to attract the notoriously imperfect?"[5]

Scripture does not answer that question. But this much we do know: When Jesus asked Matthew to come and follow, he did, and when Jesus was invited to Matthew's house, He was the "life of the party." Something about Jesus made Him desirable to the sinners of His day. What was it? What was it that made Jesus, the embodiment of holiness, so attractive to the unholy? His actions and attitudes appealed to many in the general public.

First, Jesus often took the initiative. He invited Himself to the parties; at least, with Matthew and Zaccheus (Luke 19:5) He did so. Something about Jesus seeking them out disarmed them. Second, by His willingness to interact with sinners on their turf, He broke down barriers and fostered goodwill among those considered to be spiritual outcasts. Third, Jesus was completely authentic and natural, characteristics that we appreciate. He was genuine, possessing no hidden agendas or deceit. He had nothing to sell and wasn't trying to prove anything to sinners (nor get anything from them). Jesus freely shared His humanity and found common ground with a variety of people. I am certain He listened carefully, loved genuinely, and was a true friend. Such attitudes are always appealing. He was not suspicious, prejudiced, exclusive, condemning, or unapproachable.

Jesus demonstrated other positive attitudes that would have been especially attractive to sinners. He viewed people as precious, not "scalps" to record. As a soul physician, He gravitated to soul-sick people. He genuinely liked those whom most religious people loathed. He offered them love, mercy, forgiveness, grace, and hope.

As one who challenged boundaries, traditions, and laws, Jesus fit well with those who had encountered societal scorn. Jesus clicked with society's castoffs. He offered grace without ever compromising truth (John 1:14). He accepted sinners without sacrificing His integrity. He kept the delicate balance between judging outsiders and insiders (1 Corinthians 5:9–13). And rather than being dragged down by the partying crowd (a common evangelical fear), He made disciples.

What Jesus had, most of us lack. His heart was motivated by self-giving love, while we often are dominated by self-protecting fear. We are afraid of saying the wrong thing, being embarrassed, being asked questions we cannot answer, looking like fools. And when we do have the words or formula down pat, we may lack the authenticity that helps to carry the message. Becky Pippert in her classic book *Out of the Salt-shaker* says it well:

> Our problem in evangelism is not that we don't have enough infor-mation—it is that we do not know how to be ourselves. We forget we are called to be witnesses to what we have seen and know, not to what we don't know. The key is authenticity and obedience, not a doctorate in theology.[6]

The awesome genuine life and love of Jesus was like a mag-net to those who knew they needed help. What a model for us!

GOING BEYOND APPEARANCES

We religious people tend to make quick judgments based on appearances (see 1 Samuel 16:7). The watching Pharisees did the same thing. They asked the disciples a question; actually, a cloaked criticism: "Why is your Teacher eating with the tax col-lectors and sinners?" (Matthew 9:11). The question reflected a whole series of traditions and prejudices that the Pharisees had acquired. Let us consider some of them.

Behind their question was not just prejudice, but seemingly a solid theological reason to oppose Jesus' actions. At the heart of their faith the Pharisees sought holiness and wanted to avoid defilement. They gave themselves to the pursuit of righteousness (Luke 18:11–12). They paid careful attention to cleanness and defilement, following an entire section in The Mishnah devoted to the topic (the sixth division of the Tohoroth was entitled "Cleannesses"). Defilement required ritual cleansing and elimi-nated Jews from certain religious activities. It was avoided at all costs. (Perhaps the fear of defilement kept the priest and Levite in the parable of the good Samaritan from helping [Luke 10:25–37].) Matthew 15:1–20, a major Gospel text on defilement, implies that the Pharisees' view of defilement was environmental and external. That is, defilement was essentially a product of what entered one's mouth, where one went, and with whom one came into contact. Contamination comes from contact with sinners. It can rub off. Thus, Jesus' presence at Matthew's party necessarily implied defilement.

The Pharisees sought to avoid not only evil but also the appearance of evil. They cared deeply not only about being righteous but also about looking righteous (Matthew 6:1–18). Though they might bristle at the suggestion that "image is everything," they lived as if image were important. Moreover, the Pharisees strove to keep their social slates clean not only by avoidance but also by associating with like-minded people. A good way to avoid defiling contact is to fill one's social life with "good" friends. A "holy huddle" is an effective means of avoiding worldliness, so they thought.

Because the Pharisees devoted much time to the enjoyment of sweet fellowship with like-minded comrades, they probably had neither the time nor the inclination to go out looking for the lost. John R. W. Stott suggests that the Pharisees, and we too, are merely lazy and selfish. We stand aloof from the world because, "we do not want to get involved in its hurt or dirt."[7] Instead, a common approach of religious people to the irreligious is to call them to clean up their lives and then come join us. Many misunderstand God, believing that He fundamentally despises sinners and prefers to see them suffer for their sin. Jesus, however, accepted the sinners as they were, going to them and showing grace and truth in His words and actions.

I believe that the Pharisees' question to Jesus also reflected a bit of self-righteousness. The Pharisees were largely oblivious to their own sinfulness, having convinced themselves that they were law-abiding and thus pleasing to God. They expected rewards, while sinners deserved God's condemnation and painful consequences.

Sometimes we have the same attitudes that the Pharisees had. We fear that compromising environments will defile us, and we too are vitally concerned with what people will think. We cloak such concerns under the coat of avoiding the "appearance of evil" and concern for the "weaker brother." But we have misconstrued God's teaching and missed His balance. Furthermore, we buy into the "clean up your act and come" philosophy of ministry.

CARING FOR THE SPIRITUALLY SICK

No one was as clear of His calling as Jesus. He did what He did, endured the censure He encountered, violated traditions as

He did because He had clear, divine reasons for His actions. Two short verses in Matthew 9 powerfully present three reasons for Jesus' worldliness.

First, *He cared about the spiritually hurting.* Jesus employed a proverbial statement, derived from the culture, to explain His actions: "It is not those who are healthy who need a physician, but those who are sick" (v. 12). It is a simple truism that doctors are in the business of helping the sick and frequent places where ill people congregate. And Jesus was the Master Surgeon of souls! The needs of spiritually sick people compelled Jesus to attend to them, even at the risk of infection.

Second, *He declared that compassion for people was God's priority.* Jesus quotes Hosea 6:6 (also quoted in Matthew 12:7), to explain His association with the tax collectors and sinners: "I desire compassion, and not sacrifice" (v. 13a). Once again a sharp edge is detected as an untutored itinerant preacher tells the Th.D.'s of His day to go back to the Bible. The book of Hosea is a powerful treatise on the unconditional love and forgiveness of God for His wayward people Israel, played out in the life of Hosea and Gomer. At the time of Hosea, in the eighth century B.C., Israel was practicing the prescribed rituals and sacrifices. However, injustice, immorality, and indifference to the plight of people characterized their practice. Though they continued the shell of their religion, they had lost the center. Jesus made it clear that God is more interested in compassionate deeds than religious acts.

Finally, *He got involved with the people of the world to fulfill His mission* (Luke 19:10). "For I did not come to call the righteous, but sinners," He tells the Pharisees (v. 13b). Thus it is only logical that He would not focus His ministry on the "righteous." Perhaps once again Jesus' tongue was in His cheek as He implied that the Pharisees were righteous. Surely this was their self-perception because of their zealous pursuit of religiously disciplined lives. Nevertheless, Jesus by the very nature of His call should not and could not devote His ministry to those who didn't feel that they needed what He had to offer.

It seems to me that we should have the same three motives for reaching out to the lost, even at the price of breaking traditions and making waves. The need of our culture obviously is great. God places greater stock in compassionate outreach than in compulsive religious activity. And we, like Jesus, are called to the lost. The sin-sick are plentiful but the doctors are few (Matthew 9:37). Many times we have cloistered ourselves away from sinners and have practiced "come" rather than "go" evangelism. Instead, we must incarnate the winsome attitudes of Jesus. We must understand God's heart and His call.

Bill Hybels, pastor of the large Willow Creek Community Church in suburban Chicago, reminds his audience: "You have never set eyes on anyone who does not matter to God." The church sometimes receives criticism for its "seeker-friendly" programs and approach, but few deny that the leadership and people love the lost. That motive is at the heart of the pastor, and it shows in every facet of the ministry. If we know *why* we do something, the *what* usually follows and the *why nots* are answered.

HOW TO DEVELOP CHRISTLIKE WORLDLINESS

Some may be wondering how we can grow in Christlike worldliness without falling prey to compromising worldliness, the worldliness of our culture. How can we approach the ideal of being in the world but not of it instead of being of the world but not in it? The answer is to develop spiritual sensitivity and biblical balance. Doing so will promote a healthy worldliness in our lives.

First, we must be sure we understand what worldliness is. *Healthy* worldliness means developing relationships with the people of our world motivated by Christ's compassion. *Unhealthy* worldliness means having relationships motivated by the lusts of sinful society, including materialism, hedonism, and egotism (Luke 16:14; Matthew 23:2–12). Then we must recognize and reject unhealthy worldliness—participating in and embracing as good the activities of sinful society.

In developing biblical balance, we must recognize unhealthy worldliness is found in our attitudes much more than in our actions. We should beware of superficially defining worldliness by whom we're with and where we go. Instead, our guide should be the three-part definition of worldliness in 1 John 2:16: "the *lust* of the flesh and the *lust* of the eyes and the *boastful pride* of life" (italics added). These desires are a constant temptation.

There are other ways we can achieve biblical balance and thus practice Christlike worldliness. First, we who rely on the Bible must revisit the key texts on separatism. Several have been conveniently misinterpreted. When Paul warns, "Do not be deceived: 'Bad company corrupts good morals'" (1 Corinthians 15:33), he clearly is referring to the resurrection and its implications. The corrupting company referred to is not pagan people but rather those (probably within the early church) who denied the resurrection.[8] We are warned to steer clear of those whose doctrine rejects a bodily resurrection. For a denial of the resurrection will likely impact one's morality negatively. This text is not a blanket statement about keeping away from sinners.

Similarly, looking at the context of 2 Corinthians 6:14–7:1, we can see this passage on separation prohibits *yoking* ourselves with nonbelievers; it does not prohibit *associating* with them. There is an enormous difference between yoked relationships and redemptive relationships. Jesus modeled this distinction. He yoked Himself with His disciples (Judas was an exception to this rule, a fact of which Jesus was fully aware). He did not yoke Himself with unbelievers, though He associated freely with them. Bonding ourselves with unbelievers does contradict God's command and compromises Christian character. There is a spiritual commonality that we cannot share with unbelievers.

This does not deny, however, the significant and extensive common ground that we do share with non-Christians. We really are a lot alike; diapers and dishes; downsizing and out-sourcing; elderly parents and feisty teenagers; too much month at the end of the money. We all have headaches and heartaches, taxes and death. This human commonality should be tapped for Christ's sake.

Proper biblical interpretation also can help us understand a third separation text: 1 Thessalonians 5:22. "Abstain from every form [or appearance] of evil," Paul wrote. If this is a general principle applicable to every situation, then it was not obeyed by the Lord Himself. He involved Himself in what were considered highly compromising situations that appeared to be evil. Thus God must have meant something else by this command. Again the context provides the parameters that God had in mind when this prohibition was written.

The immediate context is the proper use of prophetic utterances. It is serious business when someone says, "Thus says the Lord." Prophetic words must be examined, presumably against Scripture. That which is good should be accepted, and that which is not good should be rejected.[9] Evil, that is, human concoctions pawned off as God's truth, must be avoided. Once again, this text in context does not even address separatism as it is commonly understood.

These passages and others have left most of us with the impression that God commands us to shun sinners and encourages us to hang out with the "righteous." On the contrary, God has called us to associate with sinful unbelievers and to separate ourselves from fellow believers who are involved in gross, unrepentant sin (1 Corinthians 5:9–13; 2 Thessalonians 3:14). Though separatism from sinning Christians is supported in the Scriptures, separatism from sinning nonbelievers is not. As the apostle Paul told the Corinthians: "I wrote you in my letter not to associate with immoral people; I did not at all mean with the immoral people of this world, or with the covetous and swindlers, or with idolaters, for then you would have to go out of the world" (1 Corinthians 5:9–10).

Second, we must take seriously our Christ-given call to reach out to sinners in His stead. Remember, we are the Physician's assistants, called to heal. We must never be so busy maintaining our standard of living and the ministries of our churches that we have left little time for the lost. If we do not take seriously the responsibility to build redemptive relationships with the lost, who will? Seeking such relationships should surely figure prominently into our personal and church philosophy of ministry.

Third, with courage and wisdom we must resist the many Pharisaic impediments to Christlike worldliness. We must reject the notion that defilement is environmental and declare courageously that defilement is a matter of the human heart. Thus, no one, no thing, and no place is inherently defiling. However, wisdom requires that we be aware that we carry the potential of defilement wherever we take our hearts. Thus, we are not careless or conceited, nor do we violate our conscience. We do not play with temptation. For Christ's sake we are willing to step out of our "comfort zones" but not our "conscience zones." We accept the Bible's injunction to avoid worldliness. We take pains to pursue purity.

However, we balance the "appearance of evil" with the mandate to be ambassadors for Christ (2 Corinthians 5:20). Rather than merely tell the world to come, we must go to others, as Christ went. Let us long to build bridges.

Fourth, we must constantly pursue the spiritual maturity that motivated Jesus' relationship with "sinners." Jesus was purpose-driven; thus He was not deterred by the criticisms He received from the "righteous." Instead He was motivated by His love for lost sons and daughters and at heaven's joy as over a single lost soul that repented (Luke 15). How powerful for us to be similarly motivated! A noble purpose protected Jesus: He wanted to serve others. When we also are purpose-protected, we are less attracted to selfish temptations. The more we know Jesus and have His love motive, the more our lives will exude His grace and truth.

Fifth, we must realize that sometimes the most sinful are more likely candidates for the kingdom than the "good" or religious. We may commend "goodness" and religion in others, but "good people" tend to be blind to their spiritual needs. Those who know they are sick spiritually often will acknowledge their need of a Physician. We must not shun certain sinners as unlikely candidates for the kingdom. Heaven's population may hold many surprises.

Much of the New Testament teaches us to avoid worldly lusts as we reach out to the people of our world as Jesus did. Let us renounce separatism as a goal so that we may become active in ministry to God's precious stray sheep.

Chapter Ten
WHEN THE SICK LOOK FIT

In 1988, forty-year-old "Pistol Pete" Maravich, the holder of numerous "unbreakable" college basketball records and later an NBA All-Star, died while playing a pickup game in Pasadena, California. A health enthusiast whose last words were, "I'm really feeling good," Maravich died of a hidden heart defect. Similarly Flora (Flo) Hyman, a tall and powerful volleyball spiker, led the U.S. women's team to a silver medal in the 1984 Olympics but died of a heart attack a few years later at age thirty-one. And in November 1995, at age twenty-eight Russian figure skater Sergei Grinkov, winner of two Olympic gold medals, dropped to the ice during a practice session and died. He too had suffered a massive heart attack.

All three were world-class athletes; all had the external appearance of exceptional physical health. Each, however, had unseen fatal heart problems. They appeared to be models of physical fitness, but their well-conditioned bodies for a time masked serious sickness. Fellow athletes and fans alike were shocked.

This phenomenon occurs spiritually as well. The religious world occasionally is stunned when someone perceived to be spiritually healthy is exposed as spiritually diseased. In truth, spiritual sickness often looks like fitness to the casual observer because we are trained to evaluate fitness by a set of standards that are superficial and faulty. Therefore, subtle symptoms of spiritual sickness, masked by commendable religious behavior, often are undetected.

Consider "Jim." He has a solid doctrinal foundation, knows

and loves the Word of God, and readily distinguishes theological truth from error. His discernment is particularly helpful in "guarding the gate" of the kingdom, as he calls it. "In our culture, so many people profess to be Christians but do not have Christ in charge. Part of the problem," he asserts, "is the absence of teaching on repentance and lordship. We must teach the pure gospel, the gospel according to Jesus Christ."

Yes, Jim *is* a dedicated Christian, and his "gate-guarding" does not preclude a "love for the lost." He is zealous for evangelism and highly missions-minded. He participates regularly and enthusiastically in evangelistic outreach, even going door-to-door. And each year Jim and his wife take a portion of their hard-earned vacation time to go on short-term missions assignments. They love seeing people become a part of their church and denomination.

Listening to Jim talk, you are impressed. His language is peppered with religious phrases, and never salty. He prays sincerely and doesn't swear. His supplications seem to open up the heavenlies. Additionally, Jim has served as church treasurer with distinction. Scrupulous tithing is his personal practice and guarding God's money one of his great concerns. He deeply laments the way that folks today give so little under the guise of "being under grace, not law."

Everyone who knows Jim attests to his godly behavior. No hint of impropriety mars his reputation. His lifestyle is not just good, it shines. He avoids sin and engages in good deeds. To top it off, in his spare time Jim devotes himself to a wide variety of church clubs and ministries named after various spiritual forebearers. His earnest prayer is that "those who come behind would find us faithful."

Jim seems to be a model churchman. Few of us can match maturity and ministry with him. By all external standards, Jim would be classified as spiritually fit. But Jim has a "heart disease"—he is spiritually sick. He is a contemporary representative of the Pharisees, the people Jesus attacks in the most scathing words He ever spoke (Matthew 23). Each of the seemingly good traits I described above has an unseen and dangerous downside.

Woes to the Pharisees

Seven times Jesus pronounces "woe" upon the Pharisees. The woes can expose *our* sickness as well, we who at times are so like the Pharisees. But the woes need not lead to gloom. Rather, they can lead us to humility and repentance, as we recognize our need for Jesus to lead us. Jesus wept over those mistaken Pharisees (Matthew 23:37–38), just as He weeps for us to find our strength only in Him, not in superficial righteousness.

What appeared on the surface of the lives of the Pharisees as fitness actually masked spiritual sickness. And I have every reason to suspect, from the Scriptures and experience, that this same paradox pervades our evangelical subculture today.

Jesus, the Master Surgeon of the soul, probed beneath the spiritual skin of seemingly devoted religious leaders and diagnosed some hidden problems within. Like the three world-class athletes we met in the introduction, the "patients" showed no clear symptoms—they even appeared spiritually robust to all but the most discerning eye. But Jesus recognized and diagnosed the problem. Here in His final public address, recorded in Matthew 23, Jesus made His ultimate appeal to the Pharisees to undergo much-needed heart surgery.

Jesus bluntly pointed out seven fatal heart defects of the Pharisees. We will explore the first three in this chapter, and the final four in the next. In declaring those "woes," Jesus expressed a mixture of anger, alarm, and anguish. The woes represent a message of warning and a call to change for us today.

WOE #1: GATEKEEPERS ON THE WRONG SIDE OF THE DOOR

"But woe to you, scribes and Pharisees, hypocrites, because you shut off the kingdom of heaven from people; for you do not enter in yourselves, nor do you allow those who are entering to go in." (Matthew 23:13)

Ask any Bible-believing evangelical-fundamentalist what is necessary to get into heaven and I guarantee you will receive an answer.[1] We may leave room for sincere differences of opinion when it comes to ecclesiology and eschatology. But we are certain we know what it takes to get into heaven. Yet sometimes in our zeal to give the whole, pure gospel we become like the Pharisees, obstructing the entrance to God's kingdom.

The picture Jesus paints in this first "woe" is that of a gatekeeper. In our culture it would be like a customs agent checking passports. The gate in view is the entrance to the kingdom of

God, and the Pharisees have volunteered to be the gatekeepers. They are sure of their theology. They know what it takes to be saved and to stay saved. They feel that they can determine whether a person is sincere or not. They certainly know the kinds of people who need not apply. The Pharisees apparently thought they had the job at the gates of heaven before Saint Peter took over!

On the surface, "guarding the gate" to the kingdom seems like a good job for the spiritually fit. Those who take the job must be concerned about eternal life, know the way to eternal life, and desire that others find eternal life. Moreover, they would have to be just as concerned that those who are not fit for heaven be denied admittance. It is a cruel joke to give people the impression that they are bound for heaven when, in fact, they are not. The Pharisees sincerely believed that they were spiritual guides (Romans 2:17–20).

But Jesus did not concur with the Pharisees' self-assessment. In fact, He saw their air of fitness as spiritual sickness. First, Jesus implied that God has not solicited any applications for the kingdom gatekeeping job; the Pharisees were wrong to take a job that God had not given them. Second, no human being qualifies for this kingdom gatekeeping responsibility. The Bible makes it clear that our spiritual judgment is not very accurate. We lack insight into our own hearts, much less the hearts of others (Jeremiah 17:9). The Pharisees were guilty of letting people in whom God wouldn't and excluding people whom God would include.[2] Third, the Pharisees were obstructionists at heart, like bouncers barring the doors, standing in the way of God and His plans. For they had built their prejudices and false concepts (law, works, merit, circumcision, etc.) into the gospel.

This is not spiritually healthy behavior, and Jesus diagnosed it, calling the Pharisees "hypocrites." Their "goodness" was more theatrical than actual. Their supposedly godly efforts to guard the gate of the kingdom were actually turning people away! It was the Pharisees who refused to recognize Jesus as the Messiah and did all they could to dissuade others.[3]

This woe pictures religious people with graceless hearts who fancy themselves as kingdom gatekeepers. Do we do likewise? I think so. It is seldom that the sins of the religious in the Bible do not parallel our own. First, we must ask ourselves whether God gave us the job to guard the gate to the kingdom.

Yes, He clearly commanded us to go into all the world and preach the gospel (Matthew 28:18–20; Mark 16:15; Acts 1:8). We are commissioned to be His ambassadors (2 Corinthians 5:14–21). No doubt He has given us the opportunity to call people to come into Christ's kingdom. We are responsible to preserve the simplicity and integrity of the gospel. The apostle Paul spent a major portion of his ministry defining the gospel (Romans) and opposing various attempts to alter or add to the gospel (Galatians).

But what about this business of gate-guarding? Initially it must be noted that gate-guarding and practicing church discipline are not synonymous. We must protect the purity of the church from gross sin, as 1 Corinthians 5 informs us. But we are not to be about the business of judging those outside the church (1 Corinthians 5:9–12). Moreover, in the parable of the wheat and the tares (Matthew 13:24–30, 34–43), Jesus told His disciples not to try to sift out the genuine from the false for fear that the good would be hurt.

Our task as "evangelicals" is to proclaim the gospel and make disciples of Jesus Christ. We cannot know whether a person's profession is genuine, for we do not judge a person's heart; only God does.

A major debate in the Christian community over the past several years concerns the attempts at dialogue between Evangelicals and Roman Catholics. Seeking light, heat has been generated. A fundamental issue in the debate is justification, who gets in the gate. Some prominent evangelicals have been criticized for their theological looseness while others insist on a rigid Reformed definition. Clearly some parameters are necessary and biblical, but what is not often noted in the debate is the inability of fallen humans to judge the human heart. Genuine saving faith has been expressed as simply as "Jesus, remember me when You come in Your kingdom" (Luke 23:42) or "God, be merciful to me, the sinner!" (Luke 18:13) or as complete as the apostle Paul delineates in Romans. I fear our theological wrangling over those who get in the door may well nauseate the One who proclaimed, "I am the door; if anyone enters through Me, he will be saved, and will go in and out and find pasture" (John 10:9). Or perhaps we are not even as "good" as the Pharisees, for too many of us today don't even seem to care if people get in the gates or not.

Do we not, also like the Pharisees, sometimes turn people

away from the gospel? We fancy ourselves as heralds of heaven, while the world is turned off to God by our hypocrisy. Numerous polls of the religious life of America, no matter how much we may try to discount them, chronicle a sad spiritual condition in the church. We do not have in most places a reputation for grace, goodness, and truth. Rather our reputation (and thus, indirectly, Christ's) is of gracelessness, carnality, and hypocrisy. By our lives, our lack of witness, our personal failures, and our hypocrisy are we, those who presume to be God's gatekeepers, not shutting the gates? Something is amiss when those who presume to man the gates of heaven are repelling people.

What would Jesus say to modern Pharisees like you and I? I think He would issue some stern warnings. Jesus would tell us first to look into the mirror and check out our own relationship with Him before presuming to evaluate others (Matthew 7:1–5). "Judge yourselves before judging others," He'd say. "Spend more time in your closets on behalf of the lost than at the gates 'defending' yourselves. Beware of intellectualizing and superficializing the requirements for salvation."

We need to remember the simple gospel. A vast difference exists between the simple gospel and the superficial gospel; they often get reversed. We must beware of erecting any ungodly barriers at the gates of the kingdom. William Barclay comments, "The gravest danger which any teacher or preacher encounters is that he should erect his own prejudices into universal principles and substitute his own ideas for the truth of God. When he does that he is not a guide, but a barrier, to the Kingdom, for, misled himself, he misleads others."[4]

WOE #2: GOSPEL-PEDDLERS WHO
INCREASE THE POPULATION OF HELL

"Woe to you, scribes and Pharisees, hypocrites, because you travel around on sea and land to make one proselyte; and when he becomes one, you make him twice a much a son of hell as yourselves." (Matthew 23:15)[5]

In my background the pinnacle of success is "full-time Christian work." None hold higher esteem than zealous evangelists and those who go into foreign missions (home missions is a lesser rung on the ladder). Most of us are such woeful evangelists, unwilling even to go across the street to tell a neighbor about Christ, that we assume those who are willing to go and to talk to people about their faith must be close to God. They simply must be spiritually fit.

However, we must be careful not jump to such quick conclusions. For Jesus points out in this second "woe" that evangelism and foreign missions are not necessarily signs of spiritual fitness. People can be and often are zealous for the wrong things, resulting in greater harm than good.

Evangelism was a priority among the Pharisees of the first century, though it cannot be confirmed that the Jews of Jesus' day were "evangelistic" in the twentieth-century meaning of the term, D. A. Carson comments, "A sizable body of scholarship convincingly argues that the first century A.D. till the Fall of Jerusalem marks the most remarkable period of Jewish missionary zeal and corresponding success."6 The Jews at the time of Christ had some interest and limited success in converting pagan Gentiles to Judaism. This task was not easy, however, given the requirements of Pharisaic Judaism and the pagan life style of the Gentiles. Thus the major "outreach ministry" involved encouraging "God fearers" (nominal Jews) to fully convert to Judaism and to assume the yoke of the Torah in its entirety.7 The Pharisees were mainly concerned with conversions to their understanding of the holy life. They confused proselytism (converting people to one's particular religious opinions and culture) with evangelism (introducing people to the living God).

Yes, we are no less inclined than the Pharisees to evangelize to our particular slant and set of traditions. Even on the mission field there is "successful" proselytism without a satisfactory product, just as there was in Jesus' day. (See "Swazi Clothes and Christian Faith" for an example of that phenomenon in action.)

Notice that Jesus had no gripe with the proselytism, evangelism, or missions activities of the Pharisees. Nor did He criticize their zeal. His concern was the product and the results! For the product of the Pharisees' ministry was not sons of the kingdom but sons of hell. And to make matters worse, these sons of hell were doubly zealous agents for the Evil One. For it is common for converts to a system to be more militant and less balanced than their teachers.8

What went wrong? First, the Pharisees introduced converts to a misguided religious system instead of the living God. This system misjudged the Messiah, even calling Him Beelzebul

(Matthew 10:25; 12:24, 27), offered a way of works for salvation, and demanded obedience to humanly concocted traditions and fences. Second, the Pharisees lost sight of the fact that the evangelistic proof is in the product, not the proselytizing. Moreover, when the converts were "discipled," "they 'out-Phariseed' the Pharisees."[9] The misguided efforts of the Pharisees actually multiplied as they made followers who were hell-bound and on an even faster track than the evangelists-missionaries who converted them!

At times, we do likewise. First, it should be noted that like the Pharisees of old, most of us are not very active in evangelism and missions. This is not to say that we do not "support" evangelism and missions. We do—from giving offerings to missions and missionaries to serving on missions committees. Second, we seem to be far more concerned with converts than with disciples, with "scalps" and baptisms and statistics than with people who truly walk with God. In this regard we are not as "good" as the Pharisees, for at least they sought full commitment. We must never forget that God is looking for disciples (Matthew 28:19), true worshippers (John 4:21–24), people whose faith is deeply rooted in good soil (Matthew 13:1–23). It is spiritual sickness, not fitness, to be evangelistic and missions-minded while producing adherents who live by the Law, or without the Law in a promiscuous lifestyle.

Can we draw some practical applications? First, we should not make superficial judgments about spirituality on the basis of certain religious activities, no matter how difficult they may be or how zealously engaged in. Personality, an adventuresome spirit, and self-discipline devoid of God's Spirit can empower many seemingly spiritual activities. Second, we must be careful lest we, like the Pharisees of old, convert people to a religion, a denomination, a sect, a theology rather than to Christ. For what we seek, I trust, is not clones of ourselves but Christlike human beings. Third, we, like people in business, must keep our eye on the product. We do not help the eternal cause of Christ by transforming a culture from paganism to legalism. Though legalism may raise the standard of living among the people (and this is good), it may also lower their sense of need of God (and this is undoubtedly bad). Perhaps we are too quick to applaud "conversions" and fail to care how Christianity is played out in a life or a culture.

THE RIGHT WAY

Swazi Clothes and Christian Faith

Like the Pharisees, we can at times evangelize with a gospel that reflects our own set of traditions. There are numerous illustrations of the missionaries of the colonial countries interweaving European culture with Christianity. But I saw this phenomenon firsthand as a short-term missionary in Swaziland.

While I taught in Swaziland, some of my African coworkers told me that the early missionaries considered one of the signs of genuine Christian conversion to be people giving up their traditional Swazi dress, or lack thereof, and putting on Western clothes, including three-piece suits. Eventually Christianity became associated in the minds of some with a style of dress rather than a relationship with Christ.

Furthermore, I noticed in missions that denominations sometimes became rivals and did not cooperate on the "foreign field." I wondered if the major thrust of their work was to advance Christ's kingdom or their particular denomination (and its statistics). The goal must always be to present the pure gospel, without one's own cultural or denominational additions.

WOE #3: OATH-TAKERS WHO LOATH THE TRUTH

"Woe to you, blind guides, who say, 'Whoever swears by the temple, that is nothing; but whoever swears by the gold of the temple is obligated.' You fools and blind men! Which is more important, the gold or the temple that sanctified the gold? And, 'Whoever swears by the altar, that is nothing, but whoever swears by the offering upon it, he is obligated.' You blind men, which is more important, the offering, or the altar that sanctifies the offering? Therefore, whoever swears by the altar, swears both by the altar and by everything on it. And whoever swears by the temple, swears both by the temple and by Him who dwells within it. And whoever swears by heaven, swears both by the throne of God and by Him who sits upon it."(Matthew 23:16–22)

As a child I often sought to emphasize my honesty, or more commonly cover my misdeeds, by taking oaths. "Cross my heart, hope to die, stick a needle in my eye." "I swear on the Holy Bible. . . . I swear on a stack of Bibles." A couple of times I heard others say, "I swear on my mother's grave." These solemn statements usually worked with my peers (not as effectively with adults) to get me off the hot seat. The common assumption was that if someone would go to such lengths and use such powerful symbols to defend his or her honor, he or she must be telling the truth. Oaths work! I learned early in life that "God-talk" had the ability to convince people I was telling the truth, and sometimes to convince myself that I was telling the truth.

A time-honored practice in America is to take oaths with a hand on a Bible. On Inauguration Day the president of the United States still recites the oath of office this way. The action adds credibility and solemnity to the presidential oath, just as courtroom witnesses are deemed truthful when they end their oaths with "so help me God." Sometimes we think we need to say special words to help convince people that we are telling the truth.

Other common customs permit us to lie and get away with it. "I had my fingers crossed," we say. Crossing some body part legitimized lying. (We called it fibbing.) Sometimes we would even lie and if caught say, "Well, I didn't say 'cross my heart, hope to die, stick a needle in my eye.'" Once again such a statement could get one out of a tight spot.

We can laugh at these childish practices. However, when the

oath-takers are adults how do we feel? Surely we do not play such childish games, do we? I am convinced from my experience with five children that we adults do the same, only in more subtle and sophisticated ways. Children display our raw sin nature; adults, our revised sin nature. But to see religious sin nature, look at Pharisees, ancient and modern!

At the time of Jesus, the taking of oaths was a hot topic. Apparently people were misusing oaths and vows. Thus the rabbis stepped in and tried to help people to take their promises seriously.[10] The motive of the rabbis and Pharisees was good, a genuine desire to help people follow God's Law. But in their zeal to obey God, they concocted schemes that unknowingly resulted in their disobeying God. D. A. Carson comments, "The rabbis fought the abuses of oaths and vows among the unlearned masses. This is doubtless so. But the way they fought them was by differentiating between what was binding and what was not. In that sense, wittingly or unwittingly they encouraged evasive oaths and therefore lying. Jesus cut through these complexities by insisting that men must tell the truth."[11]

Rather than insist on truthfulness, the norm and intent of Scripture, the Pharisees invoked various pious-sounding oaths as they took vows. They made distinctions between valid and invalid oaths depending on the object cited. To swear by the temple was negotiable, but to swear by the gold of the temple was binding. Oaths on the altar were breakable, but oaths by the offering on the altar were binding.

But Jesus pointed out three obvious flaws in this oath-making system. First, those who should have been leading the people into truth were contributing to the art of evasion. Thus they merited the title "blind" (Matthew 23:16–17, 19). Second, Jesus pointed out that the seemingly pious distinctions were in reverse order of priority. It is not as much the material objects, no matter how expensive, that are weighty, as the spiritual objects— the temple and the altar. Third, Jesus succinctly pointed out that all oaths, no matter what words were used, ultimately involved God. All are therefore binding. Thus to break an oath using any set of pious words is odious. He is vitally concerned about honesty in all that we say. Jesus, therefore, closed up the loopholes and condemned the double standard. In another admonition to the Pharisees about honesty, Jesus insisted on straightforward answers without the taking of oaths (Matthew 5:33–37).

What about us? We live in a culture in which promises and commitments, even solemnly made ones, are routinely broken. Our wedding ceremonies, baptism rituals, infant dedications, and church membership covenants to varying degrees include pious oaths, which we cavalierly break. Every divorce is a major violation of the promise, "till death do us part." However, we spend most of our theological energy debating when it is OK to break our promises. We are like the Pharisees, seeking loopholes. We are masters at the art of evasion.

Many religious gatherings encourage people to take oaths to become Christians, to follow Jesus, to rededicate their lives to Jesus, to volunteer for foreign missions service or "full-time Christian work," or to keep certain promises in an emotionally charged environment fraught with peer pressure. Content is minimal. The cost factor of such oaths is usually unmentioned. The time needed to make a well-considered commitment is bypassed. And the scope of the oaths is often highly significant and far-reaching. Then we chalk up statistics, pat ourselves on the back, rejoice in God's "goodness."

The mouthing of pious-sounding promises is not evidence of true spirituality. Words are never an acceptable substitute for truth. It is sickness, not fitness, for us pastors to encourage people to make superficial promises, and then consider ourselves ministerially successful when they do so. It is sickness, not fitness, to allow any set of spiritual words to substitute for honesty and integrity. It is sickness, not fitness, when we routinely say one thing but actually do another.

We do not know the Pharisees' response to hearing these three woes pronounced upon them. Probably most were finding their fists clenched in restrained anger, disbelieving the direct attack by this young rabbi. But perhaps a few had begun to wonder if they were as spiritually healthy as they assumed. Either way, they had not heard the last from Jesus. He would declare four more woes, giving His listeners insight into the heart of a heavenly Father who desired true obedience. And along the way, they—and we—would learn about the way to true spiritual fitness.

Chapter Eleven
THE WAY TO SPIRITUAL FITNESS

mericans continue to have a weight problem. A recent study by the National Center for Health Statistics measured obesity by calculating a body mass index that takes into account a person's height and weight. The government study found that more than 50 percent of adults are overweight, defined by having a body mass index in excess of twenty-five.[1] Though we have minimal data about obesity in ancient Israel, it is pretty clear from Matthew 23:23–24 that Jesus thought the Pharisees had a weight problem. And as Jesus pronounced the fourth woe, He found this problem a major contributor to the spiritual sickness of the Pharisees.

As we continue to explore the seven woes, we will learn more about how the spiritually sick can seem fit and, more importantly, how to find the way to true spiritual fitness.

WOE #4: GNAT-PICKERS WHO SWALLOW CAMELS

"Woe to you, scribes and Pharisees, hypocrites! For you tithe mint and dill and cummin, and have neglected the weightier provisions of the law: justice and mercy and faithfulness; but these are the things you should have done without neglecting the others. You blind guides, who strain out a gnat and swallow a camel!" (Matthew 23:23–24)

In our culture, we usually place the main point last. But in the Jewish culture of His day, Jesus employed the common literary device called *chiasm* to draw His listeners' attention to this middle woe. Thus this fourth woe is the centerpiece of the seven.[2] Jesus' main point was that the Pharisees had majored on minors. They had lost any sense of great and little and thereby reversed God's priorities. They had lost the spirit of the Law in pursuit of the letter of the Law. They had gravitated toward the easier things and neglected the more important, "strained out a gnat and swallowed a camel," "devoted themselves to minutiae at the expense of the essentials of the Law."[3]

A Weight Problem

Basically they had a "weight problem." They gave much weight to small, peripheral, trifling things and little weight to the more central, decisive, and important matters. The Pharisees, for all their Bible knowledge, had failed to understand the central theme and thrust of Scripture.

Jesus highlighted the Pharisees' stewardship practices which certainly seemed impressive. The Pharisees were scrupulous tithers.[4] They were so intent on fulfilling the letter of the Law that they even counted out the leaves of their garden herbs and gave every tenth one to God. There was some debate among the rabbis of the day about the extent of the tithe. David Garland writes, "The more rigorous interpretation considered every natural growth to be subject to the tithe (cf. Lk. 18:12b); while the more humane interpretation understood Deuteronomy 14:22–23 literally—only grain, wine and oil were required to be tithed."[5] The Pharisees were determined to adhere to the rigorous rather than the humane interpretation. Why? They wanted to make certain that they met God's standards, and even exceeded them. God said to give a tenth. They gave more.

What dedication! What a sign of spiritual fitness! What synagogue or church wouldn't welcome a flock like this? The annual budget would never be an issue. The pastor could sleep easier at night knowing that there would always be ample money in the church coffers, because people had understood the blessing of giving to the Lord.

But wait a minute! Jesus was not as quick as we may be to pronounce spiritual fitness on scrupulous tithers. He noted that the Pharisees, though faithful tithers, had neglected far more important spiritual matters, namely justice, mercy, and faithfulness. These, Jesus stated, are more important than tithing. This trio of traits, plucked from the pages of the Old Testament, is straight from the heart of the Father (Hosea 6:6; Micah 6:8; Zechariah 7:9–10). He is far more concerned about caring for people than carrying out legalistic rituals, about faithfulness than fastidious concerns with defilement, and about the heart than the art of religion.

I find this exasperating. These three attributes, though I know their value, are so abstract, ambiguous, far-reaching, and unmeasurable that I can never know if I have "achieved" them. Besides, they are so hard. How will I ever know if I am just? To what extent must I demonstrate active compassion toward those in need? What does it mean and how can I measure my intimacy with God?

Jesus did not say that tithing is irrelevant, by the way. It is an important practice of those who follow God. But it is not nearly as important as justice, mercy, and faithfulness.

To drive home His point, Jesus employed a derogatory name and some humor. Once again, the Pharisees merited the title "blind guides," for they presumed to be pointing people to God but were oblivious to His priorities. But a joke sealed the case of the absurdity of scrupulous tithing without merciful "truthing." Sometimes humor penetrates where a plain statement falls flat. In this woe Jesus referred to a familiar practice of the Pharisees. They were very concerned about ingesting anything unclean, which would render them ritually impure. One of the unclean animals with which they were most absorbed was the gnat that regularly gathered around the fermenting wine. To prevent swallowing a gnat, the Jews would take pains to strain the juice through gauze, and even to drink the beverage through clenched teeth. Now the largest of the unclean animals known to the Jews was the camel. So Jesus pictured a fastidious Jew straining the wine and clenching his teeth so as to avoid swallowing a gnat, while he had a camel hock hanging out of his jaw!

Measuring Our Piety

Once again our behavior parallels that of the Pharisees in remarkable and convicting ways. Like the Pharisees, we gravitate toward acts of piety that are measurable, visible, and achievable. We like to have a sense of our standing with God, our relative standing with others, and a sense of personal satisfaction. We love "helps" such as a set prayer pattern, a 10 percent tithe, and how-to books on living a spiritual life—all to measure our piety. But we are not nearly as comfortable with standards that are qualitative rather than quantitative. Yet many of God's standards are not measurable. How does one quantify a relationship?

This fourth woe is particularly odious to Americans who like to measure everything and are uncomfortable with ambiguity. At school we receive grades; at work we get performance evaluations; in sports we have records and statistics. And everywhere we have how-to formulas that list what to do to succeed.

Like the Pharisees, we also tend to reverse the order of God's priorities. We major on minors and gravitate toward religious acts we can accomplish by gut-power. We are quite vocal about protecting our religious rights, but how many of us stand up for justice? We do protect our own interests (particularly economic), but do we defend the poor and oppressed? We may read books on social justice, but we tend to put down much money for seminars on how to handle our finances. We elevate conservative politics at the expense of social conscience. And how often do we hear sermons about mercy? Have we forgotten that mercy is a requisite for followers of Jesus Christ and especially for church leaders?[6] Like Israel of old, we come to God with sacrifices when He desires loyalty (Hosea 6:6); we want celebration when He desires a contrite heart (Psalm 51:6–10).

Like the Pharisees, we tend to get caught up in straining out gnats. Most church splits are the result of misplaced priorities. Two pastors of my acquaintance have endured considerable church conflict over the choice, taste, and color of the beverage at communion. This is gnat picking! How many times has the attention of the ministry of a church been diverted to checking out makeup and jewelry, debating the beat or instrumentation of music, or deciding the color of the carpet. We bicker about minor ecclesiastical matters while the major issues of being and making disciples of Christ are ignored.

Our true mission is to reflect, resemble, and represent Christ; to "do justice, to love kindness, and to walk humbly with your God" (Micah 6:8); and to "visit orphans and widows in their distress, and to keep oneself unstained by the world" (James 1:27). A just, merciful, and faithful heart is a tried and true mark of maturity. However, justice, mercy, and faithfulness are awfully hard to measure!

WOE #5: CLEAN HANDS AND DIRTY HEARTS

"Woe to you, scribes and Pharisees, hypocrites! For you clean the outside of the cup and of the dish, but inside they are full of robbery and self-indulgence. You blind Pharisee, first clean the inside of the cup and of the dish, so that the outside of it may become clean also."(Matthew 23:25–26)

A common trait of well-trained Christians, like myself, is an ability to look good and act right in most situations. I did not have to work hard to master the art of appearances. It comes naturally to a serious religious person. So a discrepancy can easily develop between our private and public worlds. I can look good on the outside and be rotten inside; I can seem to have righteous behavior and hide a rebellious heart. Religious people can easily hide the sins of the heart from others and even themselves, but not from God. Good external behavior has many built-in rewards and reinforcements.

A Clean Heart

The heart is another matter altogether. It is impossible to clean up the inside without divine help. Although heart intentions may slip out from time to time (especially at home), sins of the heart can be effectively eliminated from public view. Judas, the disciple-traitor, illustrates a seemingly upright religious person who hid a bad heart from everyone except Jesus. He conducted clandestine meetings with Jesus' enemies, and no one knew. He must have been highly respected by his apostolic peers or they would not have given him the money box (John 13:29). He skillfully hid his deep dark sins from people who lived with him every day for three years under grueling conditions. One would think that he would have cracked or slipped or revealed some of the "robbery and self-indulgence" of his heart. No one saw inside Judas except Jesus. Even when Jesus specifically indicated that Judas was the traitor, his fellow disciples were puzzled as to why he left the Upper Room (John 13:28).

Judas shows us the truth: A dirty heart *can* be hidden effectively from people! You can fool all the people all the time. But you cannot fool God.

One of the issues that the Pharisees of Jesus' day debated was the defilement of cups and plates. There were two schools of thought on the matter. The school of Hillel held that cleaning the inside of the vessel made it "clean." The school of Shammai argued that both the inside and outside of the object be washed in order for it to be declared "clean." Jesus used their debate as a metaphor of human character and conduct, not just cup-cleaning.

Essentially, Jesus declared that Hillel was right. Clean the inside, the part in which the food is placed, and the entire vessel is useful. Clean only the outside of the vessel, the more apparent part, and it is possible that the inside may still hide some dirt. The tendency of the Pharisees, like many religious people, was to clean up external actions without touching internal attitudes. The pious external behavior of the Pharisees masked materialism and hedonism. They appeared to be righteous people but were robbers. They appeared to be spiritual people but were self-indulgent. The outside and the inside of their lives didn't match up!

Jesus also told the Pharisees how to correct the disjunction. Clean the inside, the heart, of your life and (as Hillel has said) the outside will take care of itself. Take care of your private relationship with God first, and your public world will follow, and there will be a genuine correspondence between them.

What would Jesus say to us today? An outwardly clean life is not enough! We may know how to behave within boundaries, but what motivates our righteousness? We may avoid breaking the God-given Ten Commandments and man-made Dirty Dozen, but have we superficialized God's Law? A clean moral life is commendable. Such a life is commanded in Scripture, reinforced by society, and is good for the reputation of Christ and His church. Besides, behaving well works. However, appearances can be deceiving, even self-deceiving.[7] Moral living avoids many of the pitfalls of the rebellious and saves a lot of scars, but it does not keep us from sin.

Two Hidden Sins

Jesus highlighted two hidden Pharisaic sins: robbery and self-indulgence. Those sins remain a diabolical duo today. Overt robbery is not common among us (nor was it among the Pharisees), but at the heart of robbery is materialism, a common cultural flaw among Americans. It shows itself in greed, covetousness, a desire to keep up with the Joneses, and immediate gratification. Indeed, our economic system is built on stimulating covetousness and greed. Marketers and the media have largely institutionalized and aggrandized this quest for more things. And if materialism is our number one god, hedonism is a close second. We are among the most self-indulgent people on the face of the planet (and ironically among the most unhappy).

There are other hidden sins that religious people, like myself, continue to wrestle with. Lust, hypocrisy, jealousy, envy, bitterness, and self-righteousness are on the list. So are unforgiveness and pride. But we can hide our struggles with these from everyone—even ourselves up to a point. We can keep them private easily enough.

Jesus' solution to this woe of secret sins is for us to examine and focus on cleaning our hearts. Jesus says that defilement is a matter of the heart, not the environment. The Pharisees incorrectly saw the source of defilement as being outside the person—the company kept, places frequented, and objects touched. Defilement was environmental. But Jesus says defilement happens inside out, not outside in.

Thus heart transformation, not behavioral and environmental clean-up projects, is the key to true righteousness. Boundaries to help maintain purity are both wise and necessary, but they are not the ultimate answer. The ultimate answer is inside. It comes from inside, where the Holy Spirit resides to empower us; and it comes from above, where Christ's blood cleanses us as we confess our sins (1 John 1:9).

WOE #6: THE DISGUISE OF MINISTRY

> "Woe to you, scribes and Pharisees, hypocrites! For you are like whitewashed tombs which on the outside appear beautiful, but inside they are full of dead men's bones and all uncleanness. So you, too, outwardly appear righteous to men, but inwardly you are full of hypocrisy and lawlessness." (Matthew 23:27–28)

A sobering confession has come from Howard Hendricks, a seminary professor and leader of the Center for Christian Leadership:

> My spiritual experience has been revolutionized recently. I must confess, as many a Christian worker must, that it's very easy to become compulsively active. It is hard to learn the lesson of the barrenness of busyness. Activity simply becomes the anesthetic to deaden the pain of an empty life. And if we get off long enough, we discover we have activity without accomplishment.[8]

There are few better ways to hide spiritual deadness than with church activity. Sadly, many times we Christians minister out of emptiness, not fullness. Every church has its army of "faithful saints" who give of themselves for the cause of Christ. Many do serve Jesus out of His fullness in them, motivated by His love. But others serve to dull the pain, to fill the emptiness, to disguise the deadness they feel (or worse yet, do not feel) inside. God's people can appear beautiful but be spiritually dead.

The Ministry of Hypocrites

The sixth woe refers to another common Jewish practice. In this case the whitewashing of tombs becomes the metaphor Jesus uses to describe the hypocritical behavior of the Pharisees.

The Jews knew that a corpse was unclean and that contact with it required purification (Numbers 19:13–22). The rabbis took this teaching of God seriously and sought to make it practical for the people. Touching a corpse or inadvertent contact with a grave became one of the most feared and surest forms of defilement according to the Jews. So to warn the faithful about the presence of a grave, the practice of marking them was established (with Ezekiel 39:15 as the scriptural basis).

Avoiding defilement was a constant concern for the righteous. But maintaining one's ceremonial purity was particularly important before Passover. For to an observant Jew, it was a great loss not to be admitted into the celebration of the great act of God's deliverance of Israel from Egypt. D. A. Carson comments, "During the month of Adar, just before Passover, it was customary to whitewash with lime graves or grave-sites that might not be instantly identified as such, in order to warn pilgrims to steer clear of the area and avoid ritual uncleanness from contact with corpses."[9]

Perhaps Jesus was using this metaphor of whitewashing tombs to make an allusion to the whitewashed appearance of the Pharisees. The Pharisees apparently were fond of wearing white. Then, as now, white carried the connotation of purity and righteousness.[10] So the Pharisees' beautiful and pure-looking clothing gave the impression of piety when in fact their hearts housed impurity. The Pharisees' seeming beauty and that of whitewashed tombs are alike, Jesus said. Both shout out, "Beware, defilement is near!"

Appearance Versus Reality

Whereas the fifth woe exposed the Pharisees' faulty means of spiritual cleansing (cleaning the outside instead of the inside), the sixth woe exposes the differences between appearance and reality. The contradiction between what seems to be and what actually is true is the essence of hypocrisy, and Jesus twice mentions the Pharisees' hypocrisy. Beauty on the outside can hide ugliness within. Though they seemed to serve God, their ministry was polluted by their own selfish motives. Teachers of the Law may be lawbreakers. Purported paragons of piety may in fact be impure. Religious people can effectively disguise spiritual decay.

Religious people are commonly criticized for a difference between the inside and the outside, their Sunday versus Monday behavior. Churches sometimes surpass Broadway in their ability to turn out excellent actors and actresses. A certain set of behaviors is expected and reinforced in the confines of churchdom. Most people rise to the occasion. A whitewashed appearance is not that difficult to pull off. And usually we are unaware that we are acting!

Ministry that is done without spiritual vitality is hypocrisy. Such hypocrisy will deceive us. It will give us a sense of rightness without righteousness. It will dull the pain of emptiness so that we do not have to face it. And eventually it will become normal for us to act one way while inner attitudes do not jive. It is easy after a while to simply ignore the hypocrisy and go on.

WOE #7: THOSE WHO MURDER THE RIGHTEOUS

"Woe to you, scribes and Pharisees, hypocrites! For you build the tombs of the prophets and adorn the monuments of the righteous, and say, 'If we had been living in the days of our fathers, we would not have been partners with them in shedding the blood of the prophets.' So you testify against yourselves, that you are sons of those who murdered the prophets." (Matthew 23:29–31)

The final woe of Matthew 23 denounces the Pharisees for building monuments to the prophets of old while preparing to murder the very Son of God who stood before them. Once again what looks like spiritual fitness is actually spiritual sickness.

Building monuments for the prophets was a growth industry among the Pharisees of Jesus' day.[11] Perhaps they engaged in it simply to honor those they thought they resembled. Maybe they built monuments seeking to atone for the sins of their fathers who had persecuted the prophets by honoring the prophets posthumously. Such monument building certainly helped the Pharisees to divorce themselves from their evil ancestors and to put forth an image of piety.

The Pharisees coupled their monument building with sharp criticisms of the deeds of their forebears (v. 30). The Pharisees were swift to protest their innocence from the deeds done by their ancestors. They insisted that things would have been different if they had been alive. They were certain that they would have protected the prophets, not persecuted them. So they claimed a certain distance from their past and acknowledged their superior enlightenment. Jesus, however, turned the tables on the Pharisees by saying that their activities demonstrated their kinship with the prophet-killers of old. They were cut from the same spiritual cloth.

As Jesus concluded His diatribe against the Pharisees, passion poured through His speech (vv. 32–36). He switched from past and present sins to future judgment. Verse 32 is a transition verse, a bridge to the threat of judgment that follows. Jesus ironically invited the Pharisees to get on with their dastardly deeds and fill up the cup of God's wrath. A common belief among the Jews, supported by Scriptures, was that God could take only so much evil before His patience ended and His judgment began.[12] This belief was applied to the Gentiles. Jesus, however, informed them that they, the Pharisees, had exhausted the mercy of God.

Their coming judgment is well-deserved (vv. 34–35). The Pharisees represent only the latest chapter in a long history of persecution of God's messengers. Jesus pointed out that though the Pharisees saw themselves as morally superior to their ancestors, they were actually worse. The Pharisees were guilty of all the blood from the first martyr, Abel (Genesis 4:8), to the last, Zechariah, the son of Berechiah.

Are we any different? Not in any way! We readily take the names of spiritual greats and "honor them" by building monuments and institutions in their names. However, the truth is we would likely reject them if they ministered among us today. (See "Learning from Leaders of the Church.") Moreover, though we honor their memories, we do not approximate their character or ministry. Many of these greats of old would be appalled by what is done today under their names.

THE RIGHT WAY

Learning from Leaders of the Church

It's not wrong to esteem the great giants of the faith. Indeed, some churches find inspiration from their forefathers. Lutherans rightly admire Martin Luther, for example. But we might be surprised by what they think of our modifications.

I wonder, for instance, if Martin Luther would join a Lutheran church, or John Wesley would become a Methodist. Would Saint Francis be welcomed in the Franciscan order and would Augustine be an Augustinian? Would John Calvin teach at Calvin College?

We love to read about and reflect on the lives of the great saints of old. Their names lend credibility to our cause. But would they be as fond of us? Would those whose names we so freely attach to our institutions approve of the way we do ministry? Perhaps not. We tend to conveniently forget that many of the famous former saints were persons of extraordinary conviction and courage who initiated costly (and usually controversial) change. Some of them were rather crusty. Most were mavericks. If they reappeared and made a tour of the institutions that bear their names, I suspect that they would turn over a few chairs, deface a few signs, and issue some scathing calls for renewal.

I am certain we would find them annoying or embarrassing. Perhaps, like the Pharisees, we would even rejoice if they were to leave our earth. In our efforts to advance the church, we often honor our spiritual forebears even as we display actions and attitudes contrary to theirs. Let us have a passion and commitment like theirs, and embrace those among us whose zeal is like that of the saints of old.

If Jesus donned modern dress and visited us, I am certain we would mistreat Him in some of the same ways and for the same reasons that the Pharisees did two thousand years ago. It demonstrates extraordinary and deeply culpable historical amnesia and spiritual blindness to think we would not act today as the Pharisees did years ago.

I wonder how God views our track record today with the "prophets" He sends among us. When someone exposes our materialism or demonstrates our political naiveté or points out our scriptural duplicity or attacks our sacrosanct traditions or suggests that much of our piety is pretense or offers another way of looking at Scripture, how do we respond? We may respond in a slightly more sophisticated manner than the Pharisees. However, perhaps our "sophisticated" response is actually a lack of zeal. How easily we overlook the consistently taught principle of Scripture that the greatest enemy of the righteous is usually the religious.

FROM WOES TO WEEPING

How fitting that Matthew 23 concludes with tears and not jeers, with weeping rather than a whipping. The denunciations that Jesus issued broke His tender heart. Like a mother hen, Jesus wanted to gather these dear Pharisees to Himself and lavish His love on them. He only asked that they be honest with themselves and see their depravity and need, that they pursue authentic fitness not religious sickness, and that they embrace His message of grace and truth.

We, too, need to weep over our self-deception and ungodliness. Sadly, the woes Jesus issued fell not only on deaf ears but on diabolical hearts, Matthew tells us. Rather than repenting, the Pharisees reacted in anger and killed the Messiah.

How do we avoid these "woes" and instead snuggle under the "wings" of the Lord Jesus? How do we avoid the pseudo-fitness of religion and find true spiritual health? How do we develop a lifestyle that receives Jesus' "well-done" rather than His woe? I believe it begins with a willingness to be honest with God and with ourselves. This requires that we see portions of our souls that we would rather ignore. We must recognize our hypocrisy, duplicity, religious gamesmanship, perverted priorities, focus on the externals to the neglect of our souls, historical amnesia, and our spiritual myopia. We must repent, in humble confession (with tears, perhaps). Above all, we must not be fooled into pursuing a false spiritual fitness that masks spiritual sickness.

THE WAY TO SPIRITUAL HEALTH

How do we avoid spiritual sickness and pursue genuine spiritual fitness? First, we ought to specialize far more on spiritual cardiology than spiritual dermatology. We should not be content with right answers without right hearts. We should examine our motives as much as we seek to have proper outward behavior. Preachers should address the listeners' hearts if they want to alter behavior patterns.

Second, we should cease from making evaluations of spirituality based on superficial criteria. Ask not only about evangelistic zeal and missions-mindedness but about the spiritual health of the product. We must not be as impressed with religious verbiage as with incarnated grace and truth.

Third, we must not content ourselves with conformity to superficial standards. How many of us derive an immense sense of spiritual satisfaction from our checkbooks and appointment calendars. I, like many other pastors, have told congregations that a "foolproof" method of evaluating one's spirituality is by evaluating how you spend your time and money. But by this standard the Pharisees would have received high marks. Time and money are neither the only nor the truest tests of the heart. Justice, mercy, and faithfulness are.

Fourth, we must never let our propensity to slip into Pharisaism keep us from returning to the open arms of Jesus. I am certain that if Jesus had a talk with me, I would probably be spiritually stripped bare and scared. For on some level I can relate to every one of the woes. But after I've been appropriately dressed down, I hope I'd have the sense to run into His arms and have a good cry. I hope I would see beyond the frown on His face to the tear in His eye. I hope that I wouldn't fixate as much on His wagging finger as His inviting arms. I hope I could separate His righteous indignation from His unconditional acceptance.

I hope I would run to Jesus rather than run Him through. For in the final analysis, it is only through His power that we can have true spiritual health. Real acts of righteousness originate in Him. That relationship with Jesus is crucial, and it is the subject of our final chapter.

Chapter Twelve
THE RIGHT RELATIONSHIP

Any way you cut it, religion does not work with God. Attach any name to it that you wish—Islam, Hinduism, Judaism, even Christianity—human efforts to make one's way to God are futile. No amount of self-effort can reform the heart. No pursuit of piety or understanding of philosophy can connect one to God. No traditions have the power to produce true spirituality, and no fences can protect from transgression. No degree of separatism can shield one from sin. For that matter, no amount of moral uprightness can produce righteousness.

However, billions of people have and are giving themselves to religion in the pursuit of God. People everywhere are trying to find God or are searching for "a higher power"; they are seeking to fill what Pascal calls that "God-shaped vacuum" in their souls. Religion seems the answer to many seeking souls. For in religion is found a sense of righteousness, a reservoir of knowledge, a path of piety. Religion also offers meaningful traditions, protective fences, and guidelines for how to live a separated life.

Our human nature is inescapably religious. We desperately desire a way to relate to God. However, we seek to relate to Him as we fashion Him, in our ways and on our terms. This is not what God seeks!

At the vanguard of this movement to relate to God in our own ways are the Pharisees. As we have seen, the Pharisees pursued extreme righteousness. They modeled many good traits; in many ways they obeyed God's commands. Yet their flaws were significant, as Jesus clearly exposed. And as previous chapters have shown, we who take our faith in Jesus Christ seriously are frequently subject to the same sins as the Pharisees. If all of the exposure to the Pharisees has left you reeling spiritually, I understand, for I have spent the last two decades of my life wrestling with my susceptibility to Pharisaism.

But good news: Hope yet remains! The Scriptures do provide compelling answers to the Pharisaism that tends to grip our religious souls. The antidote to Pharisaism is clearly, powerfully spelled out in Philippians 3. The remedy to religion is relationship. The freedom to live a righteous life is found in drawing close to Jesus Christ.

ALL THE RIGHT STUFF YET STILL NOT GOOD ENOUGH

None other than the apostle Paul, "a Hebrew of Hebrews" (v. 5), learned that truth after trying to live a righteous life through religion. Paul's credentials are impeccable and stand as an unscalable monument of futility to anyone who might dare try to work his or her way to righteousness.

Our guide through and beyond the veil of Pharisaism is none other than the best Pharisee who ever lived. (I know that Jewish people would disagree with this statement. However, perhaps they have viewed Paul as we have viewed Pharisees, with extreme negative bias.) In Philippians 3:4–6, Paul summarized his pedigree and accomplishments. He delineated seven characteristics denoting what perfect human righteousness would look like for a Jew. The apostle challenged the Judaizers (the Christianized version of Pharisaism), about whom he was speaking, to a showdown. His background and accomplishments were second to none.

The apostle Paul began by citing four characteristics that seemingly would have pleased God, if religion could do so. First, he was circumcised on the eighth day. In strict conformity to the Law, he was a full-fledged Jew from the cradle. Second, Paul was "of the nation of Israel," born of pure-blooded Jewish stock; a birth member of the "chosen people" of God. He could trace his family lineage back to Abraham (2 Corinthians 11:22). Third, he was "of the tribe of Benjamin." This tribe, though small (Psalm 68:27), was renowned in Israel. Benjamin was Jacob (Israel's) favorite son, born to Rachel, Jacob's favorite wife (Genesis 30:23–24; 35:16–18). Benjamin was the only son of Jacob's born in the Promised Land (Genesis 35:9–19). Significantly, Jerusalem, the Holy City, was within the territory assigned to Benjamin

(Judges 1:21).[1] Fourth, Paul was "a Hebrew of Hebrews." He was of pure, zealous, godly Jewish stock from both parents. He spoke Hebrew and Aramaic as his mother tongue, a mark of faithfulness (Acts 22:2–3). This placed him atop the Jewish sub-ethnic pecking order above those Jews who were cultural Greeks and Romans and spoke Greek as their native tongue (called Hellenistic Jews in Acts 6:1).

Paul also cited three personal religious achievements that would impress Jews (and seemingly God). He began with the words, "As to the Law, a Pharisee." Calling oneself a Pharisee was a mark of distinction, not a curse word (Acts 23:6; 26:5). Paul was at least a second generation Pharisee (Acts 23:6). This meant that he had reached the pinnacle of religious orthodoxy and experience in Judaism. Moreover, Paul had studied the Mosaic Law under Gamaliel, the Pharisees' most celebrated contemporary teacher (Acts 5:34; 22:3).

In addition, Paul practiced his faith fervently. "As to zeal, a persecutor of the church," he wrote. Paul was passionate and intense about his religious commitment. He strongly believed in the truths that he espoused as a Pharisee and was willing to protect them at all costs, even life. So he hunted down and gave authorization for the killing of Christians. His zeal was legendary, and when it went awry, Paul's actions were diabolical.[2]

Perhaps the crowning achievement of Paul's pre-Christ religious life was that "As to the righteousness which is in the Law, [I was] found blameless." Paul paid such meticulous attention to the ritual requirements of the Law (remember this included all 613 Old Testament commands as well as thousands of traditions and fences) that no one could find fault with him. This is an extraordinary statement. There was no chink in his religious armor; no one could make an objectively verifiable criticism of his legal righteousness. This does not mean to imply that Paul thought he was sinless. Sinlessness was foreign to the Jewish way of thinking. Peter O'Brien states, "Here is a man well satisfied, reminiscent of the rich young ruler in the Gospel story (Luke 18:21) who claims to have kept all the commandments from his youth."[3]

The apostle Paul had all the right stuff religiously. He had the grounds for boasting. He had a pure, unblemished, orthodox Jewish background. He had impeccable religiosity, unparalleled zeal, and unblamable behavior. So when he ventured into the realm of critiquing religion, he did not do so as a novice or an armchair critic. The critique came from one who knew what he was talking about, who modeled Judaism in the most orthodox manner, and who had every theoretical and experiential grounds to evaluate it. No one, he wrote, could match him. Nevertheless, religion, no matter how purely and passionately practiced, is not enough.

THE WAY OUT OF PHARISAISM

The apostle Paul had planted the Philippian church during his second missionary journey (Acts 16) and visited it again on his third (Acts 20:1, 6). He was close to these believers, and they had sent gifts to the apostle more than once (Philippians 4:16, 18). His letter to this spiritually strong church contains the constant theme of rejoicing. Nevertheless, the church was not safe from Pharisaism. Like Christians today, the believers in Philippi were hearing a message that added legal requirements to their faith. The Judaizers, a group of quasi-Christians, said those who had come to Christ must keep the Mosaic Law; without certain religious practices Christians could not be saved or sanctified.

The apostle Paul rightly saw this as undercutting the essence of the gospel. Thus his tone in Philippians 3 quickly shifted from affection to stern warning. Those who would undermine the gospel he unaffectionately called dogs. Paul, obviously distraught, had a heavy burden to communicate to his beloved Philippians. In so doing, he has given us, under the inspiration of the Holy Spirit, "a foundational building block for theology and a true classic of Christian spirituality."[4] Philippians 3 offers six keys to combating Pharisaism. As we study them, we are pointed once more to the priority of nurturing our relationship with the Lord Jesus Christ.

BEWARE OF FALSE RELIGION

The way out of Pharisaism must begin with constant vigilance to avoid the lure of false religion. Religious alternatives to authentic Christianity are always available. We are, often unknowingly, surrounded by counterfeit versions of the Christian life. The apostle Paul, being deeply sensitive to perversions of the gospel, warned his beloved Philippians about spiritual counterfeits. After reminding them that joy in the Lord can always be theirs and rejoicing always can be "a safeguard for you," he issues a warning: "Beware of the dogs, beware of the evil workers, beware of the false circumcision" (v. 2).

With a rapid-fire triple warning, Paul said, "Beware, Beware, Beware." Gerald Hawthorne expresses the meaning of this warning, "'Take proper notice of,' 'pay attention to,' or 'learn your lesson from.' Thus Paul is not so much warning the Philippians to be on guard against their opponents, as he is asking them to pay careful attention to them, to study them, so as to understand them and to avoid adopting their destructive beliefs and practices."[5] When something dangerous threatens our spiritual welfare, we must pay attention.

With three stunning characterizations Paul defined those whom the Philippians must beware of. First, they must "beware of the dogs." In Bible times dogs were dirty, wandering scavengers that prowled the cities, ate whatever they could find, and attacked people. Thus "dog" is a term of derision.[6] In fact, Jews regularly referred to Gentiles as dogs. Now the apostle reverses roles, saying that the Judaizers, with their false religion, must now be regarded as Gentiles.

Second, they must "beware of the evil workers." The Jews prided themselves on being people of God's Law. They preached, practiced, and protected it. Again Paul turned the tables on the Judaizers.[7] He told them that they were evil workers, not doers of good deeds. For when deeds of the Law are done by human effort in an attempt to placate God, they are counterproductive.

Third, the Philippians must "beware of the false circumcision." Few things were more precious to the Jews than circumcision, the sign of the covenant God had made with Abraham. Nevertheless, Paul turned this Jewish rite on its head, this time with a pun. "False circumcision," or "mutilation" is in reality pagan butchery.[8] Not only does it mutilate the body but also the spirit. For what God has always sought, and of which physical circumcision was merely a sign, was the circumcision of the heart.

In contrast, the true circumcision—the genuine heirs of Abraham—"worship in the Spirit of God and glory in Christ Jesus and put no confidence in the flesh." With these three phrases, Paul defined authentic Christians. Our worship is Spirit-empowered, not conjured up by our own efforts (John 4:19–24). It is motivated internally, not maintained by traditions and rites learned by rote. It is pleasing to God, not a stench in His nostrils

(Isaiah 1:11; Jeremiah 6:20). Our glory is in Christ Jesus, not ourselves, in what He has done and is doing through us. Our confidence decidedly is not vested in ourselves, but in Christ. We trust in Christ, not religion, rituals, pedigree, experiences, or achievements.

It is not by accident that the Scriptures are so full of warnings about false religion, (Pharisaism, the Judaizers, the Gnostics, etc.) The Old Testament prophets, Jesus, and Paul didn't seem to think that legalism was benign. God's spokesmen have always thundered against those who added to the gospel or externalized religion. They refused to add circumcision, baptism, or rules and regulations to the gospel. They warned against the practice of embracing grace for salvation and rejecting it for sanctification.

Perhaps legalism is far more dangerous than we think. Paul referred to such "good works" people as spiritual scavengers, "evil workers," and butchers. Present-day Christians must be acutely aware of the religious clothes in which modern-day Pharisaism dresses. We must always beware of the danger. Constant vigilance is required to escape the subtle pull of Pharisaism.

A VOTE OF NO CONFIDENCE

A second way out of Pharisaism and religious works, is to abandon any "confidence in the flesh." The apostle Paul had once built his religious life around fleshly confidence (vv. 3–6) but concluded such superior advantages and effort were vain. Paul learned to place no confidence in his highly sophisticated, educated, and self-disciplined flesh.

The Pharisees basically devised a system by which people could work their way to God. This system was based on the Bible, with numerous human additions designed to "help" people follow God's Laws. As we have noted, however, religious systems do not work to develop true righteousness. Religion did not work in ancient Israel. Instead it was regularly corrupted into hypocrisy, formalism, and even idolatry. And though the Pharisees were among the most zealous for righteousness, their faith went to seed. They ended up crucifying their Messiah and trying to cover up their sin. Religion has never worked since.

"Confidence in the flesh" is the essence of religion (including Pharisaism, the Judaizers, and any of a thousand forms of legalism that plague the Christian landscape). It is natural to trust in one's religious acts, spiritual pedigree, Bible knowledge, witnessing zeal, prayer life, and external compliance with God's standards. It is easy to fall into a performance mentality with one's spiritual life. All of these are regularly reinforced around us by people and in us by the Evil One. But the flesh will not get us to God. God must get to us. God must live in us and through us![9]

The way out of Pharisaism must include a good long look at our souls. We must honestly acknowledge that we place all kinds of confidence in our abilities, intellect, learning, spiritual capacities, and self-effort to please God. Yet to the extent we place our confidence for spiritual success in anything apart from Christ, we will fall prey to Pharisaism.

SPIRITUAL ACCOUNTING

The third key to leaving Pharisaism is to recognize our true spiritual wealth. In Philippians 3:7–9, the apostle sounds more like a certified public accountant than a theologian. Three times in these verses he used the word "count" to describe a spiritual activity that he commended to the Philippians, and to us. The great apostle had just described a perfect list of spiritual credentials, the substance of which many would be enormously proud. He inferred that at one time this spiritual pedigree and these religious accomplishments were placed prominently in the asset column of his spiritual bank account. However, when he came to Christ, he acquired a new accounting system—one that brings inestimable wealth to the spirit.

The apostle Paul utilized several accounting procedures as the Messiah reoriented his spiritual life. First, he took all of the spiritual inheritances and accomplishments (religious background, religious achievements, morality, scholarship, reputation) that had formerly been in the asset column of his life and moved them to the liabilities side of the ledger (v. 7). These former "gains" he now counted as losses. Second, Paul put a formula into his spiritual spreadsheet that prohibited any human spiritual accomplishments from again appearing in the asset column. He told us that he counted all things to be loss.

Third, and most important, the apostle placed knowing "Christ Jesus my Lord" as the lone asset on his spiritual spreadsheet. This asset is so enormous that all other assets pale in comparison and are practically valueless. Perhaps he intended to imply that if we try to add anything but Christ to the asset column we will lose, not gain.[10] Finally, over the items which once prominently dominated his spiritual bank account, he wrote in bold-faced letters, "Rubbish!" That which he once had worked so hard to achieve was now considered revolting.[11]

The apostle Paul's new found wealth was freely given by Christ. However, it did have a price tag. When he pronounced "rubbish" over his former assets, he incurred the wrath of those who did not understand his spiritual inheritance. This resulted in suffering "the loss of all things" (v. 8). Paul knew theologically and experientially that bucking the system of spiritual wealth would have painful consequences both personally and socially. His pride would have to die and other people's pride would be pricked. Paul paid a hefty price for following Christ. Perhaps he had his property confiscated; maybe he was disinherited by his family. Surely he lost all his stature in Judaism. He even suffered heavily at the hands of the Christian church. Nevertheless, as Gerald Hawthorne noted, "Paul did not lament his loss. For him it was welcome relief."[12] Jesus has said all who truly follow Him alone will pay a price personally and socially (John 12:24–25; Luke 9:24–26).

Paul's gain overwhelmed his loss. Imagine that you were a shrewd businessperson who had built a nest egg of $50,000. Bill Gates, the multibillionaire founder of Microsoft, befriends you and later decides to bequeath much of his considerable wealth to you. What would you do? Probably you would view all the money you had worked so hard to accumulate as unworthy of your attention. You might even eliminate it from your accounting, for it is as rubbish next to your newly acquired billions. In the asset column you would have great difficulty writing an amount because the figure is too large. Instead you may simply write "Inheritance from William Gates." Furthermore, any future assets that you would accumulate from your job would seem inconsequential in comparison.

So it was for The apostle Paul, who was given an infinite spiritual inheritance by the Lord of the universe! So it should be with us.

The apostle Paul at one time bought into the spiritual invest-ment scheme of the Pharisees. Like them, he was a meticulous spiritual accountant. He managed to rise to the top spiritually via multiplying the assets he had been given and by working very hard. However, he eventually came to see that he was spiritually bankrupt. Similarly, our own spiritual investment schemes of

THE RIGHT WAY

Escape from the Dungeon

Paul offers six keys to unlock us from the dungeon of Pharisaism. They all are found in Philippians 3. The keys were offered to the believers at Philippi to escape the false, legal teachings of the so-called 'udaizers. They apply to all Christians who wish to escape from the prison of Pharisaic service to God and enter into a fuller relationship with Christ. The six are:

1. *Beware of false religion.* God's spokesmen—the prophets, the apostles, and Christ Himself—have always opposed those who added to the gospel or externalized religion (v. 2).

2. *Forsake any confidence in the flesh.* Religious acts will not get us to God before or after our spiritual salvation (vv. 3–6).

3. *Recognize your spiritual wealth.* In Christ we have our only eternal asset. We must guard and cherish our relationship with Him (vv. 7–9).

4. *Develop your love relationship with Jesus.* We know Him better by spending time with Him and experiencing life as He did (vv. 9–11).

5. *Pursue Christ passionately to know Him deeply.* Like an athlete in a race, we are to be active in seeking to deepen our relationship with Jesus (vv. 12–16).

6. *Avoid the pull of the world to libertinism.* We must be careful not to overreact to legalism by embracing license, as the world does (vv. 17–21).

hard work lead only to spiritual poverty. Fortunately, Paul and we were found by the world's spiritually wealthiest person and given an inestimable inheritance. We no longer have to work for our worth or worry about our wealth. All we care about now, like Paul, is to know better the one who has given us everything we have, Jesus, the Son of God.

Clearly the method of proper spiritual accounting for us is the same as for The apostle Paul. At the top of the asset list write "Inheritance from Jesus Christ, the Lord of the universe." It's our relationship with Jesus Christ that is paramount. What does this mean? First, on our spiritual spreadsheets we should never place our puny spiritual works in the same column as the inheritance given to us by Christ. Many times this is very difficult to do, as pride continually motivates us to think that we are working together with God to increase our spiritual wealth. But the wealth increases only by the power (and mystery) of "Christ in [us], the hope of glory" (Colossians 1:27).

Second, the focus of our spiritual wealth truly becomes the riches of Christ bequeathed to us by His grace. He will never love us more than He does right now. He will never give us more than He has already put at our disposal. My mission is to tap the riches of Christ in me. We are to live in light of our actual spiritual wealth. Our privilege is to come to know intimately the One who gave us so much.

Next to the riches of Christ, my contributions are no better than rubbish. And yet, Christ glories in every way that I use the wealth I have been given to sing His praises, to enhance His reputation, to love His people, and to represent His name. Unbelievably, he even multiplies the spiritual billions and rewards me richly for any genuine acts of devotion to Him!

RELATIONSHIP, NOT RELIGION

For as long as I can remember, I have mouthed the mantra, "I have asked Jesus into my heart, and I have a personal relationship with Jesus Christ, my Lord and Savior." Evangelicals rightly believe that true Christian faith has at its heart a "personal relationship" with Jesus. However, many of us, including myself, often mouth those words without understanding them or really applying them to our lives.

The fourth key to escape Pharisaism is developing our love

relationship with Jesus. In fact, Paul's theology can be summed up in his words, "know Christ" (vv. 8, 10). He had abandoned all human routes to righteousness and now wanted only to know Jesus. This knowing of Christ has several components that the apostle pointed out in verses 9–11.

In a single verse (v. 9), Paul defined the difference between human and divine righteousness. The goal of human righteousness is to find God. By inference, it is motivated by human self-confidence, by the assumption that we can do what is required to please God. It is based on the Law of Moses and our ability to keep the standards of that Law. In contrast, those pursuing divine righteousness seek to be found by God and in Him. They recognize their spiritual bankruptcy and long for God's mercy. This righteousness is received as a gift, not earned. It is "found" by faith in Christ.

The entire goal of Paul's spiritual life had been altered by God's grace. Paul's passion now was to know Jesus Christ. He desired to have a personal, intimate, deepening relationship with the ascended Lord Jesus Christ. This is not the same as reciting facts or creeds about Him or giving mental assent to certain historical events or even knowing a lot about Him. As in a marriage, intimate knowledge of Christ requires trust, love, loyalty, talk, vulnerability, risk, time, service, and other ingredients. Paul was willing to invest what it took to know the One who so lovingly and forcefully took hold of him (Acts 9).

The apostle Paul wanted to know three facets of Christ's life in order to develop the relationship with Jesus: His resurrection power, His sufferings, and His death. Nothing better characterizes the power of Christ than His resurrection from the dead. Paul wanted to experience this power of Christ personally. He also wanted to know Christ by experiencing sufferings for His sake. Christ's passion included betrayal, denial, injustice, rejection, persecution, and much pain. This too Paul was willing to accept for the sake of knowing Christ. Indeed, Paul did experience many similar sufferings.[13] Third, Paul even accepted "being conformed to His death" as part of the package of knowing Christ.

We come to know people best when we experience with them, even in small measure, the good, the bad, and the ugly of their lives. So also it is with knowing Christ. We come to know Him as we share in His resurrection power and as we experience

His sufferings and death. Clearly part of this is theological, for we are to reckon ourselves dead to sin and alive to Christ (Romans 6:11). Paul told us that we are "crucified with Christ" (Galatians 2:20). We are to call to mind regularly His death (Luke 22:19–20; 1 Corinthians 11:23–25). However, I believe that part of this knowledge is also experiential. We come to know Him when we experience His power working through us in ways that we know are not our own. We are drawn closer to Christ as we experience suffering for His sake. We come to know Jesus better as we struggle with sin in our lives, and as we voluntarily lay down our lives for Him. Peter O'Brien comments, "It is not in the fellowship of Christ's sufferings as such that Paul is conformed to Christ's death; rather, it is by participating in those sufferings (which he experiences in the course of his apostolic labours) *and* as strengthened to do so in the power of his resurrection that he is continually being conformed to Christ's death."[14]

THE ACTIVE PURSUIT OF INTIMACY

The apostle Paul has used two metaphors so far in describing the believer's escape from Pharisaism. We are to be watchmen, watchful and wary of false religion. We are accountants, properly calculating our spiritual bank accounts. Now Paul describes us as athletes pressing on to win the prize. Paul readily acknowledged that he hadn't arrived spiritually and didn't expect to until he was called upward (v. 14). But until that time he fully intended, like a world-class athlete, to go for the gold medal: to lay hold of Christ Jesus, actively pursuing intimacy with Him.

As an athlete (perhaps a marathon runner), the apostle is dedicated to his goal of knowing Jesus, expressed with the words "I press on" (vv. 12, 14). Like a runner in a race, Paul had his eyes fixed in the right direction (v. 13b). He did not look over his shoulder, only forward, as he strained for the finish line. He was not immobilized by the past, did not dwell on the past, live in the past, or long for the "good old days." This does not mean that Paul blocked out everything from the past as he pursued knowing Christ. We know that he never forgot the depths of his sin (1 Timothy 1:13). However, he did not dwell on his past accomplishments or failures. He did not see his future as predetermined by his past. Instead he put the past behind him, reached into the present, and pressed toward the future when he would "breast the tape." He lived to be called up to the winners' stand to receive the prize, which ultimately was union with the Lord he loved. And he admonished the Philippians, and us, to do likewise (vv. 16–17).

The fifth key to escaping Pharisaism's dungeon is to *actively* pursue intimacy with Jesus. The first half of Philippians 3 could leave one with the impression that overcoming legalism, Judaism, and Pharisaism involves simply "let go and let God." That is, give up on all the spiritual disciplines, let a relationship develop, and see what happens. Unfortunately, it doesn't work that way. Marriages, even good ones, tend to get stale if they are not continually nurtured. It takes effort to build intimacy with both fellow humans and with God. Maturity likewise doesn't just happen; it must be cultivated.

Developing a relationship with Christ often begins with holy dissatisfaction. When we look at others, we may become smug, but when we look inward and upward, we are righteously appalled. We come to a place where we are not satisfied with our present state and long to know Christ better. He is always eager to meet us at the place of need and get to know us more intimately. The place then to start, and never leave, is His love and knowledge of how He laid hold of us.

The way out of Pharisaism requires some of the disciplines of an athlete. Knowing Christ requires an active pursuit of intimacy coupled with a knowledge of our humanness and an expectation of future glory. The process is initiated by Christ, not us. His longing for relationship with us is infinitely greater than our longing to know Him. Nevertheless, to know Christ takes some of the same disciplines and efforts that are required by any athlete.

As we connect with the loyal love of Christ for us personally, we will want nothing more than to please Him. Our past accomplishments and accidents will pale in the light of this new direction for our lives. And we will not give up this pursuit until we are called to live in the heavenly Father's house.

THIS WORLD IS NOT MY HOME

The final key to leaving the prison of Pharisaism is to beware of developing a permissive attitude. Adopting a lifestyle of license is as dangerous as a life of legalism. A libertine, like a legalist, cannot live a righteous life. Yet for those liberated from Pharisaism, libertinism is tempting. Freed from the grip of law, some fall into the clutches of freedom gone to seed. The pendulum of spiritual life seems seldom to stop in the middle; rather, it swings from side to side.

Those who come out of Pharisaism have a tendency to abuse their freedom in Christ. Of this The apostle Paul was painfully aware (Romans 6; Galatians 5). So he concluded his teaching to the beloved Philippians with a warning about libertinism.

Armed with a correct understanding of himself and his Lord, Paul invited his Philippian brothers to follow his example and that of others in the congregation (v. 17). Paul's good example was not the only alternative for the Philippians, however. With great emotion he pointed to bad examples to avoid (vv. 18–19). Apparently Paul had repeatedly warned the Philippians about certain "enemies of the cross" and was even weeping as he wrote.

Who are these enemies? We cannot say with certainty, as a variety of groups have been identified by Bible scholars. But we can identify some of their characteristics. First, their teaching contradicted the blood sacrifice of Christ. The Cross could be demeaned by adding religious rituals, rules, and regulations to salvation as the Judaizers did or by giving license to sin as the libertines did. In either case, the Cross's power was cheapened. Second, these enemies, because they had opposed the Cross of Christ, were destined for eternal destruction. Reject the Cross and there is no other provision for salvation. Third, they worshipped their fleshly appetites. They lived for the lusts of the flesh and gave themselves over to self-indulgence (or perhaps they made a god out of their food laws). Fourth, they took pride in what should have been shameful to them. It sounds like the enemies of the Cross engaged in immoral behavior and relished it, perhaps like the Corinthians (1 Corinthians 5). Finally, these enemies of the Cross lived for this world, not the next. Their philosophy of life was materialistic, not spiritual; earthly, not heavenly.

The chapter ends with an impassioned, hymnlike appeal to acknowledge our alien status on earth and eagerly look forward to our glorification in heaven. Our citizenship is in heaven; earthly things ought to be secondary to us. We wait for our Savior, not the satiety of our sensual appetites. We long for freedom from the presence of sin, which God will one day grant.

In recent years the impact of legalism has lessened in many arenas of the church. But in its place has not always been a return to authentic Christianity. Rather, it seems to me that libertinism has blossomed like a weed on the land. The statistics from every source tell us that we Christians are more or less clones of our secular culture, and in some cases even worse.[15] I fear that we have gained slight insights into Pharisaism only to slip into antinomianism. If The apostle Paul were our pastor, he would be weeping! For Christ's sake, the way out of Pharisaism must not lead us into lawlessness.

THE WAY TO RIGHTEOUS LIVING

Paul has presented the way out of Pharisaism—also known as legalism and Judaism (and sometimes evangelicalism and fundamentalism). The way out begins with a warning. We must be constantly vigilant for perversions of the way of Christ. Then we must deal decisively with fleshly confidence. That is, we must place no stock in human attempts to please or placate God. Next we need to redo our spiritual accounting system. Our human assets must be viewed as potential liabilities. And Christ, our only enduring asset, should become the object of our passionate pursuit. Nothing should motivate us more than to know the One who loves us so. This pursuit, like a marriage, is a lifelong quest that will not be completed until heaven. In the meantime, we should pursue intimacy like an athlete going for gold. Finally, we must avoid the human tendency to replace one error (legalism) for another (libertinism). Instead, as faithful pilgrims we will live in this world while longing for our future home.

"THE CURE HAD BEGUN"

In *The Voyage of the "Dawn Treader"* (the third book in the *Chronicles of Narnia Series*), C. S. Lewis painted a vivid portrait of a greedy, snobby character named Eustace. It forms a fitting metaphor for our escape from the self-effort of Pharisaism to the comforting clothes of life lived in the Spirit.

In the story, Eustace was turned into a dragon, a fitting reflection of his character. When he was forced to face what he had become, he realized what a fool he had been. He longed to be undragoned and changed back into a boy. He wept and worked hard to behave differently, with some success but no loss of his dragon skin. Then he attempted to forcibly scratch off his skin. But each time he did, a new layer appeared. After several rounds of trying to strip off his dragon skin, Eustace gave up.

At this point, disillusioned and desperate, Eustace met Aslan the lion, the Christ figure of the chronicles. Aslan told Eustace, "You will have to let me undress you." The fearful boy/dragon watched in fear:

> I was afraid of his claws, I can tell you, but I was pretty nearly desperate now. So I just lay flat down on my back to let him do it. The very first tear he made was so deep that I thought it had gone right into my heart. And when he began pulling the skin off, it hurt worse than anything I've ever felt.[16]

But Aslan peeled off more than the skin and finally threw Eustace's stripped and sensitive body into a well. Then the great lion, like Christ, dressed Eustace in a brand-new set of clothes. Eustace, the rebel, had met Aslan, his savior and lord. Lewis concludes,

> It would be nice, and fairly nearly true, to say that "from that time forth Eustace was a different boy." To be strictly accurate, he began to be a different boy. He had relapses. There were still many days when he could be very tiresome. But most of those I shall not notice. The cure had begun.[17]

Appendices

Appendix 1:
HOW THE PHARISEES BEGAN

U nderstanding the Pharisees requires knowledge of the cultural and political movements that gave birth to and nurtured them. The Pharisees emerged as an identifiable group during what is called the intertestamental period, the years between the Old and New Testaments. During those more than four hundred "silent years" between Malachi and Christ, Israel was predominantly ruled by various foreign powers, exactly as Daniel had prophesied (Daniel 7). Though many of the Jewish people became assimilated into the cultures around them, some, like Daniel and the other Hebrew youths (Daniel 1; 3), refused to compromise their identity and way of life. These "purists" clung tenaciously to the Scriptures, while others, including members of the clergy (priests and Levites), compromised with the culture.

The philosophical and religious forerunner of the Pharisees is Ezra, whose intense devotion to the Law (Ezra 7:10) set the standard for the scribes that followed him. Ezra, of priestly lineage (Ezra 7:1–5), was a godly man with an intense desire to communicate and apply God's Word to common people in changing cultural settings. According to tradition Ezra was also a founder of the synagogue. Thus he defined the work, devotion, and setting that was later to be copied by the Pharisees.

HELLENISM, THE HUMANISM OF THE DAY

One of the major players in the process of "creating" the need for the Pharisees was Alexander the Great, who built his empire, which included Palestine, from 336 to 323 B.C. Though

Alexander is best known for his military conquests, his most lasting legacy in Israel was cultural. When the Greeks conquered the Persians, who had been the overlords of Palestine, Alexander enacted policies that were acceptable in Israel, particularly among the ruling and religious elite. He allowed the Jews limited autonomy and stimulated economic prosperity, which lulled them into accepting other cultural innovations. Alexander and his successors encouraged the adoption of Greek culture, literature, institutions, entertainment, ideas, names, norms, coins, and the Greek language, all of which further eroded the unique identity of the Jews. Hellenism, the humanism of the day, was as potent a temptation as idolatry had been earlier in Jewish history. Alexander's promotion of Greek culture set the stage for subsequent resistance by the pious.

Following the short-lived reign of Alexander, his empire was parceled out. Israel first was ruled by the Ptolemies (301–198 B.C.). Under these Egyptian rulers, Israel enjoyed peace, prosperity, and relative religious autonomy. The fortunes of the Jews were reversed, however, when in 203 B.C. Antiochus III (the Great), a Syrian ruler, captured Jerusalem. Thus began more than a century of Seleucid rule in Palestine. The Seleucids were much less willing to extend autonomy to the Jews and much more intent on promoting Greek culture, or Hellenism. It was during this period that the Pharisees almost surely were galvanized into an identifiable group.

A CLASH OF CULTURES

During the reign of the notorious Antiochus IV, called Epiphanes (175–164 B.C.), events in Palestine worsened, and new forces spurred the emergence of the Pharisees. A clash of cultures erupted between the orthodox and the Hellenistic Jews. The cultural right resisted Hellenism; the cultural left advocated acculturation. The clash came to a head over the selection of the high priest. The orthodox viewed the priesthood as a spiritual office attained by divine call. Others connived to make the high priesthood a political office given to the highest bidder. Antiochus, who wanted to transform Jerusalem into a model Greek city, agreed the post should be a political office. He awarded the position to those he thought best supported his goals. Some Jews rebelled, and Antiochus, being pressured by Rome, decided to take more decisive, and brutal, action against the orthodox.

The actions Antiochus inaugurated in 167 B.C. sought to remove all traces of orthodox Jewish faith. He tried to link the Greeks' Jupiter with God. He offered swine in sacrifice upon the altar in what is commonly referred to as the "Abomination of Desolation." He forbade Jews,

> under penalty of death, to practice circumcision, Sabbath obser-vance, or the celebration of the Feasts of the Jewish calendar. Copies of the Scriptures were ordered destroyed. The laws were enforced with utmost cruelty. An aged scribe named Fleazar was flogged to death because he would not eat swine's flesh.[1]

The abominable behavior of Antiochus IV Epiphanes was the straw that broke the back of Seleucid power in Palestine and launched the Maccabean Revolt.[2] When it was over, the Mac-cabees, under Judas Maccabeus, had wrested control of Palestine from the Syrians and placed it in the hands of Jews for the first time in four hundred years. In December, 164 B.C., the temple in Jerusalem was rededicated and an eight-day celebration, the Feast of Dedication, also known as Hanukkah or the Festival of Lights, was inaugurated as a lasting remembrance among Jews. Though conflict from without was lessened, conflict within Israel continued between the orthodox/conservative and the Hel-lenistic/liberal. This conflict occasionally resulted in bloodshed.

ENTER THE PHARISEES AND SADDUCEES

In this setting, the Pharisees became prominent. The Mac-cabees eventually founded a political dynasty,[3] and during the reign of John Hyrcanus I (134–104 B.C.), Josephus cited the Pharisees as an official party.[4] He notes that the conservative Pharisees had a falling out with Hyrcanus when they resisted the king's claim to be a priest as well as a king. So Hyrcanus sided with the more liberal Sadducees. This resulted in Sadducean dominance of the ruling elite and Pharisaic prominence with the masses.

Thus about 150 years before the public ministry of Jesus Christ, the two great parties of Judaism that we read about in the New Testament, the Pharisees and the Sadducees, were recogniz-ably born. Both were prominent at the time of Christ and Pharisaism continues to this day.

The Pharisees were the party that continued the ideology of

the patriotic Maccabean movement that had first taken a stand for the Law and the religious integrity of Judaism. The Sadducees became the party of the priests and Levites, and toward which the Hellenistically inclined Jews gravitated. The Sadducees stressed the centrality of the Temple and the rituals. The Pharisees' base of operations was the synagogue. (The differences between the two are detailed in chapter 3.)

The fortunes of the Pharisees and the Sadducees in the century before the birth of Christ shifted with the occupants of political power in Israel. Alexander Jannaeus (103–76 B.C.), the Hasmonaean warrior-king, embarked on a policy of territorial expansion (using many foreign mercenaries) and showed little respect for his priestly responsibilities. Thus he further alienated the Pharisees and grew to despise them. Openly Alexander defied the Pharisee's scruples and even had eight hundred Pharisees crucified while he caroused with his concubines. Josephus tells us, however, that surprisingly on his deathbed Alexander instructed his wife to distance herself from the Sadducees and reign with the help of the Pharisees.[5] Salome Alexandra (76–67 B.C.) took her husband's advice and befriended the Pharisees, thus averting further civil strife. She initiated what is referred to as the "Golden Age of Pharisaism."

During this time the Pharisees had considerable political clout, social influence, and religious impact. Politically they were the neck that controlled the head of state. Josephus implied that the Pharisees possessed the royal authority whereas Alexandra had only its burdens.[6] Judicially, they insisted that the perpetrators of the crucifixions under Alexander be executed. Socially, they emphasized education, based on the Scripture.[7] Religiously, they exerted their influence in the synagogues throughout the land. Although the Pharisees were lay Scripture students, they eventually supplanted the priests as the authoritative interpreters of the Law. The Pharisees truly dominated the spiritual heartbeat of the nation.

TENSIONS BETWEEN PHARISEES AND SADDUCEES

Tension continued between the Pharisees and the Sadducees. The Pharisees harbored resentment for those who had been killed by Alexander Jannaeus, and the Sadducees were ever-suspicious of Pharisee gains in political power. Throughout this period, both parties vied for control of the Sanhedrin. The ongoing "culture war" between the two major parties compromised the nation and contributed to the political takeover by the Romans led by Pompey in 63 B.C.

During the final decades before the birth of Christ, the two greatest rabbis emerged, Shammai and Hillel. Shammai was the conservative. His rulings were stringent and sometimes harsh. On the issue of divorce (Matthew 19:9), Jesus seems to side with Shammai's unaccommodating interpretation. Hillel was the moderate. He was known for his compassion and sought to reconcile scriptural law with the actual situations of life. Some scholars have even suggested that Jesus was a disciple of Hillel.

Appendix 2:
SOURCES FOR THE STUDY OF THE PHARISEES

O ur knowledge of the Pharisees derives from three primary sources, though each is considered by some scholars to be flawed. The first source is the writings of Jewish historian Flavius Josephus,[1] who delineates many of the beliefs, behaviors, and contributions of the Pharisees, as well as their shifting political fortunes. Josephus has his detractors. His Pharisaic credentials are suspect, as is his character and patriotism. He advised compromise with the invading Romans in the late 60s A.D. and was subsequently rewarded by the brutal conquerors of Israel. Thus he is regarded as a traitor, an opportunist, and an egoist. Nevertheless, he does record numerous invaluable snapshots of the Pharisees of the first century.

The second source of information about the Pharisees is the late second century compilation of Rabbi Judah the Patriarch (or Prince) known as The Mishnah ("to repeat"). This monumental work is a topical collection of the legal rulings of Judaism for the years between approximately 200 B.C. and A.D. 200. The Mishnah to the Jew can be likened to the New Testament for the Christian. It highlights debates between the two greatest Pharisee rabbis, Hillel and Shammai, and their respective schools. However, because of its late date, anti-Sadducee bias, and favor toward the school of Hillel, some scholars advise caution in using The Mishnah to reconstruct the characteristics of the Pharisees around the time of Christ.[2]

The third primary source of information about the Pharisees is, of course, the New Testament. Like Josephus and The Mishnah, the New Testament documents have their critics. Jewish scholars protest their anti-Jewish and anti-Pharisee bias. Few, however, can deny the early date of these writings and that they depict life in Israel around the time of Christ from the perspective of the early Christians, almost all of whom were Jewish and understood Judaism. The most prolific writer of New Testament documents, The apostle Paul, affirms his card-carrying Pharisee credentials.[3] He is imminently qualified to evaluate the Pharisees. As an evangelical who affirms the reliability of the biblical documents, I fully accept the New Testament accounts as factual. However, I hasten to add that our negative bias against the Pharisees has caused us to seriously misread these accounts. I further contend that the New Testament portrait of the Pharisees is not as negative as a superficial reading would suggest.

All three primary sources provide valuable and reliable information, and, taken together, they present a consistent portrait of the Pharisees.

Appendix 3:
SPIRITUAL FRUIT GONE TO SEED

Authentic spirituality produces good fruit.[1] False spirituality, however, results in no fruit, bad fruit, or the fruit turning to seed. The Pharisees did not produce the fruit that God sought.

Here is a brief description of each of seven types of bad fruit of the Pharisees, with associated Scriptures. As we look closely, we can see some of the ways our own spirituality can go bad.

SIGN-SEEKING

In the past, God gave signs to strengthen the faith of the timid. He did this with Moses (Exodus 3–4) and Gideon (Judges 6:17–24), for example. But Jesus made it clear that signs and miracles "are never to be performed or demanded or as a sop for unbelief," as Carson notes.[2] When we ask God to show His power or love by outward manifestations, we may be presumptive or demanding, as the Pharisees were. True faith needs no signs from God and true spirituality needs no miracle answers. Sight often stifles rather than stimulates faith—a phenomenon modeled by the Pharisees.

Scripture passages: Matthew 12:22–45; 15:39–16:4; John 2:18–22; 6:22–59.

NAME-CALLING

Spirituality has gone to seed when the religious resort to name-calling in order to discredit opponents. When we call our adversaries names, we turn them into objects of ridicule rather than those who deserve respect and honest evaluation. Name-calling was commonly employed by the Pharisees as they tried to discredit Jesus. Scripture admonishes us in numerous places (particularly Proverbs and James) to choose our words carefully and to use kind rather than cutting words.

Scripture passages: Sexual innuendoes, John 8:41; racial slurs, John 8:48; social stereotypes, Matthew 11:18–19; psychological labeling, John 10:20; and spiritual put-downs, Matthew 9:34; 12:24; John 7:20; 8:48, 52; 10:20.

BROW-BEATING

Similar to name-calling, brow-beating involves intimidation and aggressive tactics designed to win an argument or control an opponent. The Pharisees did this, thinking they were helping God deal with those who they believed did not see things God's way. When we Christians ignore, downplay, or stereotype questions from unbelievers, our "fruit" is rotten. When we ridicule or intimidate fellow believers who have less Bible knowledge or different views, we have no spiritual fruit.

Scripture passages: John 7:12–13, 45–52; 9:1–41; 11:45–53, 57; 12:42–43.

MONEY-LOVING

The Pharisees' materialism, hinted at in the three parables of Luke 15 and stated directly in Luke 16:14, affects many Americans, including Christians. Jesus said that money is a great trap for religious people, gripping their emotions and priorities (Matthew 6:19–34). We must remember that money does not assure our future. Our hope must be on God alone, and our riches should be viewed as gifts from Him, to be used for good deeds (1 Timothy 6:17–18).

Scripture passages: Matthew 6:1–4; 12:11–12; 19:16–26; 23:14, 16–26; Luke 8:14; 11:39–41; 16:14; 18:11–12; 20:47.

TRAP-SETTING

There is a place for asking questions and giving tests to determine someone's qualifications and abilities. However, the Pharisees and some modern-day religionists have the wrong motive: They want to discredit an opponent or humble someone in order to exalt themselves. Christians can do this when they act as inquisitors at church board meetings or at question-and-answer forums with a pastoral candidate. Instead of getting information, the motive is to control or trap the person. Some set traps to display power or cleverness.

Scripture passages: Matthew 16:1–4; 19:1–12; 22:15–40 (testing Jesus on taxes, the resurrection, and the greatest commandment); Luke 10:25–37; 11:53–54; John 8:1–11.

TRUTH-TWISTING

In this advanced form of spiritual fruit gone to seed, truth becomes secondary to the cause. The end justifies the means; thus truth can be twisted to reach the goal. That clearly was the case as the religious leaders maneuvered toward the execution of Jesus. They would even tell lies to get rid of Him. When we readily accept rumors or even circulate rumors about those we think are disobeying God, we are no different. If we distort their words, twisting what they say out of context; when we condemn them without ever having talked with them face-to-face, we are twisting the truth to accomplish what we deem is God's way.

Scripture passages: Matthew 26:57–68; 28:11–15.

DEATH-PLOTTING

Religious people are sometimes pushed to acts of violence while convinced they are doing the will of God. Spiritual fruit gone to seed contains unimaginable cruelty and unspeakable crimes. Thus we have the entrenched fighting between Protestants and Catholics in Northern Ireland and the massacres of "Christian" Hutus and Tutsi in Rwanda and Burundi. Among most sophisticated American Christians, physical and verbal fighting has become the murder weapon of choice in the church.

Scripture passages: Matthew 12:14; 16:21; 17:22–23; 20:18–19; 21:33–46; 22:1–14; 23:33–39; 26:1–5, 14–16, 57–68.

NOTES

Chapter 2: A Common Caricature

1. William E. Phipps, "Jesus, the Prophetic Pharisee," *Journal of Ecumenical Studies* 14 (winter 1977): 29.
2. See William Davies, *Introduction to Pharisaism* (Philadelphia: Fortress, 1967); Robert Herford, *The Pharisees* (Boston: Beacon, 1962); N. T. Wright, *The New Testament and the People of God* (Minneapolis: Augsburg Fortress, 1992); and E. P. Sanders, *Judaism: Practice and Belief* (London: SCM, 1992).
3. D. A. Hagner, "The Pharisees," vol. 4 of *Zondervan Pictorial Encyclopedia* (Grand Rapids: Zondervan, 1975), 746.
4. Merrill C. Tenney, *New Testament Times* (Grand Rapids: Eerdmans, 1978), 93.
5. Jesus even affirmed the relational aspect of the Pharisees' soteriology when He commends a lawyer (who may well have been a Pharisee) who asked about eternal life (Luke 10:25–28).
6. Josephus, *The Life of Flavius Josephus*, Sec. 38, in *The Works of Josephus*, trans. William Whitson (Lynn, Mass.: Hendrickson, 1982), 100.
7. Josephus, *Wars of the Jews*, in *The Works of Josephus*, 434.
8. Josephus, *The Antiquities of the Jews*, in *The Works of Josephus*, 281.
9. Tenney, *New Testament Times*, 192.
10. "Pharisee," Colin Brown, gen. ed., *The New International Dictionary of New Testament Theology*, vol. 2 (Grand Rapids: Zondervan, 1986), 810.
11. Steve Mason, *Flavius Josephus on the Pharisees*, (New York: E. J. Brill, 1991), 170.
12. Ibid., 376.
13. Hagner, "The Pharisees," 749.

Chapter 3: Your Best Friends

1. G. K. Chesterton, The Secret of Father Brown (Mattituck, N. Y.: Amercon, n.d.).

Chapter 4: When Rightness Leads to Wrongness

1. See Luke 15:6, 9; Romans 12:15; and 1 Corinthians 12:26.
2. Similarly, Augustine pleaded, "Lord, save me from that wicked man, myself." John Knox, perhaps the greatest preacher in the history of Scotland, confessed, "In youth, in middle age and now after many battles, I find nothing in me but corruption." And I have several times

watched with wonder as evangelist Billy Graham befuddles his media interviewers with remarks about his failures.

3. See "A Time to Seek," *Newsweek*, 17 December 1990, 56, where Kenneth L. Woodward writes, "In their efforts to accommodate, many clergy have simply airbrushed sin out of their language. . . . Heaven, by this creed, is never having to say no to yourself."
4. J. C. Ryle, *Five Christian Leaders of the Eighteenth Century* (Banner of Truth n.p.: 1960), 138.
5. William Lawrence, "Through Pain to Glory," Berean Sunday School Class, Northwest Bibe Church, Dallas, Texas, 4 June 1995 (audio tape).

Chapter 5: When Bible Knowledge Blinds and Binds

1. Philip Yancey, "We Have No Right to Scorn," *Christianity Today*, 15 January 1988, 72.
2. See Acts 15:1; 20:28–30; 1 Timothy 1:3–11; 2 Timothy 3:1–4:5; Titus 1:10–16; 2 Peter 2; Jude.
3. E. P. Sanders, *Judaism:Practise and Belief 63 bce–66ce* (Philadelphia: Trinity, 1992), 415–816.
4. See 1 Kings 3:9; Philippians 1:9; 1 John 4:1–6.
5. Cf. Matthew 7:28–29; 21:23–27; Mark 1:21–28; Luke 5:17–26; John 7:14–24.
6. John R. W. Stott, *Christ the Controversialist* (Downers Grove, Ill.: Inter-Varsity, 1976), 97.
7. Everett Ferguson, *Backgrounds of Early Christianity* (Grand Rapids: Eerdmans, 1993), 505.
8. For instance, piety could be measured by fasting, so they must have wondered along with John's disciples why Jesus was so undisciplined (Matthew 9:14). They had extended the Old Testament teachings about priestly ceremonial washings to all of God's people by developing numerous traditions about ritual cleansings (Mark 7:1–23; Matthew 15:1–20). When Jesus' disciples didn't wash their hands before eating, the Pharisees wondered why such a "clear" implication of the scriptural text would be violated so cavalierly (Matthew 15:1–20).
9. Stott, *Christ the Controversialist*, 96.
10. Charles Swindoll, *Growing Deep in the Christian Life* (Portland, Ore.: Multnomah, 1986), 31.
11. John White, *The Fight* (Downers Grove, Ill.: InterVarsity, 1978), 55.

Chapter 6: When A Private Relationship Becomes A Public Show

1. For instance, three of Islam's Five Pillars are almsgiving, prayer five times a day, and fasting during Ramadan; Hinduism focuses on the way of works, the way of knowledge, and the way of devotion.
2. William C. Varner, "Jesus and the Pharisees: A Jewish Perspective," *The Newsletter Publication of Personal Freedom Outreach* 16, no. 3 (July–September 1996):12.
3. John R. W. Stott, *Christ the Controversialist* (Downers Grove, Ill.: Inter-Varsity , 1976), 205.
4. R. T. France, *Matthew: Evangelist and Teacher* (Grand Rapids: Acedmie, 1989), 131. Almsgiving was specified in the Law; see Exodus 23:10–11; 30:15; Leviticus 19:10; Deuteronomy 15:7–11.
5. William David Davies and Dale C. Allison, *A Critical and Exegetical Commentary on the Gospel According to St. Matthew* (Edinburgh: T & T

Clark, 1988), 579;

6. D. A. Carson, *The Expositor's Bible Commentary*, vol. 8 (Grand Rapids: Zondervan, 1984), 164.

7. Kathleen Kern, *We Are the Pharisees* (Scottsdale, Pa.: Herald, 1995), 61. Jesus uses the word *hypocrisy* in Matthew 6:2, 5, 16; 23:13–15, 23, 25, 27, 29.

8. William Hendriksen, *New Testament Commentary: Exposition of the Gospel According to Matthew* (Grand Rapids: Baker, 1982), 320.

9. Craig L. Blomberg, *Matthew*, vol. 22 of *The New American Commentary* (Nashville, Broadman: 1992), 117.

10. See Genesis 16:13; Psalm 139; Mark 10: 40–42; John 21:17; Hebrews 4:13.

11. Hendriksen, *Gospel According to Matthew*, 322.

12. William L. Coleman, *The Pharisees' Guide to Total Holiness* (Minneapolis: Bethany, 1977), 62–63.

13. Davies and Allison, *A Critical and Exegetical Commentary*, 588, 610–11.

14. See 1 Samuel 1:26; Nehemiah 9:4; Jeremiah 18:20; Mark 11:25.

15. Hendriksen, *Gospel According to Matthew*, 322.

16. Charles Swindoll, *Strengthening Your Grip* (Waco, Tex.: Word, 1982), 152.

17. Ibid., 149.

18. Israel Abrahams, *Studies in Pharisaism and the Gospels*, ed. Harry Orlinsky (New York: Ktav Publishing, 1967), 125.

19. Leviticus 16:29–34; 23:26–32; Numbers 29:7–11; Deuteronomy 9:18; 1 Kings 21:27; Nehemiah 9:1ff.; Psalm 35:13; 69:10; Daniel 9:2–20; 10:2–3; Joel 2:12; Jonah 3:5.

20. 1 Samuel 7:5–6; 2 Samuel 12:16, 21–23; 2 Chronicles 20:3, 5ff.; Ezra 8:21–23; Nehemiah 1:4; 9:1ff.; Isaiah 58:6, 9; Jeremiah 14:12; Daniel 9:3.

21. Hendriksen, *Gospel According to Matthew*, 341.

Chapter 7: When Tradition Twists Truth

1. Merriam-Webster's Collegiate Dictionary, 10th ed. S.V. "tradition."

2. Jaroslav Pelikan in an interview in *U.S. News and World Report*, 26 June 1989, 57.

3. Donald A. Hagner, *Word Biblical Commentary: Matthew 14–28* (Dallas: Word, 1995), 430.

4. Jacob Neusner, *From Politics to Piety* (Englewood Cliffs, N.J.: Prentice-Hall, 1973), 86.

5. Under the section regarding cleannesses (Tohoroth), a portion of The Mishnah is devoted to the issue of "Hands" (Yadaim). The Pharisaic traditions dictated when the hands had to be washed: before every meal and between each course. They decreed what kind of water had to be used for the cleansing procedure: water kept in special stone jars, protected from contamination, water that was to be used for no other purpose. Since the vessels that housed the water that was used for the hand-washings could also become defiled, special procedures for the washing of cups and pitchers and pots were also devised (Mark 7:4).

6. William Barclay, *The Gospel of Mark* (Philadelphia: Westminster, 1975), 164–65.

7. Cf. Exodus 21:15, 17; Leviticus 20:9; Deuteronomy 27:16; Proverbs 20:20; 30:17.

8. John R. W. Stott, *Christ the Controversialist* (Downers Grove, Ill.: Inter-Varsity, 1976), 138.
9. Cf. 1 Corinthians 8:7; 2 Corinthians 11:2; James 1:27; 2 Peter 3:14; Revelation 14:4; 21:27.
10. Frank R. Tillapaugh, *Your Ministry Can Break the 20/80 Barrier* (Denver: Shared Vision Network, 1994), 37; T. H. Olbricht, in *Dictionary of Christianity in America* (Downers Grove, Ill.: InterVarsity, 1990), 922.
11. Similarly, we can think certain services and programs are crucial for ministry. Some Christians still make the Wednesday evening prayer meeting the barometer of spirituality. Attendance is a sign of spirituality and nonattendance a mark of complacency. However, attendance at meetings, if it breeds smugness, is a sure route to spiritual blindness. In addition, some who have enjoyed the traditions of children's church and children's choirs, or youth clubs, such as AWANA, Christian Service Brigade, Pioneer Clubs, may believe they are essential to a child's spiritual growth. Neither they nor even a specific adult program, such as "body life," small group meetings, and "seeker services," is innately more spiritual nor biblical than any other.
12. P. Westermeyer, "Music, Christian, " ed. Daniel G. Reid et al. *Dictionary of Christianity in America* (Downers Grove, Ill.: InterVarsity, 1990), 786–87.
13. Leith Anderson, *Dying for Change* (Minneapolis: Bethany, 1990), 43.

Chapter 8: When Fences Become the Focus

1. Eugene J. Lipman, trans. *The Mishna* (New York: Viking, 1973), 446.
2. Ibid., 79–80.
3. Cf. Matthew 12:1–8, 9–14; Luke 13:10–17; 14:1–6; John 5:1–9; 7:21–24; 9:1–41.
4. In Exodus 16:29 and Jeremiah 17:22, one's home was cited as the base of acceptable Sabbath day activities. And Numbers 35:4 used the distance of a thousand cubits from the city wall as the proper extension of the city limits. Combining the texts, one can arrive at a distance of one thousand cubits from one's home to be an acceptable Sabbath day's journey.
5. John MacArthur, *The MacArthur New Testament Bible Commentary: Matthew 8–15* (Chicago: Moody, 1987), 283.
6. The Scriptures condemning alcohol include Isaiah 28:1–8; Romans 13:13; 1 Corinthians 5:11; 6:10; Galatians 5:21; Ephesians 5:18; 1 Thessalonians 5:6–8; 1 Timothy 3:3, 8; and 1 Peter 4:3. Some of the Scriptures that allow or commend drinking of alcohol are Numbers 28:7; Deuteronomy 14:22–27; Psalm 104:14–15; Ecclesiastes 9:7; Matthew 26:27–29; John 2:1–10; 1 Timothy 5:23.
7. Proverbs 20:1; 23:29–35; and Isaiah 5:11–12 describe the deceptiveness; the consequences are described in Genesis 9:20–27; 19:30–38; Proverbs 4:17; 20:1; 21:17; 23:19–35; Isaiah 5:22–23; Hosea 4:11; and 1 Corinthians 11:27–30.
8. Cf. 1 Samuel 18:6–7; 2 Samuel 6:14–16; Psalm 30:11; 149:3; 150:4; Luke 15:23–25.
9. D. A. Carson, *From Sabbath to Lord's Day* (Grand Rapids: Zondervan, 1982), 70.
10. Cf. Matthew 9:3, 11, 14, 34; 10:25; 11:19.
11. Robert C. Roberts, "The Fruits of the Spirit," *Reformed Journal*, February 1987, 10.

Chapter 9: When Separatism Leads Us Astray

1. Colin Brown, *Dictionary of New Testament Theology*, vol. 2 (Grand Rapids: Zondervan, 1979), 810.
2. *Today in the Word*, devotional booklet (Chicago: Moody Bible Institute, 8 March 1996), 15.
3. William L. Coleman, *The Pharisees' Guide to Total Holiness* (Minneapolis: Bethany, 1977), 46–48.
4. Philip Yancey, "Where the High and Mighty Meet the Down and Dirty," *Christianity Today*, 11 January 1993, 80.
5. Ibid.
6. Rebecca Manley Pippert, *Out of the Saltshaker* (Downers Grove, Ill.: InterVarsity, 1979), 24.
7. John R. W. Stott, *Christ the Controversialist* (Downers Grove, Ill.: InterVarsity, 1976), 189.
8. Craig L. Blomberg, *I Corinthians: The NIV Application Commentary* (Grand Rapids: Zondervan, 1994), 300.
9. Ibid. 114.

Chapter 10: When the Sick Look Fit

1. Evangelical Christians choose from many tracts that give the formula in simple, transferable language. "The Four Spiritual Laws"; "The Bridge Illustration"; "Steps to Peace with God"; "How to Share Your Faith Without an Argument" are among the many widely distributed salvation guides available. Probably one of the most often-asked evangelistic questions is, "If you were to die tonight and were ushered into the presence of God, why would He let you in?" I have used this question numerous times and know exactly the answers I am looking for.
2. Cf. Matthew 9:9–13; 21:15–17; Mark 7:24–30; Luke 15; 19:1–10; John 4:1–45; 8:1–59.
3. Cf. Matthew 9:33–34; 11:19; 12:23–24; 21:15.
4. William Barclay, *The Gospel of Matthew*, vol. 2 (Edinburgh: Saint Andrews, 1956), 289.
5. The previous verse, Matthew 23:14, suggests an added "woe." However, this woe is not found in the earliest manuscripts of the Bible. It may or may not be among the words spoken by Jesus on this occasion. But we do know from the other Gospels that Jesus did say those words (Mark 12:40; Luke 20:47), condemning the Pharisees for having long prayers yet preying on widows and other needy people. It is possible, even probable, to have what appears to be an excellent prayer life and be spiritually sick; we can exploit others privately yet seem spiritual through our public displays, including public prayers.
6. D. A. Carson, *Matthew*, vol. 8 of *Expositor's Bible Commentary*, ed. F. E. Gaebelein (Grand Rapids: Zondervan, 1984), 478.
7. Scot McKnight, *A Light Among the Gentiles* (Minneapolis: Fortress, 1990), 107.
8. Craig L. Blomberg, *Matthew*, vol. 22 of *The New American Commentary* (Nashville: Broadman, 1992), 344.
9. Carson, *Matthew*, 479.
10. David E. Garland, *The Intention of Matthew 23* (Leiden, England: E. J. Brill, 1979), 133–34.
11. Carson, *Matthew*, 279.

Chapter 11: The Way to Spiritual Fitness

1. Charles Leroux and Graeme Zielinski, "The Big Fact: Overweight's Now the Norm," *Chicago Tribune*, 16 October 1996, 1:5. The study found that 59 percent of men and 49 percent of women were overweight.
2. In *chiasm*, the poem or argument follows an A B C B A pattern. The central point is designed to be emphasized.
3. David E. Garland, *The Intention of Matthew 23* (Leiden, England: E. J. Brill, 1979), 137.
4. John MacArthur, *The MacArthur New Testament Commentary: Matthew 1–7* (Chicago: Moody, 1985), 383–84.
5. Garland, *Intention*, 137.
6. Cf. Matthew 5:7; 9:13; 12:7; 18:33.
7. Cf. 1 Samuel 16:7; Jeremiah 17:9; John 7:24; 2 Corinthians 5:12; 10:7; Colossians 2:23.
8. Howard Hendricks, "Leadership, Evaluation and Development (LEAD) 1, Leadership Center Conference, audio tape, Dallas Seminary, 17–21 October 1988.
9. D. A. Carson, *Matthew*, vol. 8 of *Expositor's Bible Commentary*, ed. F. E. Gaebelein (Grand Rapids: Zondervan, 1984), 482.
10. Garland, *Intention*, 157.
11. Ibid. 163.
12. Cf. Genesis 15:16; Daniel 5:25–28; 8:23; Romans 2:5; 1 Thessalonians 2:15–16.

Chapter 12: The Right Relationship

1. In addition, the tribe of Benjamin led the armies of Israel (Judges 5:14; Hosea 5:8). and gave Israel its first lawful king, after whom Paul (Saul) had been named (1 Samuel 9:1–2). A Benjamite, Mordecai, brought national deliverance with the help of Esther; and the tribe, along with Judah, formed the new core of Israel after the Babylonian Captivity (see Ezra 4:1; Nehemiah 11:7–9, 31–36).
2. Cf. 1 Corinthians 15:9; Galatians 1:13–14; 1 Timothy 1:13.
3. Peter O'Brien, *The Epistle to the Philippians* (Grand Rapids: Eerdmans, 1991), 379.
4. Moise Silva, *Philippians* (Chicago: Moody, 1988), 165.
5. Gerald Hawthorne, *Philippians*, vol. 43 of *Word Biblical Commentary* (Waco, Tex.: Word, 1983), 124–25.
6. Used figuratively, *dog* is always a term of reproach (cf. Deuteronomy 23:18; 1 Samuel 17:43; 24:14; Proverbs 26:11; Isaiah 56:10–11; Matthew 7:6).
7. Silva, *Philippians*, 69.
8. O'Brien, *Epistle to the Philippians*, 357.
9. Romans 7 is a companion text to Philippians 3. In a common vein, Paul declared in Romans that "nothing good dwells in me, that is, in my flesh" (v. 18). Significantly, Paul, someone with such great spiritual capacities, declared the whole system bankrupt.
10. Hawthorne, *Philippians*, 135–36.
11. "Rubbish" translates the vulgar Greek word *skuballa*. It is variously interpreted as food scraps, muck, dung, excrement ("The portion of food rejected by the body, as not possessing nutritive qualities" [Lightfoot], "The refuse or leavings of a feast, the food thrown away from the table" [Lightfoot], "Half-eaten corpse or lumps of manure" [Hawthorne].

12. Hawthorne, *Philippians*, 139.
13. Cf. Romans 8:17–18; 2 Corinthians 4:8–11; 11:16–33; Philippians 1:29–30; 2 Timothy 3:12.
14. O'Brien, *Epistle to the Philippians*, 407.
15. According to George Barna's research, born-again Christians are now slightly more likely to divorce than the general population (27 percent versus 23 percent for the general population); See Maja Beckstrom, "Researcher Takes Religious Pulse in U.S.," *Houston Chronicle*, 17 August 1996, 3E. And Os Guiness in *Dining with the Devil* regards the church as the primary secularizing force in America today.
16. C. S. Lewis, *The Voyage of the "Dawn Treader"* (New York: Collier, 1970), 90.
17. Ibid., 93.

Appendix 1: How the Pharisees Began

1. Charles F. Pfeiffer, "Between the Testaments," *The Open Bible* (Nashville: Nelson, 1985), 1337.
2. The revolt began when Mattathias, an elderly priest, and his five sons, defied the orders of a Syrian emissary, killed him, and then headed for the hills. They gathered other people zealous for the Law of God—the hasidim, or "pious ones,"—and launched a nationalistic movement against the Syrians and Hellenistically-minded Jews. Following the death of Mattathias, the firstborn son Judas, known as Maccabeus ("the Hammer"), became the military leader. Using guerrilla warfare tactics, the Maccabees defeated the Syrians. The apocryphal books of 1 and 2 Maccabees tell some of the events of this revolt.
3. Their dynasty was called the Hasmonaean dynasty, named for an ancestor of Mattathias. See Hershel Shanks, *Ancient Israel: A Short History from Abraham to the Roman Destruction of the Temple* (Englewood Cliffs, N.J.: Prentice-Hall, 1988), 183.
4. Josephus, *Antiquities of the Jews* in Book 13, chapter 10, *The Works of Josephus*, trans. William Whitson (Lynn, Mass.: Hendrickson, 1982), 281.
5. Ibid. chapter 15, section 5, 287.
6. Ibid., chapter 16, 287.
7. Pfeiffer, "Between the Testaments," *The Open Bible*, 1339.

Appendix 2: Sources for the Study of the Pharisees

1. Josephus, *The Works of Josephus*, trans. William Whitson (Lynn, Mass.: Hendrickson, 1982).
2. Nicholas Thomas Wright, *The New Testament and the People of God* (Minneapolis: Fortress, 1992), 183; and E. P. Sanders, *Judaism: Practice and Belief* (Philadelphia: Trinity, 1992), 413.
3. Acts 22:3; 26:5; Philippians 3:5.

Appendix 3: Spiritual Fruit Gone to Seed

1. See Matthew 7:15–20; John 4:36; 15:1–17; Romans 7:4; Galatians 5:22–25; Colossians 1:10; James 3:17.
2. D. A. Carson, *Matthew*, vol. 8 of *Expositor's Bible Commentary*, ed. F. E. Gaebelein (Grand Rapids: Zondervan, 1984), 294.

Moody Press, a ministry of Moody Bible Institute,
is designed for education, evangelization, and edification.
If we may assist you in knowing more about Christ
and the Christian life, please write us without obligation:
Moody Press, c/o MLM, Chicago, Illinois 60610.